The Tragedy of Islam

The Tragedy of Islam

Admissions of a Muslim Imam

Imam Mohammad Tawhidi

Published by Reason Books

Reason Books International
786 Adelaide Post Office
Adelaide, South Australia
5000, Australia
www.ReasonBooks.Global

Ordering Information:
Special discounts are available on quantity purchases by individuals, corporations, associations, and others. For details, contact the publisher at the address above.

Tawhidi, Mohammad.
The Tragedy of Islam: Admissions of a Muslim Imam / Imam Mohammad Tawhidi

ISBN 9781925880212

First Edition

Websites:
The official website of Imam Tawhidi: www.ImamTawhidi.com
The official website of this book: www.TragedyofIslam.com
Foundation website: www.TawhidiFoundation.com
Reason Books International: www.ReasonBooks.Global

REASON BOOKS

INTERNATIONAL

Table of Contents

Acknowledgments

I give thanks to God almighty for protection and the ability to complete this book.

Although this period of my life was filled with many ups and downs, I thank the Islamic extremists who threatened and physically assaulted me, as well as destroying my vehicle and house. This book wouldn't have been possible without the passion born out of the obvious need for change.

A very special thanks to the government departments and officials that provided me with security throughout my travels across the Middle East, as I searched for physical copies of sources and references used within this book.

I would also like to thank my wonderful friend L.A. of Shankland, and my two advisors S.L.P. and J.A. of South Australia for reviewing this book.

Writing a book such as this is a surreal process. I'm forever indebted to the brilliant Kate Leeson of South Australia for editing this book.

Special thanks to my partner for her support. Even though she entered my life towards the final stages of this book, she was as important to this book being completed as I was. Thank you so much, dear.

This humble work of mine is dedicated to all the men, women, and children who have been murdered, oppressed, and mistreated across the ages as victims of Islamic extremism and terrorism.

And to my Uncle Faris, the colonel who was kidnapped and burned alive by ISIS as he bravely served his country in the Iraqi Army in 2015.

About the Author

Imam Tawhidi is an Australian Muslim scholar, publicly ordained Islamic authority, thinker, educator, speaker, and one of the leading voices in the global movement of Islamic reform. He has dedicated his life to ideologically tackling the spread of Islamic extremism.

He was born in the Holy City of Qum, Iran, into a spiritual family with a history of decades of participation in Islamic seminaries, and had memorized much of the Quran by the age of ten. Imam Tawhidi returned to Australia in 2015, after his journey in the Islamic seminaries of Iran and Iraq. He is considered an internationally active personality, being fluent in Arabic, English and Farsi.

He has delivered speeches at conferences, parliaments, mosques, Islamic centers, churches, synagogues, temples and universities across the Middle East, Europe, America, Asia, and Australia. Imam Tawhidi is licensed by Islamic leaders of the highest order to lead and represent the Muslim community. He enjoys healthy international diplomatic relationships with numerous government officials and provides regular advice on counter-terrorism.

Imam Tawhidi was recognized by the Senate of Canada on Wednesday June 13th of 2018.

***

> It is hard not to imagine that Islam in Australia is going to be heavily
> influenced by this 'Imam of Peace'
> for some years to come. – The Spectator

Glossary

Allah – The Arabic word for "God."

Ayatollah – A title literally meaning "sign of God", awarded to Shia Muslim experts on Islam.

Caliph – An elected or appointed leader of Muslims. In Shia Islam, there can only be one caliph on earth at a time.

Caliphate – An Islamic state under the leadership of a caliph.

Fatwa – An Islamic ruling or verdict issued by a recognized Islamic jurist or authority. It is considered a scholarly opinion that must be followed and emulated.

Grand ayatollah – A Shia Muslim expert on Islam who has announced that they are an Islamic leader and who has a following.

Grand imam – In the context of this book, "grand imam" means an imam who is highly revered and more prominent than a regular imam.

Hadith – A narration, report, account, chronicle, or record of the traditions, sayings, and doings of Prophet Mohammad.

Hijrah – The migration of Prophet Mohammad and his companions from Mecca to Medina in the year 622.

Imam – In the context of this book, imam means Islamic leader. In Shia Islam, the word imam also means an infallible descendant of Prophet Mohammad, such as Imam Hussain.

Islamic government – A government based on Sharia Law, which is not necessarily governed by a caliph. Examples include the Islamic republics of Pakistan and Iran.

Islamic scholar – A recognized scholar on the Quran, and other Islamic teachings and scriptures.

Islamism – A fundamentalist and hardline brand of Islam that revolves around a militant ideology and interpretation.

Islamist – A Muslim who believes in utilising violence or militancy in order to spread fundamentalist and hardline brands of Islam. Muslims of both Shia and Sunni denominations can be Islamists. Islamists are activists who aim to establish the rule of Sharia Law.

Jihad – The fundamental Islamic obligation to fight for the cause of God.

Jihadist – An Islamist Muslim who engages in the act of jihad.

Jurisprudence – The study of law. In this case, it is religious law. For example, Sharia Law is a combination of different sources of Islamic jurisprudence.

Jurist – An expert on jurisprudence and the theory of law.

Kaffir – The Arabic Islamic terminology to describe a disbeliever in Allah and or the Islamic religion.

Mufti – A Sunni Muslim jurist who is qualified to deduce Islamic laws from the Quran and hadith and present them as authoritative legal opinions.

Quranic – An attribution to the Quran. For example, Quranic verse means a verse from the Quran.

Salafism – A hybrid of Wahhabism.

Sayed – In the context of this book, a sayed is a descendant of Prophet Mohammad.

Shaikh – An honorific title given to Arabian "leaders" or Islamic scholars regardless of nationality.

Sharia Law – Islamic law that is derived from the religious precepts of Islam, mainly the Quran, its various interpretations and the hadith.

Shia and Sunni – Shia Islam and Sunni Islam are the two Islamic denominations which all Islamic schools of thought and sects stem from. Sunni Islam is the larger denomination, and its adherents believe the fathers-in-law of Prophet Mohammad are his rightful successors. Shia Islam is the smaller denomination and its adherents believe that prophetic succession was passed onto Mohammad's son-in-law Ali, and continues through his offspring who are the grandchildren of Mohammad.

Terrorism – There is no single definition of terrorism. In this book, the word "terrorism" refers to any use of violence and intimidation against civilians or opposition in the pursuit of political and/or religious aims, whether it be government - or non-government - sanctioned violence.

Terrorist – In this book, a terrorist is an individual who orders or personally uses violence against civilians or opponents in the pursuit of political and or religious aims.

Wahhabism – A fundamentalist and extremist Islamist movement founded by Muhammad ibn Abd al-Wahhab, an eighteenth-century preacher and activist.

Necessary Explanations

My usage of the phrase **"the majority of Muslims"** does not refer specifically to Sunni Muslims, but refers to the majority of all Muslims regardless of denomination and/or school of thought.

The phrase **"grand Islamic authority"** is not an indication of a position or status within Islamic society. It is used in this volume merely as a description to distinguish between an Islamic authority and a senior Islamic authority. While "authority"usually refers to somethinga person has, and not something a person is, the word "authority" here refers to the status of a Muslim scholar who has been given such authority from a superior religious authority.

The words **"historic report"** refer to a report from within the sources of Islamic history. The historical Islamic sources I have cited were all authored by prominent Muslim historians who are revered and glorified within Islam and Islamic educational institutions.

The words **"Islamic scripture"** do not refer to a specific book, but refer to all texts considered by Muslims to be the obligatory doctrine of God, mainly the Quran and books of hadith.

The phrase **"authentic hadith"** is not my personal evaluation of the hadith; it is rather the grade that accompanies the hadith in its original Islamic scripture. All reports, scripture and hadith used in this volume are graded as "authentic." If the word "authentic" is mentioned, my purpose is to stress its authenticity, and not imply that other hadiths are not authentic.

An Important Preface

It is highly likely that you will one day hear that I have been murdered. Therefore, before we begin, I believe it is necessary to clarify certain matters regarding this book, which I believe will be matters of concern for the reader. There will be many who will make claims about what I have set out to do by writing this book, and thus I wish to make clear the goals I hope to achieve.

Audience and Purpose

This book is written for both Muslims and non-Muslims who have failed to obtain an explanation of why Islam, as a religion, is struggling to find a place within the West. The first chapter is a necessary review of the last two decades of my life, and what has led me to make such statements and confessions, then the second chapter begins to shed light on the tragedy of Islam. *This is not a book that "bashes" or attacks Islam and Muslims. It is rather intended to be an informative volume that presents my personal development and educational journey within Islam and the Islamic seminaries throughout the Middle East.*

I understand that English is a second language in numerous European countries suffering from Islamic extremism. Therefore, I have intentionally written this book in straightforward English for the benefit of all English-speaking people.

Sectarianism and Internal Islamic Conflicts

Although I was educated and trained by both Shia and Sunni Islamic schools and religious authorities, I have avoided falling into the trap of sectarianism when writing this book. I strongly oppose sectarianism, and as a reformist Muslim scholar, my difficulty is with fundamentalist elements which have led to the current situation of the religion as a whole. I have no regard for minor disputes between sects, and I criticize and expose the wrong within all Islamic denominations based on facts and solid historical evidence. Moreover, I have dedicated an entire chapter to the difficulties within my own denomination, Shia Islam.

Methodology and Approach

When I began writing this book, I intended it to be only about Islam and the ideological challenges it faces in our era. However, I also believe that it is important for the reader to gain an understanding of who I am, where I came from, and how I developed into a reformist Imam.

Although I do intend to write about my journey in detail sometime later down the track, in the first chapter of this book I have shared a number of episodes from my life that will allow you to recognize what I have gone through in the past, how I became the person I am today, and why I have chosen to make these dangerous admissions.After discussing my personal journey, I will begin to shed light onto the ideological difficulties within Islam.

This book identifies the main theological and doctrinal problems within my religion, simply because identifying the problems is the first step to offering possible solutions.This book is by no means a complete chronicle of the present failings in my religion. It does not contain *everything* that is relevant to modern Islam, because that would be impossible. Its main focus is the problems and complications which form the foundations of Islamic scripture, history, theology, and jurisprudence.It concludes by shedding light on the reform movement within Islam and the prospects of genuine reform.

Notes on the References

I have used the most authentic Islamic scriptures as sources, from both Islamic denominations, Shia Islam and Sunni Islam. What you will read in the chapters discussing the difficulties within Islamic thought will most likely be new to you. This is because the Muslim institutions do not and will not translate certain parts of religious scripture to preserve and maintain the reputation of the religion, as I will explain. Therefore, I have translated the teachings as accurately as possible, as Arabic is my mother tongue.

I have repeatedly called for my detractors within the Islamic clergy to nominate a qualified person to debate me publicly, and to refute my statements if they can. More than a year has passed, yet no-one has come forward. I am sure this silence is because they know that such a debate can only expose the dark secrets they wish to conceal. The most chilling of these secrets is that the books they promote are the religious fuel that powers violent Islamic terrorism.

The sources I have used are unavailable as hard copies in the majority of countries, which is why I have spent over 100 hours compiling online links to the original Arabic and Islamic scriptures for the reader's convenience. These are available on my website: www.ImamTawhidi.com/References or
www.TragedyofIslam.com.

A Note for Muslims

This book is about Islam, but it is not an Islamic book. The prayer of blessings upon the Prophet Mohammad and his family will not be included in this volume. Readers are free to observe this practice whenever names you may revere are mentioned.

When mentioning Prophet Mohammad, I have maintained a balance throughout this book. I have referred to him as "Prophet Mohammad" and at times simply as "Mohammad." I have also presented what both the majority and minority of Muslims believe regarding their Prophet.

Introduction

For years, I have publicly explained the complexities of my religion and advocated the need for serious change. I have done this via media releases, public forums, articles, social media and addresses to community groups and government organizations. I have also engaged where possible with Muslim and non-Muslim religious figures, academics, politicians and members of the general public. Many times, I was advised to "write a book." I have now accepted this advice and offer the following work for your consideration.

The aim of this book is to provide a different side to present-day arguments as to what Islam is and the current popular narrative. Not only am I an Islamic scholar, but I am ordained as a third-generation imam and Islamic authority. As such, I feel that there is a particular responsibility on me to speak out against the extremists and fundamentalist ideologies that have infested my religion.

For much of my life, I subscribed to the vision of Islam presented to me by my religious teachers. While being devoted to my religion, I undertook the long process of study to become an accredited imam. It was during this period that I came to question the interpretations of Muslim doctrine that many religious scholars promote as "true Islam." The revelations revealed to the Prophet Mohammed contained in the Holy Quran are in fact not the only basis of many contemporary Islamic practices. The source materials for much of their teachings are books written centuries after Mohammad's death. These theological and jurisprudential works are in fact in contradiction with each other. Deeply troubling to me were the bigoted, violent, and extreme interpretations that these scholars were using to indoctrinate young minds. I was lucky enough to liberate myself from extremist ideologies, and I wish the same for many of my co-religionists.

Both Muslims and non-Muslims have a vital role to play. At its simplest, we must support the modernizers against the "traditionalists," and relentlessly drive the extremists from our societies. In particular, we must rid ourselves of the doctrine of "multiculturalism at all costs" as it has provided extremists with useful cover. Islamists have found themselves able to claim victim status in a society that they hope to destroy and supplant. Tolerant democracies have offered an opportunity to Muslim immigrants, to attain a better and safer life for themselves and their families. How we have got to our present state, where we have had terrorist attacks on our soil, lies in our own misconceptions regarding the nature of the mind set of extremists; and here I am witnessing the same jihadists my family fled from, now moving into our neighborhoods.

It is obvious that our governments are at variance with the views of the majority of citizens as to what constitutes a sensible immigration policy. This is a dangerous mindset for governments to hold, as it opens the possibility for Islamic extremists to make major political gains. This sadly is not confined to Australia; it is common to most of the tolerant democracies.

My goals are to do all I can to strengthen the force of reformists and modernists within Islam, and to warn my fellow Australians and the citizens of other democracies of the dangers in their midst.

CHAPTER 1

Highlights of My Journey

1997 — I **arrived in Australia** at the age of 12
I lived in Western Australia and complted by initial studies in a private Muslim school.

2007 — I **return to Iran** to complete my Islamin studies.
Due to my Australian citizenship, I was seen as an asset and eventually radicalized by the institutions of the Iranian regime.
I became a close ally, travel partner, and advisor to officials within the Iranian regime.

2011 — I **ended my relationship with the regime** and withdrew from its institutions.
From here onwards, I faced challenges, interrogations, imprisonment, and beatings by the regime. The Grand Ayatollah Shirazi ordained me as a Muslim imam with an outstanding grade.

2013 — I **travelled to Iraq** where I continued my advanced Islamic studies and worked at a Shirazi-owned TV station.

2015 — I **returned to Australia** and began preaching amongst the Muslim community.

2016 — I began to **distance myself from the Islamic hierarchy** and call for reform within Muslim communities. I began forming relations with local and federal governments.

2017 — I made my **reformist agenda** clear, and made use of my international and diplomatic relations to tackle Islamic extremists and establish peace within a number of communities.

A Timeline of My Life

An Islamic Childhood

"Allahu Akbar, Allahu Akbar": these are among the earliest sounds that I can remember as a small child. I would awake to my father calmly repeating these words during his prayers, meaning "God is the Greatest." The living presence of God was with me from my earliest childhood memories. My father, Imam Abdolmuttalib Tawhidi, would make sure that I was awake at dawn to offer my morning prayers. I would stand behind my father and follow his lead in every part of the prayer. It was from my father that I learnt foundational beauty and peace.

I was brought up to love and respect all those around me regardless of the color of their skin, their ethnic origins, or the name by which they called God. I spent the early years of my life in Iran, in the Holy City of Qum. Every day I could look out upon the glorious architecture of this holy city, and the shrines of the descendants of Mohammad. The green gardens and the sparkling fountains all shaped my perceptions of the religion of my ancestors. This provided the physical backdrop for the first twelve years of my life. It was also where I was introduced to a mass of other races and cultures. Walking along the narrow and winding alleyways that meander between the great holy sites exposed me to different faces and a babble of different languages, as the faithful from Iran, Afghanistan, Pakistan, Lebanon and many other places came to make their devotions at the mosques and shrines.

My wise and gentle mother was and still is a strong influence in my life. I truly believe that she epitomizes the Arabian belief that "Heaven lies beneath the feet of your mothers." Indeed, I had the luxury at that time of being her only child. The story of my birth wasn't as pleasant as that of many children within my circle. As a refugee in Iran, I was detained immediately after birth due to my father being unable to afford the hospital bill. I was finally given to my mother several days after birth.

My enlightened father practices the tolerance which he preaches, and as I grew older my respect for him rose as I discovered the true horrors he had endured throughout his life. He was sentenced to death for his opposition to the tyrannical dictator Saddam Hussain. I now look back and praise the Lord that the sentence was not carried out. My family has a history of opposing tyrants. My renowned grandfather Shaikh Yasin al Rumaithi was considered the "Voice of the Faith."* He was a eulogist who delivered sermons highlighting freedom. Three of his sons, Taha, Adil and Aqeel, were executed by Saddam's regime, which left him with a heart condition until he died in 2005.

As I was growing up I heard my mother speak about how Saddam Hussain's intelligence services had camped in her house, waiting for her activist brothers' arrival so that they could imprison them. One day, the officers became impatient as my wanted uncles never returned home, so they resorted to arresting my uncle Amir, who was twelve at the time, along with my mother. As my twelve-year-old uncle stood in the interrogation room shivering in fear, not knowing what tragedies could pour upon him that night, he heard a loud sound – the sound of an Iraqi officer slapping my young mother across her face for no apparent reason at all.

My uncles however endured torture and pain under the regime of Saddam Hussain. Ahmad was only twenty-one when he was forced to join the war against Iran. He was severely tortured by Saddam's army generals the moment he refused to abide by their inhumane orders to mass murder innocent Iranian civilians. He was then thrown into a prison cell, only to find that his brother had been thrown in there before him. My uncle Ahmad bled to death in the lap of my uncle Ra'ad.

Uncle Jasim suffered the most. He was a senior police officer during the time his brothers were wanted for rising against Saddam Hussain. He was forced to falsely testify against his own brothers and sign documents that supported their executions. It did not take long before it was his turn. He was also found guilty of assisting the opposition, whose crime it seems was helping the poor and protecting the innocent. The morning arrived when Jasim was dragged to court and forced to stand in front of a merciless judge with a history of harsh sentencing. The judge looked at my Uncle Jasim and said, "You have testified against yourself that you have been involved in conspiracies

* According to Grand Ayatollah Sayed Mohammad Baqir al Sadr.

against the regime of Saddam Hussain." My uncle responded by tearing his jail uniform open to reveal the evidence of torture on his body that he was subjected to when he refused to falsely testify against himself. His torture marks noticeably shocked even this judge. My uncle's back had been ironed with a clothes iron. Out of shock or sympathy, the judge dismissed his case.

Jasim was the first person in my family to seek asylum in Australia, and Amir and my parents then followed through family sponsorships. Upon arrival in Western Australia, I was enrolled in a private Muslim school, the Australian Islamic College; with Muslim, Christian, Hindu, and Atheist teachers. I loved each one of them, and I considered school my second home. During my break times, I explored different cultures and I learnt words from different languages my friends would teach me. I was never a quiet boy to say the least. I was always outspoken and confident, perhaps one of my Scorpio characteristics.

Every Sunday my father and I would head out fishing, and I can safely say I was captivated by this pastime. I fell in love with the flow of the Murray and Swan rivers, and the tides of the rich Australian oceans. Fishing for me was not only a sport, it was also one of the things that taught me patience and appreciation. It was my favorite activity during the Holy Month of Ramadan, as time flew by quickly without feeling the long day of fasting!

With my father being a senior Islamic faith leader and my mother a student of Islam, I received an Islamic upbringing. I had memorized a large amount of the Holy Quran by the age of ten, including the second and largest chapter. I prayed five times a day and was taught to give charity to the poor. Alongside my daily attendance at a private Muslim school, I attended Saturday classes known as "Madrassah" at Al-Taqwa Mosque in Western Australia, where we were taught Islamic studies, and that Islam is the perfect way of life. My parents were proud of raising such a devout Muslim child.

My father concentrated on serving the Muslim community, and had a great passion to aid new arrivals to Australia, those who were genuine refugees. My father and his good friend Mr. Hosseini established Western Australia's first Shia Muslim mosque. The building was originally a church named St. Mary's Church and, out of my father's respect for the Christian majority and his love for St. Mary, it was named St. Mary Mosque. A very long and detailed story lies behind this mosque and its demolition in 2017. All I will say at this stage is that St Mary Mosque played an essential role in my Islamic upbringing as a child living in Australia.

Mecca and the House of God

One morning in 2006, my mother spoke to my father about visiting Mecca to perform her obligatory Hajj pilgrimage, the religious trip to Mecca performed by over four million Muslims each year. My father was unable to accompany my mother on this trip, and because the rulings of Hajj require a female to be accompanied by a male, I was given the opportunity to visit Mecca. My visit to Mecca was life changing. The group tour was led by Ayatollah Shaikh Jafar al Baqiri, a relative of ours who resided in Melbourne during the last decades of his life. This trip to Mecca lasted 14 days, and paved the way for me to become more attached to my religion. On our first stop in Medina, I visited Masjid al Nabawi, Prophet Mohammad's mosque and burial site, along with Al-Baqi, the demolished shrines of his household.

Islam teaches that prayers offered in Prophet Mohammad's mosque are rewarded much more than prayers offered anywhere else.

Mecca is a rich city that reflects the history and development of Islam. Muslims believe its land is pure and sacred as it embraces the Kaba – the cuboid stone structure that is considered to be Allah's holy home. Our tour bus stopped in front of the hotel where we were to stay for the next seven days. With the millions of pilgrims flooding the city and the congregational prayers at the Kaba, a queue extended to the front door of our hotel located one kilometer away. On my first day in Mecca, because of my sense of awe, I was extremely anxious entering the mosque that contains God's home. The glory and ambience of the building captured me instantly.

During my first evening in Mecca, tens of our group members were speaking about their visit to the Kaba as an indescribable and unexplainable experience. I knew my time was coming, and that I would have to enter the holy mosque, but I wanted to enter with the right mindset and appropriate approach. The next morning, I performed my washing ritual and made my way towards the house of God, the Kaba. When I was younger, I was taught that every step towards the Kaba carries great rewards and every prayer performed around it is equal to a thousand or more prayers elsewhere.

I stood before God in the holy mosque, wearing nothing other than two pieces of cloth covering my body, representing complete detachment from the materialistic world and a connection to a high level of spirituality. This practice reminds us that at the beginning of creation we owned nothing, and that we will return to meet God wearing simple and humble material.

After completing my prayers, I began walking towards the glorious Kaba, feeling the gravity of the black cube drawing me towards it. I found myself gravitating towards and rotating around the house of God with four million other pilgrims. I felt breathless, gasping for air as I got closer to the Kaba. It was such an intense feeling. It became seriously hard to move and/or breathe as I reached the location of the "Black Rock," a rock believed by Muslims to have descended from paradise.

We were taught that it's a great honor to reach the Black Rock, which was mounted onto the Kaba by Prophet Mohammad. I was eager to touch the rock, and I knew I was going to achieve this. I looked at the bottom edge of the Kaba and noticed the base had a two-inch edge formed from thick marble tiles. Being younger and only weighing about fifty kilograms, I believed it would be a good idea to walk across the edge of the base of the Kaba and reach the Black Rock to avoid the wave of people. As I stepped on the edge, I was dragged down by an Indonesian female pilgrim who tried to climb up on the edge with me. I quickly got back onto the edge and moved towards the Black Rock. Finally, I was right above it. Being less than a meter from the ground, I threw myself onto the crowd made up of millions of pilgrims, all wanting to touch the Black Rock. The wave of people pushed me towards the Black Rock. I landed with my back towards the rock, sealing it completely. AllI had to do now was turn around and fulfil my wish of touching it. The one mistake I shall never forgive myself for was wearing a robe on that day. My robe became stuck between the people around me, preventing me from turning around to face the rock. I managed to touch the rock eventually, and the problem was now to get out of this wave of humanity. I felt myself beginning to suffocate. Luckily, I was dragged out of the crowd by a large African man whom I thanked profusely.

As I was completing my prayers, I noticed an elderly man from Pakistan who had lost the group he had come to Mecca with. I could not understand what he was saying but he showed me his hotel card, so I knew where he was residing – he was in the city. I did not know the route to the hotel, and he had difficulty walking. We walked all the way back to his hotel after some assistance from members of the public. When we reached the hotel, I entered to make sure it was the one he was residing in with his friends. He came in behind me to confirm that it indeed was the very hotel he was looking for. He had a smile on his face and insisted that I joined him for dinner. I excused myself as my mother was awaiting my return, but as I turned around he placed his hand on my shoulder, and I turned around to find him raising his hands towards the sky and praying for me. I felt very humbled by this gesture of his and sometimes I tell myself that this good deed might have been the reason behind the good I have been blessed with in later years.

We slept a night in Muzdalifah, one of the locations all pilgrims must visit. Upon waking up to offer my dawn prayers, I heard clapping followed by loud and happy cheering voices. Suddenly, Saudi Arabian authorities flooded the scene to arrest those who were celebrating. Moments later we learnt that Saddam Hussain had just been executed, and those celebrating were victims of the oppressive Ba'athist regime. They were Shia Muslims, and their happiness angered the Sunni and Saudi authorities who cherished their relationship with the Iraqi dictatorship.

An incident that I shall never forget occurred during this trip to Mecca. I was returning to the hotel after having lunch in a nearby restaurant and ran into the disgraced Grand Mufti of Australia, Taj El-Din al Hilaly. I discovered that he was residing in the same hotel as our group from Australia. We waited for the lift to come down, and as we both entered the lift, he asked what floor I was in. I responded saying level 5. He then pressed number 5 and number 14, which was the top floor. He then smiled at me and said, "I'm sleeping on the fourteenth floor, much closer to God." This is when I realized that we as a Muslim community in Australia had serious problems. In my heart I told myself, there are taller buildings in Israel. I wonder if he thinks Jews are closer to God when residing on the 30th floor. If you haven't heard of Hilaly, he was Australia's first Grand Mufti, and the one who compared "uncovered" Australian women to cat meat.

We had also travelled to Medina before Mecca, where I first gazed on the dome of the mosque and mausoleum of Prophet Mohammad. This time I was standing in front of the Prophet Mohammad. I noticed a fence surrounding the grave with a Sharia Law police officer roaming the inside with his shoes on; I had never seen such disrespect, as we were taught to take our shoes off in revered and holy locations. I managed to pass through the crowd and get close to the grille of the holy grave. As I reached out to touch the window of the grave, the Sharia police officer struck my hand with a baton and yelled "Shirk!" which means "Paganism!" According to Wahhabism, seeking aid from the dead is paganism, even though the spirit of the dead will always remain alive. I exited the Mosque of Prophet Mohammad to walk to Al-Baqi Cemetery, where Mohammad's family and household are buried. I saw the site that was demolished by fundamentalists, who believe that building domes over graves is a pagan ritual; but it somehow seemed perfectly acceptable for the Prophet Mohammad to have a grave and a dome only a few steps away. I realized that hatred towards the offspring of *their own Prophet* Mohammad was deeply entrenched in their Wahhabi ideology, leading to the complete demolition of one of Islam's most important shrines.

In Al-Baqi Cemetery, I saw my mother walking towards a group of females who had joined a tour group from Australia. I noticed that the group was completely segregated, with men separated from the women. Furthermore, I noticed that the clergyman of the group had disappeared. So, I asked one of the organizers why the group was segregated. He answered that Saudi Arabian authorities accuse Shia Muslim clergymen of engaging in sexual activities with females within the group. So, they separate the two genders to prevent such accusations and to avoid giving extremists an excuse to tarnish their reputation. It was after this incident that I realized that the hatred towards us as a Shia Muslim minority was very real.

I returned to Australia a more religious and astute Mohammad Tawhidi, who knew much more than he did before travelling to Medina and Mecca. I spent many hours enlightening my friends and family about this inspiring and awakening pilgrimage to Mecca. I have not been to Saudi Arabia since, nor do I plan to go.

My Second Pilgrimage: Iran

Australia was always home, and my social life in Australia was very healthy. The mixing of males and females is highly frowned upon within Muslim culture, which meant most of my friends were male. Alongside all my social engagements as a developing teenager in Western Australia, I was deeply influenced by one of our Shia Muslim community clerics. I have chosen to keep his name private throughout this chapter considering the change of career he underwent, and shall refer to him as "the Sayed."*I saw him as my second father. I loved him deeply and still regard him as a dear person. It was he who paved the way for me to pursue religious studies. Every weekend, I would spend time at his house located within our suburb, Ballajura, in Western Australia. He was one of my father's closest friends. I along with my childhood friends, a group of approximately 12 to 15 boys, would gather at the Sayed's house to learn about Islam. It was a very friendly atmosphere, highly educational and very rewarding. The Sayed encouraged me to begin delivering short sermons and eulogies during community events and gatherings and, although I knew it was not going to be my career, it made both me and my parents happy.

Although the Sayed was a Shia Muslim cleric, I also had frequent

---

* "Sayed" is a title given to a Muslim cleric who is also a descendant of Prophet Mohammad.

engagements with my coordinator from high school, who in recent years has taken on the role of an imam. He was and still is a fundamentalist, and an extremist Muslim. I was taught the basics of Islam in his lessons. Once I left the Islamic college to attend a public Australian school in 2006, I lost contact with him, although we did initiate contact with each other ten years later, during early 2017, as he unsuccessfully attempted to persuade me to stop criticizing fundamentalist Muslims in the media, because he believed that "doing so does not serve Islam."

In 2006, the Sayed came to visit my father one evening to discuss an idea he had in mind. The idea was to begin educational Islamic tours from Australia to Iran, and that our group of around 20 people would be the first group to participate in this educational tour. My father was very supportive of this idea, because he thought it would be a valuable experience for us young men to go to the Middle East and see what life is like there. My father believed that our group had a lot to learn about life in the Middle East, and that a short trip would increase our appreciation of the privileges and advantages we had in Australia, as opposed to what our parents had when growing up in the Middle East.

My father asked me what I thought about a short trip to Iran during the school holidays. I was very excited and positive in my response, especially knowing that I would be engaging in studies to increase my knowledge of Islam. My friends and I got together and spoke about this trip for over two weeks as we anticipated boarding the plane to travel to the holy lands of Qum and Mashhad. I gradually began to prepare my travel luggage, making sure I took everything I needed with me on this holy trip. Eventually the time came for me to board the plane, and after a long and tiring flight from Perth, Western Australia to Tehran with two stops on the way, we reached Imam Khomeini Airport just after midnight. The doors of the plane opened and I could feel the coldness of the Persian winter embrace us. The moment we stepped foot out of the airport, I felt the cold breeze penetrate my bones. It was indeed cold, very cold.

Luckily, Sayed had arranged a taxi van which was waiting for us outside the airport. We walked in a group like penguins, shivering in the cold while carrying our heavy luggage. We all crammed into the freezing van and begged the driver to turn on the heating because the leather seats were also extremely cold. The van exited Tehran airport and I began to notice and read the road signs in Persian. My tears began to flow when I read a sign say "Qum," and my body began to shake. My face was soaked with tears by the time we reached the city, and many may wonder why this happened to me. I have a deep spiritual connection with the city of Qum. It was where I was born, and where I spent many productive years. In Qum, I lived in times of hardship, I passed the tests of life, and it made me a man. My body shakes every time I remember myself walking in the alleyways of that city, and breathing its air. I will never be able to describe the love I have for the city of Qum, never. It is something that lives within me every day. I submit that love is not something we can control, and I am emotionally attached to Qum.

We reached Qum before dawn, and it was snowing. I set foot on the road, and bent down to touch the ground with my hands once again. We were also hungry, thus Sayed decided to eat kaleh pacheh, because that was the only thing available to eat at the time. Kaleh pacheh is a dish of boiled cow or sheep's feet and/or head; although other cow parts, such as the brain, head and stomach (tripe) may also be used. I took a look at the plate and said, "No, thank you," and I exited the shop to wait in the cold. I have never gone anywhere near that dish, or anything similar to it, to this very day.

The Shrine of Fatimah Masumeh, located in Qum, Iran.

We heard the call to dawn prayer, and we headed to the Holy Shrine of Qum, located no more than a couple of minutes away. The shrine marking the gravestone of Fatimah Masumeh is considered to be the second most sacred place after Mashhad to Shia Muslims in Iran. Fatima Masumeh was a descendant of Prophet Mohammad who is therefore honored as a saint, and her shrine in Qum is considered one of the most significant shrines in Islam. Every year, thousands of Muslims travel to Qum to honor Fatima Masumeh and ask her for her blessings. Fatima Masumeh is honored in many hadiths, or teachings, from Shia imams that proclaim the benefits of visiting her shrine in Qum. Islamic scriptures teach that a visit to the shrine of Fatima Masumeh guarantees paradise. Being a practicing Muslim who was also born only two roads away from her shrine, I have always felt spiritually and emotionally attached to her. And here I was once again with a group of friends, standing before her tomb, offering my dawn prayers.

We headed towards one of the most prominent seminaries, located just off the "Jihad Roundabout" (Meydan-e-Jihad), known as Imam Khomeini Islamic Seminary. This university was made up of two sections, one for permanent students and another for short and temporary courses. The latter was the section of the university where we were to spend the next month. We were all taken to our dormitories, and shown our beds. All twenty of us were placed in three large rooms. The next morning our course began on the ground floor. We were all taught four lessons a day by Shia Muslim clerics who spoke in English. Even though some of my friends missed several classes, I did not miss one lesson during the entire trip. I was amazed and inspired by the entire religious and spiritual atmosphere. I fell in love with the entire program and contacted my father during the third week in Iran, asking him if I could stay and pursue my studies. My father's response was positive; however, he suggested that I return to Australia to prepare myself before making such a big and serious decision that could – and did in fact – shape the direction of my life.

We travelled to fascinating cities such as Isfahan, Mashhad, Shiraz, and Tehran before heading back to Australia. Each one of these cities had sacred shrines that have motivated me to live a strictly religious life. The shrine in Tehran belonged to Imam Khomeini, whose character in those early days I grew to love very dearly, and the shrine in Mashhad was the tomb of Imam Redha, Shia Islam's eighth successor and a descendant of Prophet Mohammad.

When our one-month short-term study course in Qum ended, we returned directly to Australia. I had very much adapted to the spiritual lifestyle and atmosphere of Iran, but I deeply loved Australia. I began to yearn to return to Iran in order to complete my studies. My family did not have the financial means to support my overseas education; therefore, I began to work in a fruit and vegetable shop (Morley Fresh) to save enough money to travel back to Iran. I initiated contact with Al Mustafa International University, informing them of my intention to return and become a full-time student in Iran. I was told that I had to wait for a response from the university. Five months passed, and I received no response. My father, who had many friends still residing in Iran, asked one of them to pay the university a visit to check on my application on my behalf. Now that a friend of ours was following up my application in Iran, I had two remaining tasks: to work, and to wait.

One morning in 2007 my father's phone rang as we were at the dining table eating dinner. I reached out for the phone and handed it over to my father. Overhearing the conversation, I realized that it was his friend in Iran who was following up my university application. My father made a gesture with his hand that confirmed to me that I had been accepted. This was the happiest I had ever been in my entire life. Relocating to Iran in order to engage in Islamic studies was the most important choice I had made, and I will forever be proud of this decision.

The Sayed, who led our group to Iran in 2006, received this news and gathered members of the Muslim community in Western Australia to announce to them that I, being the son of the state's leading Shia imam at the time, would be relocating to Iran to pursue advanced Islamic studies. This meant that out of the entire group that had travelled to Iran to study Islam, I was the only one to return. This was seen by members of the community not only as good news, but also a religious blessing. After waves of praise and encouragement, I bid farewell to the gathering that had composed my relatives and friends, some of whom I had known from Iran from the age of three.

I began to gradually prepare my bags and organise my luggage. I had purchased a vehicle to get to and from work and, in order to support me, my father purchased it from me for the same amount I had paid for it. With more encouragement from friends and family, I returned to Iran to pursue my dream.

My Return to Iran

I landed in Tehran at 2:22 am on February 3, 2007. Amar, a taxi driver my family friends had arranged to meet me at the airport, took me to the Holy City of Qum. I told him to take me to the Imam Khomeini Islamic Seminary, located at Jihad Roundabout, because I was familiar with that institute and its people. I had depended on them to assist me in finding the department I would need to attend later that morning. The reception was open 24 hours, and Amar helped me unload my luggage and waved goodbye to me. Now I was all alone. I entered the reception and informed them that I had come to study permanently. I was transferred to another location, a student dormitory, where students from all countries waited for their interview with the university committee.

I spent over five months in a dormitory with prospective students from Russia, Iraq, Azerbaijan, Turkey, Africa, the UK, and the USA. The room I was placed in included six other students waiting their turn, with the entire building holding over 50 other students. It was not a pleasant time. Many had applied to study in this university simply because there was no other option for them in life. They had either come from war-torn countries, or fled their families. Some were converts to Islam. Fights would break out between them, and some students were extremely violent. Some of those who were calm during the day annoyed me with their loud snoring during the night. There was a clear clash of too many cultures and traditions within one building. One student would purposely burp very loudly to show his appreciation of the food, while another would pass wind, as in his culture it was very similar to sneezing. I couldn't wait to be transferred to the university dormitories where I heard that the conditions were a lot more livable and amicable.

I returned one day to the dorm to find my locker had been broken into, and an amount of $20 had been stolen from me. I maintained my calmness and reported it to the administration. A week later, I was transferred to Al-Mahdi Institute, where students entering the Islamic seminary are required to reach a level of fluency in the Farsi language. I had imagined I would be transferred directly to an Arabic university because of my Arabic background, but I was required to perfect my Farsi language first. By now it was nearly 2008.

Al-Mahdi Institute can be safely described as an ideological training base, operated by retired members of the Iranian intelligence services. It consists of three floors and an underground level. The rooms in the underground level and first floor are used as classrooms and a large mosque, while the remaining floors are utilized as dormitories.

Al - Mahdi School, in Qom, Iran.

Although its job is to teach Farsi to students so that they can understand Islamic texts, and more importantly the speeches of the supreme leader Ali Khamenei, it also monitors and investigates foreign students as they are completing their extensive Farsi course.

For me, this appeared to be a make-or-break situation. This institute was nothing like what was described to us. The bed bases were hard wooden boards, and all of the students slept on bunk beds. The common showers were semi-operational and in the worst condition possible. Cockroaches and other insects climbed up and down the walls in the showers and toilets. Mice infested the building, the food was military-style, soaked in what Persians call "kafoor" (camphor in English), an ingredient added to food in the army to lower men's sexual drive.

The most difficult part of Al-Mahdi was the fact that our room contained 12 students, all varying in age and culture. Some were not genuine students. They were convicted criminals who had escaped their countries and sought refuge within the Islamic seminary, and were prepared to engage in its educational system only for the sake of shelter and food. There were no washing machines in this institute, and most students could not afford to wash their own clothes or blankets in commercial laundromats, and therefore would wash them in the showers and hang them on the balcony rails. I, on the other hand, came from a more affluent life in Australia, and I began to wonder whether I could stay in this institute much longer. With the growing political tensions around Iran, several students were arrested after being revealed to be spies. They had infiltrated the Islamic seminary in Iran to report back to their home countries about their own citizens being groomed as Islamic missionaries.

Al - Mahdi School, in Qom, Iran.

During my first week, I struggled to live and sleep comfortably. I found that having so many students and cultures in one room did not prove to be a very successful idea. Here too, the students burped and passed wind as contentedly as they would sneeze, while others would try on my western clothing without my permission for the purpose of mere photography. By the end of my first week, and on Friday which is the only weekend day in Iran, I woke up to the loud sound of sheep bleating. I thought that I was dreaming, but unfortunately I was not. I raced outside my dorm to find out what the chaos was all about, but I was too late. Three sheep were already slaughtered in the middle of the school courtyard, with their blood gushing on the ground. The school was preparing for a feast.

I contacted my father and informed him of the harsh living conditions in this institute, which sadly was the only pathway to any accredited Islamic university in Qum. My dreams were being shattered as the days passed. I became stressed. I had come a long way and expected some hardship, but it seemed to me that the administration had purposely allowed such an atmosphere to dominate the institute in order to create missionaries who would be able to endure all conditions of life, regardless of where they are sent to preach. My father told me that the matter was purely my own decision, and I was welcome to return to Australia at any time.

One evening during this difficult time, I decided to go for a long walk alone. My heart was full of love for the Iranian government, specifically its supreme leader Ali Khamenei and its former leader Khomeini. I was ready to sacrifice my life for the Iranian regime and I believed that, although it would be tough, six months of patience in the institute would be worth it, since what I would achieve through the course would outweigh the struggle. Therefore, I made the decision to stay and pursue my Islamic studies. While my family and relatives back home in Australia thought I would not last long in Iran under such conditions, they seemed impressed with my patience and determination as the years passed.

I managed to get along with everyone else by finding a common ground, this being that we were all amateur Islamists who subscribed to an extremist ideology. We all loved Hizbullah, and were prepared to join them at all costs. We detested the USA and cursed it daily along with Israel and the UK. The ideology of the Iranian regime was simply part of my religion, to the point that we would twist the religion to benefit the Iranian regime. My father did not raise me as a radical, but my community, friends, surroundings, and teachers did. I never knew that I was a believer in an extremist ideology, because I simply thought that was the only way to be. This ideology had become normality for me in Iran, and we were all taught to become soldiers of religion, who would return to our countries, in my case Australia, and preach Islam – the hardline Iranian revolutionary type of Islam. I also came across other students from Australia and elsewhere in the West, which made life a lot easier.

Our Farsi language classes in Al-Mahdi Institute began at 8 am and paused at 12 for noon prayers and lunch, then continued from 3 pm to 5 pm. The entire curriculum focused on indoctrinating the students and teaching us material that presented the Iranian regime as God's righteous government on this planet; however, it was presented in Farsi. They were hitting two birds with one stone by teaching us the language and the history, merits, supposed achievements, miracles, and glory of the Islamic government of Iran.

The Islamic lectures, school, and mosque programs I had attended in Australia had preached a much more basic version of this indoctrination, so the path was already paved for my brain to be controlled by the regime-dominated educational atmosphere. I was completely radicalized, and willing to kill anyone who spoke a single word against Ali Khamenei, whom I saw as the link between myself and God. Even as a new student, I was expected to wear military-style cargo pants to look like one of the Islamic revolutionary guards. Although it was never official, the Iranian intelligence authorities enjoyed seeing foreign students adapt to their traditions and allowed it to continue. In other countries, an individual would be immediately questioned and possibly even arrested for dressing like the police or military personnel.

The Farsi Course was rather easy for me to complete, as I was born in Iran and was familiar with the language. Farsi consists of at least 50% Arabic, which made it even easier for me to master, as Arabic is my mother tongue.

The entire educational program in Al-Mahdi is designed to last for six months; however, it took us over two years to complete the program. There are many holidays in Iran. Iranians celebrate the births of 12 divine successors of Prophet Mohammad with a three-day weekend, and the martyrdom of 11 of them with longer weekends. The Prophet and his daughter Fatima's births and deaths are also commemorated with week-long holidays. The three holy months of Ramadhan, Muharram, and Safar, which usually fall around May, October, and December, are long holidays.*The Iranians themselves have their own national weekends when they celebrate the Persian Nowruz festival for two weeks, and other days marking the country's

* The dates of Ramadhan move every year as it is based on the Islamic lunar calendar, which is shorter than a solar year.

1979 revolution and war victories. They also took us on excursions to other Iranian states to introduce us to their culture, food, and religious cities.

Thursday nights are sacred nights, and English-speaking students at the institute would all gather to recite their prayers. When I was invited to attend this event for the first time, I saw Sheikh Mansour Leghaei, the former Sydney-based cleric who had just been deported from Australia. Even though I had never met him before, he hugged me very hard once he heard that I was from Australia, and wanted to get to know me better. He began to criticize and curse the Australian government for deporting him. Two months later, I bumped into him on the street. He greeted me and pointed to a government building and said, "These people know me. If you need anything just come here." I later discovered that the building he pointed to was an office for the Iranian intelligence services. I never saw Mr. Leghaei again, and today he prides himself on being one of my most ruthless critics.

I began to change drastically while studying at Al-Mahdi. Many things occurred before my very eyes during the first few months of my studies that proved to me that the Iranian regime was indeed a corrupt system. Female students, while segregated in female-only institutes, were regularly sexually assaulted by Islamic clerics, and administrators of the educational institutes who had access to students' portfolios preyed on them by accessing their details to find out whether a female student was single, divorced, or married.

Female students during an excursion to Al-Mahdi School.

On the third floor of the Al-Mahdi Institute, which I studied and resided in, elderly Islamic studies students from India and Pakistan would engage in sexual activities in the empty dorms with young male Azerbaijani students. One of these young men, who has now developed into a prominent scholar in Azerbaijan, was referred to as "Motorbike," because "he would give anyone a ride" when most teachers and students were worshipping in the lower ground floor mosque. The piety of the students was judged based on their loyalty to the regime and its supreme leader Ali Khamenei, and not by good actions. I realized that if you were a proud and outspoken patriot who reported to the intelligence agencies about other students, you could get away with literally anything.

The male teachers in this institute also preyed on younger male students. I remember asking one of my teachers, Mr. Behbehani, for the Wi-Fi password and he responded saying, "Open it so that I can give it to you." When I gave him a death stare, he said, "Open your Wi-Fi on your phone so that I can give you the password." He was exposing his vulgar nature indeed, as he was in fact referring to his desire to sexually assault me.

One of the disgraceful incidents that has been buried and is never mentioned within Al-Mahdi Institute involved one of my former friends, Mohammad, aged 27, from Nepal. He had spent at least five years studying a 6–12-month Farsi and Islamic Studies program at Al-Mahdi due to him being tongue-tied from birth. He needed extra time to improve his pronunciation of the language. During this time, he got to know a young girl aged 16, who was the daughter of a religious martyr killed during a visit to Iraq. Mohammad was dark skinned, dressed like an American rapper with baggy jeans and extra-large shirts, and also spoke English. Regardless of his difficulty in speech, he did attract the eyes of many Iranian women who admired westerners, especially those who had the "American style." Mohammad ended up impregnating the 16-year-old girl in 2008, and was instantly expelled from Al-Mahdi Institute and deported back to Nepal, not as a form of punishment, but to remove him from the scene of the investigation and lessen the level of shame that was about to shower upon the institute. The institute then entered into a financial arrangement with the girl's parents and settled the case with 40,000,000 Iranian rials, less than $15,000 USD, considering the Iranian economic situation. Her parents agreed not to approach the media regarding this incident as it would bring shame to the religion. But Mohammad was not happy that he was deported, so he wrote a letter to the Iranian President Mahmud Ahmadinejad, asking him to intervene and allow him back into Iran to complete his Islamic studies. Months later, Mohammad was back in Iran from Nepal and continued his studies as though none of this ever happened.

With all of this corruption taking place before me, a struggle remained within me to accept it as normality, both religiously and culturally. Therefore, I began to justify everything I saw although I knew deep down that it was wrong – according to my Australian upbringing, of course. However, I was in Iran, and on my way to becoming an Islamic scholar; therefore, I put my Australian values aside, not willingly, but because I had been brainwashed to.

My Encounter with Iran's Supreme Leader

In October 2010, Ali Khamenei visited the Iranian Holy City of Qum for the first time in ten years. At the time, I was studying at Al-Mahdi Institute. I was infatuated with Khamenei and his "aura"; I was a follower of his teachings and loved his existence. I was approached by the dean of students at the time, and was asked to meet with a cleric in the Imam Khomeini University, located in front of the main "Jihad Roundabout" in Bajak, the Holy City of Qum. I attended the university and met with the cleric who was the main motivational speaker of the Iranian Sepah, also known as the Islamic Revolutionary Guard Corps. He invited me to attend a gathering in the Holy Shrine of Qum, where the supreme leader Ali Khamenei would be delivering a speech to scholars and students of the Islamic seminary. The plan was to take a student from every country, and I was chosen to represent the students from Australia.

I attended the event, with around 500 other people from Iran and abroad. The Quran was recited as we all waited patiently for Khamenei to deliver his short speech. When refreshments were served, I was seated exactly thirty-three seats away from Khamenei himself. I counted the seats as I was enamored by his character and personality. When the event had finished, I inquired how I would be able to get in touch with Khamenei himself. My former Iranian-American friend, Mr. Bagheri, assisted me in writing a letter to Khamenei, as I had not yet mastered the Farsi language. The lines of my letter were filled with praise and respect towards him and his status as leader. I took the opportunity to introduce myself and my humble projects and activities. At the bottom of the letter, I included my contact details and the names of eminent ayatollahs who could verify the content of the letter. I handed the sealed letter to the brother of the late Ayatollah Ahmadi Faqih, and requested that he hand it to Khamenei in the upcoming Friday prayers, as they travelled from Qum to Tehran to attend the Friday sermon each week.

A month later, I received a call from Khamenei's office in Qum. The caller greeted me and requested that I visited the office located in

Safa'iyeh Street, and that it was with regards to the letter that I had written. After my classes had ended for the day, I raced to the office of Khamenei to see what the response was. Eagerly waiting, I was sent to an office located in the underground level, where I saw a humble and elderly man waiting for me in his office. I introduced myself, and he opened the safe and reached for an envelope. He told me to take the envelope to the Islamic bank located on the same street, in front of the office of Ayatollah Makarem. Although I did not request money in my letter, I accepted it as a blessing from my then "spiritual leader". When I reached the Islamic bank, I handed the document that was in the envelope over to the female bank teller. Noticing that I was a foreigner, she asked me if I had come with a vehicle. I answered no, I came on foot. She advised me to hire a taxi as I should not be carrying this amount of money on my person in public. I did not know how much the amount was, but I began to feel that Khamenei, or his office, wanted to gift me a large amount of cash. The bank teller took a cloth bag and began to fill it with stacks of money. After the transaction was completed, Khamenei's office had gifted me an amount equal to $10,000 USD.

It was the first time I had received such a large amount of money. I purchased comfortable sleeping mattresses for myself and eight of my friends in the dorm. I gifted $2000 to a struggling teacher of mine who was getting married the following week, and purchased myself a rather large library of Islamic books which I have today. I kept around $5000 in my bank account for security, and used the remainder of the money to receive heart check-ups, as I was born with ventricular septal defect (VSD), a hole in the septum between my heart's two lower chambers, and dental treatment as I was coping with painkillers because visiting a dentist is quite expensive in Iran. Down the track, the Iranian intelligence services froze my bank account at Tejarat Bank and took the remaining $5000 – another matter to be mentioned in the coming pages.

My De-Radicalization and its Costs

My de-radicalization process began in a very unusual way and in two stages. First, I distanced myself from the Iranian regime and Hezbollah's affiliates, but I was still a fundamentalist Islamist. The second stage was liberating my mind from fundamentalist ideas. The first stage happened in early 2010 and continued until 2012, and was similar to switching support for political parties, but the second stage was extremely difficult as it was a period of gradual, slow, and quiet change; a process that I had to undergo alone over a period of two years.

When I was a fundamentalist among members of the Iranian regime, I did not engage in any research to verify whether the information I was being taught was true or not, simply because I believed it to all be true as it was presented to us with a religious and divine coating.

Myself in a private meeting with Hassan Khomeini, Grandson of Imam Khomeini.

My drift away from the Iranian regime began with an unforeseen meeting that was about to change my entire life. In an ancient market called Guzar Khan, in Qum, Iran, I heard the sound of a eulogy that was very attractive to my ears. I walked towards the sound to discover that it was a cassette being played in one of the stores that sold CDs and cassettes. I inquired about the reciter of the eulogy. The shop owner told me that the reciter was his friend, and that he was going to meet him for dinner that day. After I had told him that I had come from Australia, he invited me to join them for dinner and to meet the reciter of the eulogy. The reciter was and still is a very prominent reciter, but I shall conceal his name for his own protection.

Bazar of Gozar Khan, Qom Iran. Picture: Fars News.

I attended their dinner gathering in an Islamic center. I met the reciter, and found him to be very humble, welcoming, and charismatic. He was in his mid-20s at the time, and very mature for his age. As we began to speak, he inquired about my presence in Iran. After I informed him that I was a student at Al-Mahdi Institute and that I was a follower of the Supreme Leader of Iran, Ali Khamenei, his eyes and cheeks turned red. The entire room went silent, and it remained silent for at least another two minutes while we all continued eating dinner.

I did not understand exactly what had happened at the time, but I knew that it had something to do with what I had said. A man named

Haider, who now resides in Sydney, broke the silence by saying, "You follow Khamenei? I will rip Khamenei's mother in half!" I was shocked, stunned, baffled and knew that I had come to the wrong place. I didn't know these people and never imagined an opposition to the Iranian regime even existed. But I knew they were the bad guys, and I quickly finished my dinner and left the building. I walked back to my dormitory very slowly, pondering and reflecting on what had just happened. The reciter, a highly respected eulogist amongst scholars, had just remained silent as Ali Khamenei, the highest Islamic authority within both the country and the faith, was rudely insulted. This raised a question within me: Why did they hate Iran's Supreme Leader so much?

The next day, and out of curiosity, I returned to the center. I acted as though the day before had never happened. This time I was not here to make friends; I was here to analyze this strange community of highly religious individuals, some even descendants of Prophet Mohammad himself. I noticed that most of the people attending this massive Islamic event had family members who were imprisoned and/or had been executed. I became curious to find out exactly why. I asked the reciter whom I had gotten to know the night before about a portrait of a man on the wall. He told me that the portrait was of "Grand Ayatollah Sadiq Shirazi," and it was the first time I had heard this name. I said, "May he rest in peace." The eulogist responded, "No, he's alive. Have you not met him yet!?"

I thought to myself, a "grand ayatollah" would rank like the pope in the Catholic Church, so how does this eulogist expect me to have met him? I responded, "No, I haven't." He said, "Would you like to meet him tomorrow?" I said, "Yes, sure." We set a place and time, and he took my mobile number. He called me the next morning and asked where I was. I said, "I am at Al-Mahdi school." He said, "Come to such and such a location carefully, and make sure the sons of b*****s don't follow you here, because they will f***k you if they find out you came here."

I got dressed quickly, and although I felt deeply that I should not be going, I trusted that my Australian citizenship would protect me if anything should happen. After all, I was just visiting a Muslim scholar in an Islamic country with an Islamic government. I was taken to the office of the Grand Ayatollah Sadiq Shirazi, where it was difficult to move around because of the large number of people who flooded his office. Hundreds upon hundreds were lined up to kiss the hand of one man, Sadiq Shirazi. I asked myself, who is this man that attracts so many people each day? And why does his office have no sign on it? And why is everyone here against the regime?

A massive chapter within the current situation of Shia Islam and my faith was missing for me, and I was just about to discover it. It was almost my turn to enter the room in which Grand Ayatollah Sadiq Shirazi was sitting. I entered the room and saw a man in his 60s, white bearded and calm. He smiled peacefully at whoever entered the room and raised his right hand to greet them from where he sat. I approached him and kissed his hand – because that is what everyone else was doing, and I didn't want to stand out as being disrespectful in any manner. I had never met a grand ayatollah before. I was not going to make independent decisions either at that time, so I was happy to be guided. The grand ayatollah pointed at me and invited me to sit beside him. I didn't know why. Perhaps it was because I was dressed somewhat differently so he wanted to hear from me, or perhaps he thought I had travelled a long way just to see him and wanted to give me the opportunity to meet him. He welcomed me and said, "Thank you for visiting me. What's your name?" I replied, "Mohammad." He asked, "Where are you from?" I replied, "Australia, but I was born in Iran." He continued, "When are you going back to Australia?" I said I had no plans yet because I was still studying here. He enquired, "Oh, you're a student here?" I answered, "Yes, I study at Al-Mahdi and will soon be transferred to study in an Islamic university here." He responded by saying, "May God bless you. My prayers are with you." He then gestured to his assistant and whispered in his ear. He bid me goodbye, and as I walked out, his assistant gave me an envelope with a gift – money, around $10, as a form of support to foreign students because many students were struggling financially. I took the gift, thanked his assistant and walked outside. The reciter saw me exiting the room and said, "How was the meeting?" I said, "It was very moving and special, but I have to get back to the school as they will become suspicious of me." He said, "It's prayer time now, so they will assume you have gone to pray your noon prayers outside at the sacred shrines. Why don't we offer our prayers in the mosque nearby and I will introduce you to the grand ayatollah's son, Hussain?" I agreed. After prayers, his son Hussain welcomed me, and asked me what my name was. I answered, "Mohammad." He said, "Mohammad what?" I replied, "Tawhidi." He said, "That is a beautiful name." After informing him that I was an international student, he praised my efforts to migrate to a Third World country in order to acquire religious knowledge.

Back at the dormitory, I innocently informed my teacher and roommates that I had visited Grand Ayatollah Shirazi. Their reaction can never be put into words, but the closest thing to describe their reaction would be that it was a shock that turned them into my vicious enemies. From that day onwards, life in Iran was never the same. The entire school was warned about me, and my friends stopped talking to me. I returned the next day to my dorm to find my cupboard broken into and my laptop stolen. Although I reported it to the dean of students and the principal, I discovered later that the school had planned to break into my cupboard to search for books, CDs, or photos of Shirazi. I didn't know what to do, so I contacted my father for advice. My father scoffed and said, "Mohammad, by visiting Sadiq Shirazi you have just visited their number one enemy."

I tried really hard to prove my loyalty to the Iranian regime. I began to wear shirts with the image of Ali Khamenei printed on them. I did everything I could think of, but that was it for me. They treated me as though I had a relationship with Satan himself. I was completely outcast. But the matter didn't end there; it escalated to bullying. They tried to make me flee the country by bullying me. The dean of students, Mr. Sanjary, would instruct senior students to pressure me to return to Australia voluntarily. The senior students would follow me wherever I went, and if I stopped they would bully me by pushing and shoving me with all their strength, causing me to fall. They would light cigarettes and throw them down the back of my shirt, and would drive beside me with their motorbikes and pull my shirt, slamming me to the ground in public. They stole my money, laptop, and phone and left me with basically nothing.

The school also began to pressure me. So, I went to the office of the supreme leader Ali Khamenei and complained to his representative. I began to cry in his presence and requested that he put an end to all of this. He understood the "mistake" I had made by visiting Sadiq Shirazi, and informed me that he would order them to put an end to the bullying, which he did in fact do and I continued with my studies normally. However, although the school's administration had stopped bullying me, the students didn't. They beat me up in the streets and accused me of being a traitor.

Even after the intercession of the representative of Iran's Supreme Leader, the dean of students, Mr. Sanjary, was still uncomfortable with my presence for no apparent reason. Knowing he was a member of the Iranian intelligence services, I had to take calculated measures to protect myself. Therefore, I followed a student he was close to, Amir, and whom he had appointed as a student captain. I personally filmed Amir engaging in indecent behaviour in public, and kept the video recording to myself. I then heard rumors from other students that Chinese students were engaging in homosexual activities in the showers. So, I hung a pair of my jeans in one of the shower rooms, and placed a recorder in its pocket. I managed to obtain an audio file of their entire session. Less than a week later, Mr. Sanjary called me to his office and accused me of a very serious crime. He gave me two options, to leave Iran or to face prison in the morning. He had organized students to falsely testify against me. I knew I was innocent, and I had already envisaged that something like this would occur.

I returned to him with the audio file of the Chinese students and the video of Amir. I said to him, "If you don't leave me alone, copies of this will be distributed to the Greens Party [the Iranian opposition]. I am almost finished with my Farsi language course, and if you try to harm me in any way, you will regret it." Mr. Sanjary understood that I was ten steps ahead of him, and I made him suspect that I had more cards up my sleeve. If news was to surface that there were homosexual activities in Iran's Islamic institutes or that its head students were engaging in indecent practices in public, it would be on the front pages of every opposition newspaper and magazine. I was forced to do this for my own protection, as I wasn't prepared to be imprisoned or expelled over false accusations.

Mr. Sanjary then sent an Afghan-Australian student from Sydney, Australia, to corner me and make me promise that I would never visit Sadiq Shirazi again. I did so out of fear. However, he still physically abused me whenever he could, and would keep an eye on my movements. One day in winter, he saw me going into the showers, and decided to bring the hose (which the cleaners used to wash the floor of the showers) and pour cold water on me from over the shower door.

I continued to remain patient and successfully completed the entire Farsi language course at Al-Mahdi Institute, and thus received my certificate.

To speed my transition from the school, the dean of students invited me to his office. He said, "You speak Arabic well, there is no need for you to continue on to the 'Basics of Islam' course. You can go straight to an Arabic university that will accept you." I applied to Aalul-Bayt University, and was accepted immediately. I finally felt free. This was going to be a new beginning for me at an actual university with a professional study atmosphere. I moved to the dormitory of the university, and I felt much more comfortable there. There was more freedom in this university, and therefore I began to visit Ayatollah Shirazi more frequently, but discretely. Interestingly, I began to notice other students from my university at his office as well. But I was skeptical as they might have been spies for the university's administration, which was in fact the case. I was called into the university's office within the first month and questioned about my visits to Sadiq Shirazi's office. I informed them that I visited all of the grand ayatollahs out of interest. They were much more lenient than Al-Mahdi's officials, but they requested that I no longer visit this particular ayatollah as "he is a deviant man."

My research into Sadiq Shirazi showed that he is a descendent of

Prophet Mohammad, and comes from a lineage of Islamic leaders dating back at least 100 years. His brother, Mohammad Shirazi, was a staunch opponent of Khomeini and rebelled against him after he executed nearly 5000 people without trial. That was the day that the Shirazi family began to rebel against the Iranian government, because they do not believe in mixing politics with religion. Therefore, they do not recognize the religious authority of Ali Khamenei who is considered to be a politician rather than a scholar, which was and still is the case. However, it bewildered me that an ideological disagreement could lead to such waves of hatred between individuals of the same denomination and school of thought, particularly because they had once been good friends. I later discovered that Sadiq Shirazi was actually under house arrest, and not allowed to leave his house. Despite this, he visits sacred shrines that are close to his home.

I developed friendships with members of the Shirazi Institute and engaged in advanced theological lessons there during the evenings. When I mentioned Shirazi at the university, everyone around me cursed him, but when I mentioned Ali Khamenei at the Shirazi office, they all wished him guidance. This said a lot about the two sides.

I began to analyze what I was being taught by both schools of thought, the Shirazi Institute and the regime's university, and to figure out what their motives were. It became clear to me that the universities were nothing more than institutes to groom missionaries to spread the ideology of the Iranian regime, while the Shirazi office was spreading true Islam without any politics or agendas involved. I ideologically switched sides and became a follower of Sadiq Shirazi. The majority of Iranian Muslims who oppose the tyrannical dictatorship are followers of Shirazi. The Shirazi school of thought within Shia Islam can be described as a non-political school that is open to other religions and nations. They have a large presence in the West and do not have an agenda to spread violent Sharia Law or take over countries. They also believe in Islamic laws, such as polygamy and child brides for instance, but they are not uniquely Shirazi beliefs; they are basic Islamic beliefs. Nevertheless, it is also a reality that a conservative Islamic authority cannot possibly be an Islamic authority without believing in the permissibility of these matters.

While studying for my Bachelor's degree, I began to introduce more western students to Shirazi as an alternative option, and in a short time I created a group of students who opposed the ideology of the Islamic government of Iran. One night, I led a delegation of thirty students to Shirazi's office and, because we returned late to the dorms, the security guard became suspicious of us, and me in particular. Therefore, the school appointed a Nigerian student to monitor me within the dorms. His name was Harun, and his room was next to mine. He would follow my movements and even record my conversations. I obviously knew this was happening, but it didn't matter to me as by now I was convinced that the Iranian regime was a tyrannical regime. I became a well-known opponent of the Iranian regime and disagreed on political matters with my teachers in the classrooms. I had a group of students, around fifty, who supported my ideas. The university administration was now alarmed that I was de-radicalizing students, or what they considered to be reversing their brainwashing of the students. Because I am an Australian citizen, it was extremely difficult for them to treat me like they would treat a regular Iraqi or Iranian student, even though I was born in Iran.

One morning, I received a call to attend the principal's office. As soon as I walked in, he said, "Mr. Tawhidi, pack your bags and go back to your country!" I replied, "Sure," and walked away to do exactly that. The principal expected me to beg him not to send me back to Australia, but I knew deep inside that he knew making me return to Australia would be a foolish decision on his behalf. The principal then sought advice from a Lebanese-Australian student who had come from Sydney to study in the same university, and who was loyal to the regime. His name was Hamza, and he told the principal, "The university should not expel Mohammad Tawhidi. His father is a senior cleric in Australia and it could tarnish the image of the Islamic seminary and anger other scholars who will no longer send you students from abroad." Until today, I have no idea why Hamza did me such a favor, but it was kind of him. The university then took measures to intimidate me into silence. In the span of one week, they expelled seven of my close associates who were from Canada, the United States, and the United Kingdom.

One of my Danish friends, out of frustration, pulled down and stepped on the portrait of Imam Khomeini, the founder and leader of the Iranian regime. He then went into hiding in Iran, as other students from America, the UK, and Australia began to search for him, promising to break the leg he used to insult the portrait. He contacted me seeking assistance, and I managed to smuggle him out of Qum to Mashhad, where he took a car and left the country for Iraq. He now lives in New York, allegedly as an ex-Muslim.

The university contacted me one Saturday morning and requested a meeting with me in the evening. I knew this was going to be a set up, so I contacted my family in Perth, Western Australia and told them that if they didn't hear from me by the end of the following week, they should report to the Australian authorities that I had been detained by the Iranian regime. However, I did not go to the meeting on Saturday, and waited until Monday arrived because the Australian Embassy was closed. I took a taxi to the Australian Embassy in Tehran and met with Australian Ambassador Marc Innes-Brown. I informed him and his first secretary, Mark Betts, of my current situation. He responded to me saying, "We can't help you, really. You need to not get yourself into trouble." I didn't expect much from the ambassador, but I had to try to notify Australia.

Two days later, on Wednesday morning, I approached the university principal, Shaikh Bakshi, and apologized for not being able to make it on Saturday. The university principal told me that I would receive a call soon. My phone rang at around 1 pm and an Iranian intelligence officer requested that I attend a certain location with my Australian passport. The location was Setad-e Khabari, Rah Ahan, in Qum. It was a building beside the city's railway station with a long, white sliding door made out of metal. I didn't know that the call was from the Iranian intelligence services, but I discovered this when I approached the building. I honestly thought it was an external university department. I knocked on the glass window, and a receptionist opened the window. I informed him that I had been asked to come here. He looked through the names then looked back at me and said, "You were supposed to come on Saturday. Why didn't you come?" I apologized and said that I couldn't make it. He responded saying, "Listen, you donkey skull, when we tell you to attend, you attend on the day we tell you to. You don't attend on the day you wish to." He then opened the door and I entered. I had to hand over my cell phone and passport, and enter an interrogation room. The room had plenty of bright sunlight and two doors. The first door led to the reception area, while the second door was where the interrogators entered. The receptionist followed me into the room and told me to sit down on the couch. It was yellow, and very comfortable. He turned the heating on and locked the door as he walked out. I remained seated for around 45 minutes. I began to sweat excessively and realized that this was one of their tactics to intimidate and pressure me. But I remained calm and didn't show any sign of worry. I looked at the ground and showed no sign of fear or discomfort, although inside I was eager to know what their plans were. Suddenly, I heard a voice I was familiar with, and I turned my head towards the window to see that a famous lecturer, also a follower of Shirazi, had just finished being interrogated and was being released. This made me burst out with laughter because this very lecturer used to warn me about the intelligence services, so seeing him being released seemed hilarious at the time. Before I had finished laughing, the second door opened and an intelligence officer walked in. He was bald, short, and had dark bags under his eyes. He wore a suit with no tie, and his very yellow teeth stood out to me. He sat in front of me with my passport in his hand and without greeting me he began to say, "Your name is Mohammad Tawhidi, and you're an Australian citizen studying here, correct?" I said, "Yes, that is correct." He said, "What is your nationality?" I said, "Australian." He said, "No, I mean your country of origin." I said, "Australia." He said, "You're speaking to me in Farsi with an accent. Then what is your background?" I said to him, "The passport you are holding is an Australian passport and it states that my nationality is Australian. Therefore, I am to be treated as an Australian, not as an

Iranian-born person." He asked, "Where were you on Monday?" I now knew that I had been followed to the embassy, or that the Iranian guard standing outside the embassy had snapped images of me and reported my visit to the ambassador. I said, "I was in Tehran." He said, "And where did you go within Tehran?" I said, "I visited the Australian Ambassador." While tapping his pen on his other hand, he said, "And what did you and the ambassador discuss?" I said, "We discussed the beauty of Iran and its amazing government." He said, "Do I look like an idiot? I am also a cleric. You went to the Australian Embassy to do what?" I said, "To drink Australian coffee."

During this time, the receptionist brought tea for both of us. The interrogator demanded that I drank my tea before it got cold. I said that I was fasting, although I really wasn't. I said this simply because I was worried they might poison me. He said, "Well you're going to be here for a while so I suggest you break your fast." I said, "I am a lecturer and I can speak for long hours without drinking fluids. I will manage."

He then asked, "Why do you attack the Iranian regime on Facebook?" I said, "My Facebook page was hacked. They weren't my words." He said, "Why do you visit Shirazi? He is an opponent of the holy and sacred Islamic regime!" I said, "I am sorry, I never knew this." He then said, "You will need to sign this paper." I read the paper; it said, "I, Mohammad Tawhidi, will never enter the house of Sadiq Shirazi ever again."

I took his pen and wrote beneath it, "I, Mohammad Tawhidi, will go wherever I like and visit whomever I like." And I signed it. After reading what I wrote, he said, "For our department, clashing with you is as simple as drinking tea." When he directed this threat at me, I responded saying, "Sometimes tea can burn your throat on the way down." The interrogator then reminded me of the financial gift I had received from Iran's supreme leader, and questioned whether my opposition to his regime was a form of thank you.

Even though I was worried about their plans for me on that day, I wasn't going to show them that I was afraid. He threw the paper at me and said, "Sign it now." So, I eventually did. He got up and said, "Wait here." He went inside and returned after approximately 30 minutes. He

said, "Here's your passport. You may leave through the front door."
He made copies of my passport, and I was banned from leaving the
country until 2013. After this incident, I decided to put an end to my
preaching against the regime, and to focus solely on my studies.

Throughout the entire period of 2009–2012, I attended Islamic
lessons both at the Iranian regime's university and privately at the
Shirazi Institute. I was exploring the differences between the Iranian
regime and its opposition. My study schedule, other than the month of
Ramadhan, would reach 16 hours a day, and I achieved the status of a
Muslim scholar in three years. When I sat my final exam at the Shirazi
Institute, I passed it with a grade of 100%. In June 2010, Grand
Ayatollah Sadiq Shirazi ordained me as a scholar and crowned me as an
imam in a public event held at his home. I continued my studies within
the regime-run university as an ordained scholar, despite being advised
not to.

Grand Ayatollah Sayid Sadiq Shirazi ordaining me as a Muslim cleric/scholar.

Now that I was dressed as a Muslim scholar with my white Islamic turban, the students that were bullying me during my days at the Al-Mahdi Institute began to spread rumors that I was a "fake shaikh." This was not because I had not completed my studies, but because they considered the grand ayatollah who crowned and ordained me as an Islamic scholar an apostate. I also knew that my annual educational visa was about to expire, which meant that I would be forced to leave Iran. I kept a very low profile during this time, hoping that all of the political and religious tensions would calm down. Al-Mahdi Institute had issued my first student visa at the beginning of my studies there, and issued the second visa before I graduated and transferred to Aalul-Bayt University. The university renewed my student visa once again, and in order to guarantee myself another annual visa from Iran's Education Department and Immigration Ministry, I began to work for one of the regime's most notorious grand ayatollahs: Grand Ayatollah Makarem.

Despite all the tension between myself and the Islamic seminaries, I wasn't a noticeable figure. This meant that most high-ranking officials had not heard of me or my situation. I approached a well-known scholar who knew Makarem's son, Masoud, and asked him to endorse me in Makarem's office. I despised Makarem, but working for him meant that I had a strong backing in Iran and that I would be protected.

Grand Ayatollah Makarem's office assigned me as the Head of the English Department in 2011-2012. I was responsible for the translation, editing, and publication of Makarem's books and lessons, along with what was published on his website and social media accounts. I worked with two other colleagues, both named Mohammad, which made us three Mohammads. One day a caller to the department requested to speak with Mohammad, and all three of us went to the telephone at the same time.

Grand Ayatollah Makarem saw that I wasn't only a translator who translated from Arabic to English, but also a scholar who eloquently crafted the context of his works in English, as I understood the subject matter. Other translators would translate word for word without giving too much importance to the fluency or context of the subject. He was very impressed with the feedback he received from his English-speaking followers on my work. However, I never placed my name on any of the works published because my critics would surely pressure Makarem to fire me.

Myself preaching on Iran's National Broadcaster

My position in the office of Grand Ayatollah Makarem led me to becoming a regular guest on national television, preaching Sharia Law and presenting a series interpreting and explaining jurisprudential teachings in English, targeting Muslims in the West. Although many students knew that I was an opponent of the Iranian regime, the Iranian public didn't, and neither did Ayatollah Makarem's office. My previous preaching of Sharia Law on television presented me as a reasonable scholar, a fundamentalist fanatic, just as they desired.

The Iranian intelligence service does not generally pressure nor interrogate employees of ayatollahs affiliated with the regime, so I gathered that, because I worked for Makarem, the Iranian authorities assumed that I had changed my political views and preaching.

Makarem placed me on an extremely high salary compared to all of his other employees. I was possibly the second highest paid individual throughout his entire jurisdiction. I was receiving approximately $500 a fortnight, with gifts of $1000 on celebration days. Even though $500 a fortnight doesn't sound like a lot of money to those living in the West, it is a very large amount compared to the student allowance granted by the university, which equated to less than $30 a month. The following are a few electronic payment receipts sent to my email from the headquarters of Grand Ayatollah Makarem Shirazi.

Masoud Pirani

pirani@makarem.ir

Electronic receipts of my payments from the office of Grand Ayatollah Makarem.

کاربر گرامی، انتقال وجه بین بانکی (پایا) با مشخصات زیر:

مبلغ:	سه میلیون ریال ساعت کاری اسفند ماه 1390 + مانه التعاون ساعت کاری های گذشیه + 1.000.000 ریال عیدی
از حساب شماره:	۰۱۰۰۹۸۲۸۲۹۰۰۷
به نام:	مسعود پیرانی
به حساب شماره:	IRAV۰۱۸۰۰۰۰۰۰۰۰۰۵۲۹۰۳۷۱۹۸۹
به نام:	محمد توحیدی
نزد بانک:	بانک تجارت (کد) ۰۱۸

با موفقیت ثبت و عملیات کسر از حساب صورت پذیرفت ، همچنین دستور واریز به حساب مورد نظر شما برای بانک مقصد ارسال گردید. لازم به ذکر است. مدت زمان عملیات واریز به حساب به عملکرد سامانه پایاپای الکترونیکی (ACH) وابسته میباشد.

ضمنا، شناسه تراکنش انجام شده در "سیستم بانکداری اینترنتی" و در "سیستم متمرکز" به ترتیب به شرح زیر میباشد:

شماره پیگیری سیستم بانکداری اینترنتی: ۱۵۶۱۷ / ۱۰۰۶۰۱ ۲
شماره رسید سیستم متمرکز: ۹۰۱۲۳۸۰۱۹۲۵۶۱۹۸۱ / ۹۰۱۰۰۲۲۸۰۱۹۲۵۶۱۷
تاریخ و زمان: ۱۳:۰۳:۴۸ ، ۲۸/۱۲/۱۳۹۰

MP Masoud Pirani   ↩ Reply | ∨
Mon 26/12/2011 10:32 PM
You ∨

کاربر گرامی ، انتقال وجه درخواستی شما با مشخصات زیر:

مبلغ:	پنج میلیون و دویست هزار ریال
از حساب شماره:	۰۱۰۰۹۸۲۸۲۹۰۰۷
به نام:	مسعود پیرانی
به حساب شماره:	IRAV۰۱۸۰۰۰۰۰۰۰۰۰۵۲۹۰۳۷۱۹۸۹
به نام:	محمد توحیدی
نزد بانک:	بانک تجارت (کد) ۱۸
شناسه پرداخت:	
شرح تراکنش:	فاکتور ترجمه آذر ماه

با موفقیت ثبت و عملیات کسر از حساب صورت پذیرفت ، همچنین دستور واریز به حساب مورد نظر شما برای بانک مقصد ارسال گردید.لازم به ذکر است .مدت زمان عملیات واریز به حساب به عملکرد سیستم انتقال وجه بین بانکی (سانا) ولابسته میباشد...

ضمنا، شناسه تراکنش انجام شده در "سیستم بانکداری اینترنتی" و در "سیستم متمرکز" به ترتیب به شرح زیر میباشد:

شماره پیگیری سیستم بانکداری اینترنتی: ۱۵۲۲۳ / ۱۷۴۵۰۸
شماره رسید سیستم متمرکز: ۹۰۱۰۰۲۲۰۱۹۱۸۲۸۲۷۵
تاریخ و زمان: ۱۳:۲۰:۰۳ ، ۰۲/۱۰/۱۳۹۰

Electronic receipts of my payments from the office of Grand Ayatollah Makarem.

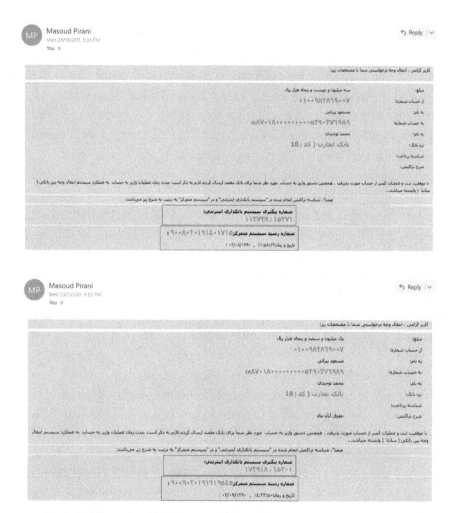

Electronic receipts of my payments from the office of Grand Ayatollah Makarem.

Ayatollah Makarem wanted to buy me as a person, and he saw me as a potential asset for his empire. I also used my salary to support other students within the university. This was one of the reasons why many began to accuse me of being funded by Israel, the UK, or the USA, because they saw me sponsoring other students without knowing where my income came from – and neither could I disclose it.

Imprisoned for Exposing a Scam Artist

Towards the end of 2012, I was presented with a lengthy English translation of Makarem's Farsi exegesis of the Quran. I was told to review it and prepare it for publication. I skimmed through the entire work and realized that something wasn't right. We had been scammed. Makarem's office had paid a translator over $6000 USD when all he did was copy the Farsi text into Google Translate and forward the English translation from Google. Every page included characters such as "(?)" which indicates that Google Translate didn't recognize or understand the Farsi word being used.

I was frustrated and demanded that the translator be brought in for questioning. After contacting him, we were told that he was visiting his home town in the USA, and that he would return in 20 days. When the dishonest translator returned to Qum, we called him in for a meeting and, lo and behold, it was a former friend of mine who had just been caught red handed, trying to scam his own Islamic authority whom he considers a "link between humanity and God." I shall refer to him as Mr. HW.

I looked at Mr. HW and said, "Nice job, buddy!" and he was astonished to see that I was in such a place holding such a position! He came to the meeting thinking he could convince a few Iranians with broken English that the translation was perfect, but to his surprise I had been examining his translated document for the previous 20 days. In an awkward meeting for him, I pointed out a few of the flaws within his translation both to him and his employers. Wishing to stop me from continuing, he claimed that seven other people had translated it with him and that he was not responsible for the entire translation. We demanded that he return the $6000 USD to the office, or that he correct the entire document.Mr. HW was and still is a cleric with close ties to people who are related to the Iranian intelligence services. Before I knew it, and a few days later, I was picked up from the street by four police officers as I left Makarem's office to go home.

I was thrown into a cell and, before the solider closed the door, I told him to not touch me. He opened the door and held me by my neck, then grabbed hold of my shirt and threw me against the wall, saying, "We made Montazari sit down. Who the hell are you?" Montazari was an opponent of the Islamic regime who was once the second in line to rule Iran after Khomeini. The guard then kicked me in my stomach with his right leg and slapped me very hard across my right eye with his left hand.

This time I was in a different intelligence headquarters, but the same interrogator came to interrogate me. It appeared to me that he was responsible for my case within the intelligence department. After having slept the night in the cell, I was told to wake up by the prison guard and prepare myself for breakfast. I was given a boiled potato. I peeled the skin off and ate the inside of the potato only, placing the potato skin on the crooked steel plate. The interrogator called me into the interrogation room at approximately 8 am. This time I sat on a chair and faced him while he sat on a couch, and no tea or water was offered. He began by asking me what I was doing in Makarem's office, and I informed him that I was working in the English Department. Up until this stage, I never knew why I was detained, but when he asked me what my job was exactly, I knew that Mr. HW was behind it.

I told the interrogator that my job was to translate from Arabic to English. He said, "No, you also work on Farsi to English." I denied this, and said that I only work on Arabic to English. Then he said, "You recently worked on a Farsi to English translation" – and this was when it clicked in my mind that Mr. HW had reported me to the intelligence services. I responded, "No, I never worked on this document or translated it. I was simply reviewing someone else's translation." He then began to show me documents containing screenshots of my Facebook posts, all containing Farsi translations in blue pen on the side of the paper. I was questioned about every Facebook post he could gather, and then asked why I even had a Facebook account, as Facebook is banned in Iran. My response was, "I saw that the grand Islamic authorities had Facebook accounts, therefore I thought it was legal to have one." This answer was convenient at the time. The circumstances all began to add up and point at Mr. HW.

Mr. HW was a Facebook friend of mine, my Facebook account was private, and out of my 30 friends on Facebook he was the only one who was in Iran, knew Farsi and would be able to translate it in such a way. Also, the content I was being questioned about went against the conservative Islamic values of the Iranian regime which Mr. HW stood for. I wondered how all this happened so quickly after our meeting with Mr. HW, and how particular the interrogator was when questioning me in regard to the translation from Farsi to English. Mr. HW's work was the first and only Farsi–English work I had laid a hand on in Makarem's office. Therefore, I was now certain it was Mr. HW who sent the intelligence services to detain me.

After the interrogation, I was sent back to my cell, which contained only an iron bed with a torn and stained mattress, a toilet and a sink. I wasn't given any lunch, and when dinner time arrived, I began to call through the cell for the guard to bring me food as I was hungry. The guard came and said, "No food for you." I said, "Why?" He said, "Because you waste food." I said, "What do you mean by waste food? I ate the entire potato." He said, "No, you were supposed to eat the entire potato including its skin! This food is bought using the money of the Islamic government. This is the money of God which you are wasting." I turned my back towards him and sat on the bed. After 21 hours had passed, I was released. In Qum, Mr. HW tried to avoid me in every way possible, as he didn't think that I would be released so soon, or at all!

Mr. HW had fabricated a case against me of treason and plots against the Iranian regime, which could have constituted the offence of "rising against the government" – an offence punishable by death. Luckily in this case, the regime officials either forgot or did not realize that I was born in Iran, otherwise they could have granted me Iranian citizenship solely for the sake of imprisoning or hanging me. I was relieved that, due to my Australian citizenship, I was saved from such an ordeal. Years later, Mr. HW found himself unable to live in America because his Iranian wife was not able to gain residency in the US. Therefore, he relocated to Sydney, Australia.

After I had developed diplomatic and government relationships in Australia, I sent Mr. HW a message through another imam, informing him that I was going to inform the Australian Security Intelligence Organisation about Mr. HW and his close ties with the Iranian intelligence services, what he did to me, his close friendship with Hizbullah and his affiliation with Sheikh Mansour Leghaei. This sent an alarming message to Mr. HW as he never expected me to become the person I am today. He then sent me a message on Facebook requesting that I get in touch with him. I responded saying that I could only meet with him in person, but he never responded because he wasn't prepared to do so. Until today, Mr. HW has not even apologized to me for what he did, and neither will I be able to ever forgive him for the torture I endured, especially when he knew that I was innocent.

The university exams were two weeks away, and I decided to continue my studies as well as my work at Ayatollah Makarem's office. I extended my visa one more time, which gave me an extra year to live in Iran. I completed my exams, but the university refused to give me my certificates; they still lie in my student portfolio under the number 41145. Therefore, knowing that my visa was valid for another year, I decided to withdraw from the Al-Mustafa University. After all, it was merely an establishment set up to radicalize and jihadize Muslim men and groom them into being missionaries, and is not recognized as an educational institution by any reputable university outside of Iran. I saw it for what it really stood for and withdrew honorably. I demanded documents upon my withdrawal in order that none of the extremist supporters of the Iranian regime could accuse me in the future of being expelled by either Al-Mahdi Institute or Aalul-Bayt University, which were both administered by Al Mustafa International University.

My Final Year in Iran

After withdrawing from the regime-run university by the end of 2012, I found myself free, and with a visa ending in December 2013. I resigned from the office of Grand Ayatollah Makarem after informing them of what Mr. HW had done to me, and my disappointment that they were not prepared to question the intelligence services about why this had happened. I no longer subscribed to the faith taught by the Iranian

regime and its Islamic universities, and I found myself unable to co-
exist with groups that supported the Iranian regime, even though they
dominated the entire city. As a matter of fact, many casual students in
Al-Mustafa University were and still are actual Hizbullah militants.

Without a place to turn to, or a dormitory to reside in, I found
myself homeless. I could not inform my immediate family of my
situation as they would be deeply worried, and I did not want to leave
Iran either. Therefore, I began to eat what I could afford until I was
completely broke. I began to visit mosques and Islamic centers that
offered meals after their events, and would request to take more home.
I spent four months sleeping on cardboard in the vicinity of the Holy
Shrine in Qum. Despite the fact that I was homeless, I maintained my
outer appearance and was very cautious to conceal my situation, as
supporters of the Iranian regime could take advantage of any sign of
weakness or instability. During this time, one Pakistani cleric, Shaikh
Ahmad, residing in Iran and who was also a friend of mine, knew of my
situation as I had told him. He also administrated an Islamic center and
would invite me regularly for meals and offer me other forms of
hospitality. One Saturday morning, Shaikh Ahmad informed me that
two men from Australia had come into his center looking for me, and
requested that I leave the area for my own safety.

Meanwhile, my friends at Shirazi's office had suspected something
was out of the ordinary with my situation because I had not visited
them nor Grand Ayatollah Shirazi for a considerable amount of time.
They initiated contact with me and inquired about how I was doing,
even though I had tried to avoid them. News had reached them that I
was in trouble, homeless, and broke. The office of Shirazi offered me a
private room within the dormitory of their educational institute and
supported me, modestly, in every way possible. Because Shirazi was
oppressed by the Iranian regime and under house arrest, he couldn't
provide me with a visa, but luckily, I had organized that already. I
remained in Iran and served Shirazi's office as a form of thank you.

By this time, I had made several public statements that supported an
enlightened brand of Islam. The clerics at Shirazi's office knew of my
intentions and, even though they were not on the same page as me,

they still welcomed me; after all, it was Shirazi who ordained me as an imam. I associated myself with Shirazi's office because, out of all of the ayatollahs, he was the most moderate and peaceful one.

During my final year in Iran, I began to develop healthy relationships with the offices of numerous grand ayatollahs and Islamic authorities, and acquired a large number of licenses and certifications from them after attending their advanced lessons. Now that I was not part of a government-run institute, nobody questioned my movements, and I was free to explore the scholarly works that were foundations of the Islamic faith. I kept my reformist agenda to myself, until I was in a strong position to express my opinions. Perhaps this explains why I did not accept the position of deputy to any grand ayatollahs or marry into their families.

Relocation to Iraq

By the end of 2013, I decided to relocate to Iraq and continue my advanced studies within its Islamic seminaries. I relocated to the Holy City of Karbala, and studied under the authority of its most prominent Islamic authorities between January 2014 and December 2015. Because I am also an Iraqi citizen, I did not require a visa to stay in Iraq. It was an open environment where students were not restricted by any government laws or policies. The two cities of Najaf and Karbala contain the leading Islamic seminaries within Shia Islam. However, Qum is and will always be viewed as a place for students to gain their basics in Islamic studies, unless of course they study independently and outside the boundaries of the curriculum of the Islamic universities.

At the beginning of 2014, I assisted in the founding of Imam Hussein TV 3 in the Holy City of Karbala, Iraq, and began to coordinate its research department and present television programs in English. Out of the two main schools of thought within Shia Islam in the twenty-first century, I began to promote the non-political school of Sadiq Shirazi over the tyrannical and terrorist Iranian regime of Ali Khamenei. I was studying from 8 am to 4 pm, then working at the TV channel headquarters until bedtime, which is where my residence also was at the time.

ISIS and the Fall of Mosul

Six months later, when ISIS took control of Mosul in June 2014, I was temporarily based in Baghdad and literally less than 1 hour away from ISIS territory. The Iraqi government along with the rest of the Iraqi nation didn't know how strong ISIS was, or if Mosul was the only area it intended to capture. The country was shaken and many ministers fled the country. Many citizens of the USA, UK, and other western countries fled Iraq through Baghdad Airport because they believed that if ISIS captured Baghdad they would all be held as political hostages.

I was also afraid. This event horrified me, but I decided not to flee the country. I immediately returned to the Holy City of Karbala, a sacred Shia Muslim stronghold that would be very difficult for ISIS to conquer. Now I was around 2 hours away from ISIS, and it is from here that my stance against Islamic extremism and fundamentalism became public. I made sure that the TV channel, including its social media platforms, primarily focused on preaching peace and tackling Islamic extremism. I began reporting from within Iraq regarding the security situation and the spread of the Islamic State. It didn't look like it was going to end quickly, and ISIS began to spread rapidly throughout both Iraq and Syria.

I remained in Iraq, both studying and tackling the ideology of Islamic extremism through TV networks. Later in 2014, I was walking with my mother in the crowded holy city when there was an explosion nearby. I will never forget how the earth moved beneath my feet, and how I lost my mother for a few minutes among the stampede of thousands of frightened people running for their lives; because in many cases, if a bomb is detonated in one area, a second explosion will follow, which increased the pushing and shoving among civilians.

In January 2015, my Uncle Faris who was a colonel in the Iraqi Army went missing, and we later received a call from Baghdad informing us that ISIS had captured and burnt him alive. Despite all the government warnings not to travel on the roads leading to Baghdad at the time, I insisted that we received Faris' body and made sure that he had an honorable burial. My uncle and I received his remains and held a funeral that my entire family attended to mourn his tragic death.

My uncle Faris, kidnapped and burnt alive by ISIS.

In December 2015, I felt that it was time for me to end my eight-year journey within the Islamic seminaries of Iran and Iraq by returning to Australia, which also meant that my work at Imam Hussein TV would be over. Although I knew that I would be preaching "Down Under," I knew that it wasn't going to be anything like the preaching of a typical Islamic cleric, and I had a strategic plan to make my message of peace and anti-extremism more effective.

After experiencing these events, losing a dear uncle and surviving ISIS terrorism, I was living in pain. This pushed me to enter the **second** stage of my de-radicalization phase, and I was about to not only liberate my mind from the fundamentalist ideologies taught to me, but to turn around and tackle them.

It all began the second I realised and felt deep down in my soul that I had been cheated and that my mind had been in the possession of barbarians who taught me corrupt and extreme ideologies, disguising it as knowledge that would benefit me in life and the hereafter.

Back to Australia (2015)

Throughout the last two centuries, moderate Muslims have been collectively tackling the extremist Wahhabi fundamentalist ideology in every way possible, but have failed to bring an end to the barbaric ideology. As a Muslim preacher, I could easily have claimed that the extremists do not represent the religion of Islam, and continued to preach peace like many Muslim clerics. I wasn't prepared to do that as honesty is an important principle within my life. Therefore, I made it clear that ISIS, Al-Qaeda and the like declare that they represent Islam, and they do in fact represent mainstream Islamic teachings. In my opinion, the only successful way to tackle the growth of such an ideology is by identifying it. The books of Bukhari and Ibn Taymiyah, which are highly revered by the majority of Muslims, include chapters about jihad. They are not about "struggle jihad." but the actual "jihad of war."

I believed and still believe that the only way to tackle such a growing extremist ideology is through diplomatic relations, by raising awareness about the dangers of extremist Islamism and the jihadization (radicalization) of youth within major Islamic institutes, and pressuring relevant authorities to take reasonable action against private Islamic school curriculums, international excursions to Islamic governments, along with other matters such as radical preachers being invited into the West from the Middle East. This mission required that I become familiar with all methods, protocols, and etiquettes of diplomacy; most importantly, it required patience. Lots of it. Attitudes, perceptions, interests, priorities, agendas, and life and career experiences vary from one politician to another. One member of parliament would genuinely believe in the policies I proposed for his or her upcoming election campaign, while another from the very same political party would sit and ridicule my ideas throughout our entire meeting.

Engaging in these meetings, sometimes publicly, raises many eyebrows within the Muslim community. According to most Muslim scholars throughout the globe, Muslim scholars need to prove to the senior scholars of the state that they are worthy of preaching and leading a community. This matter didn't apply to me as many of the Shia Muslim scholars in Australia support Hizbullah and the Iranian regime, two terrorist bodies which I have denounced.

My father on the other hand was well known among the Shia Muslim scholars in Australia and, whether he agreed with my opinions or not, this did not change the fact that I came from a lineage of Islamic scholars and leaders. It was important however for me to prove my level of education. Therefore, I established the Islamic Association of South Australia upon my arrival in Adelaide in 2016, along with an Islamic education program which operated from the University of South Australia. I chose Adelaide, South Australia, simply because it has a lower rate of Islamic extremists than Sydney and Melbourne. The latter cities have played an important role in producing soldiers who travel abroad to join ISIS.

I have developed healthy friendships with numerous politicians and government authorities within Adelaide and Sydney. I have also engaged in interfaith events, building bridges between moderate Muslims and other religious communities. Without mentioning the names of any political parties, numerous politicians welcomed and embraced me and my mission of peace, which encouraged me to continue on my journey. However, these political figures were prepared to support me in every way possible, but wanted everything to remain discreet. I refused because I believed that tackling Islamic extremism wasn't a crime, and there was no reason to do it discreetly. Secondly, the citizens who voted for these politicians had every right to know about their official meetings with me. I maintained a healthy friendship with them, but I was never prepared to engage in any official work with any of them.

I had aspirations to launch another TV channel in Australia. However, I paused this project for another time within the near future, and sought to bring attention to my mission of peace in Australia by sharing my opinions on national media channels and agencies. I caught national attention when Channel 7's *Today Tonight* program interviewed me regarding matters concerning Islam and Islamic extremism. Indeed, Australia had never seen a Muslim imam as outspoken as myself – something I am proud of, because deep inside I know that my loyalty belongs to Australia and this was a simple way of giving back to such a great country. I was humbled when many Australians rushed to my social media profiles to describe me as "a breath of fresh air." As my interview requests became more frequent, I found myself appearing on a wider variety of TV channels such as Fox and Sky News. In my opinion, what attracts the media to me the most is the fact that time keeps proving all of my warnings to be true.

In February 2017, I appeared on *Today Tonight* on Channel 7 and warned the Australian nation and government that Islamic extremists were hoping to set up a caliphate in Australia. My claims were ridiculed by the mainstream media along with the majority of the Muslim community. However, less than a week later, Muslim extremist and electrician Haisem Zahab, aged 42, was arrested in Sydney, Australia, after researching and attempting to design a laser warning device along with missiles for ISIS. Today, extremists in Lakemba, Sydney, publicly say, and on camera, that they want to establish Sharia Law in Australia and everywhere on Earth.

Many other events in 2017 confirmed my warnings about the extent of Islamic extremist activity in Australia. On May 23, 2017, the South Australia Police and the Australian Federal Police arrested a 22-year-old extremist Muslim woman from South Australia. She was charged with one count of knowingly being a member of a terrorist organization. On June 5, 2017, during the Holy Month of Ramadhan, 29-year-old Islamic extremist Yacqub Khayre shot dead receptionist Kai Hao in the foyer of a serviced apartment in Melbourne. He took another female escort hostage in an apartment while contacting both the police and the media, making references to both ISIS and Al-Qaeda. He was shot dead after wounding three police officers.

In July 2017, Australian police thwarted a plot to bomb an airliner. Four Muslim men were arrested by the Australian Federal Police and raids were carried out on their properties. On October 31, 2017, Tamin Khaja pleaded guilty to planning a terrorist attack on civilians in Sydney. On November 27, 2017, 20-year-old extremist Muslim Ali Khalif Shire was arrested for plotting a mass shooting in Australia and a major terrorist attack on New Year's Eve.

Alongside these terrorist attacks, some Muslim leaders have ongoing ambitions to purchase gigantic blocks of land and to transform them into Muslim-only neighborhoods. At the same time, Muslim preachers such as Ibrahim Saddiq Conlon have publicly announced that certain parts of Australia should fall under Sharia Law. My warnings were accurate and correct, not because they were predictions, but because I live within the Muslim community, and I know the plans of the Islamic extremists.

I was also active internationally between 2015 and 2017. On February 22, 2017, I volunteered to defend Jakarta's Christian governor Basuki Purnama (Ahok) at a blasphemy trial in Indonesia, because I truly believed that organizations promoting the ideology of the terrorist leaders responsible for the Bali bombings were plotting to replace him with an Islamic extremist governor.

My Marriage and Divorce

During my journey, I met a woman whom I can safely describe as one of the best people I had come across in my life. We got married in Iraq, as she was originally from one of its holy cities. She was the daughter of a respected scholar, and was a direct descendant of Prophet Mohammad. Because our marriage was traditional, only after marriage did we realize how different we were. She insisted on wearing a full burqa, while at times I would publicly wear a suit and tie instead of my religious robes and turban. My views, opinions, and the diplomacy work that I was and still am involved in were seen as unacceptable by her family.

Even though my wife came from a conservative family, I knew that her journey to Australia would have allowed her to see what life is like in the real world, giving her the freedom to release herself from the chains of her ignorant society. Within her ultra-conservative Muslim family, my friendships with Jewish and Christian faith leaders were considered out of bounds for a Muslim imam. With all of our disagreements on life, where to continue living and how, as well as interference from other family members, we agreed that a divorce was best for both of us. Her father was shocked that we had made this decision, as we were less than one year into the marriage.

When we went to legally file a divorce in the Iraqi Supreme Court, the guide at the door directed us to the "newlyweds' area," and was surprised to learn that we were there for a divorce. On our way out of the court, he apologized and told us that he had never seen such a friendly group coming to file for a divorce, hence he thought that we were there to register a marriage.

I don't blame my ex-wife or her family for such a difficult period of my life. Instead, I blame our outdated traditions that are negatively influencing the lives and minds of this innocent generation.

Looking at all of the difficulties and challenges that I endured throughout the last two decades, I am very grateful that none of them have had a negative impact on me. I have seen people murdered in front of me, and I have lost dear people and valuable things in life, but I have always had the ability to move on with a clear mind – something I consider to be a blessing. Some of my friends wonder how I manage to prevent life's difficulties from negatively impacting me, and my secret is: never have great expectations of anything or anyone, because if they fail to meet your expectations, you will be left hurt or disappointed.

Australian Islamic Leaders Ambush and Assault Me

I am subjected to waves of death threats by Islamic extremists. In addition, in March 2017 I was ambushed and assaulted by two Islamic leaders within Australia. For personal reasons, at this time I choose not to mention the names of those guilty of this crime.

On Friday March 24, 2017, I agreed to meet four leaders of Adelaide's Muslim community in order to discuss my programs in Australia, specifically Adelaide, along with the statements I had been making in the media – which over time turned out to be true. The meeting was organized by Leader 1, and was held at the University of South Australia's Magill Campus at 5 pm. Leader 1 is widely described as "one of Australia's most prominent and respected Muslim leaders." The meeting included myself, my secretary, and the four Islamic leaders. When we reached the carpark of the university, I had a strong gut feeling that I should begin recording the interview for my own safety. I switched on the audio recording application on my mobile phone and placed it in my pocket.

The meeting began in a very friendly manner, as we shook hands and sat comfortably beside each other around a table. The tension began when Leader 3 decided to aggressively interrogate me regarding an inaccurate media report issued by the ABC in the year 2016. The report suggested that I threatened violence after a man pulled a Muslim woman's scarf off her head in public. I had condemned and denounced this report previously, and a news article published in The Advertiser set the record straight by correcting the errors. After complaints against the ABC, they also corrected their article.

After Leader 3's interrogation was over, Leader 2 demanded that I refrain from criticizing extremist Muslims in the media, because it wasn't "in the best interest" of Australia and the Muslim community. I peacefully and respectfully disagreed by informing him that I would continue to criticize extremist Muslims and warn Australia about any potential terrorist threats. Moments later, Leader 2 stood over me as I remained seated in my chair and, while pointing his finger towards my face, said "Respect yourself." My secretary immediately sprung from his chair and requested that Leader 2 remained seated and not disrespect the imam (myself). Leader 2 then responded to my secretary, saying: "Who the f**k do you think you are? Sit down! With my shoe [in Arabic]! With my shoe!" – an Arabic statement that implied a threat to hit us with his shoe. Such a comment is also regarded as being highly insulting in Middle Eastern culture.

During this altercation, I stood to calm things down and to make my way outside of the meeting room. Leader 3 raced to shove me against the table while twisting my fingers backwards. I then shouted, "do not touch me, do not touch me," and told Leader 2: "Don't threaten anyone and respect yourself!" They then stormed outside of the meeting room except for Leader 1 as he had an appointment scheduled in the same university building. I demanded that Leader 1 call Leaders 2, 3, and 4 to return and apologize to me for physically assaulting me and threatening both me and my secretary. Leader 1, one of "Australia's most prominent and respected Muslim leaders" refused to do so, and therefore we also left the building. I immediately contacted an Australian intelligence organization and informed them of the ambush and assault. I attended a police station the next day to file a statement and press charges.

I contacted Leader 1 within an hour of the meeting with the following text message:

> I knew that I couldn't trust any one of you, which is why I had everything being recorded. Leader 3 grabbed and twisted my hands which is physical assault. We were threatened to be hit by a shoe in the University of South Australia. I was physically abused and manhandled and also insulted. This is not good for you, or Leader 2, or the University of South Australia.

Leader 1 responded with: "It's unfortunate you say this because I trusted you …" I then responded:

> I met with you to have a peaceful verbal conversation. But when we are ambushed and I'm assaulted, and we are threatened to be hit by Leader 2's shoe, I don't think you are being fair to me. They made a big mistake doing what they did to me this afternoon.

When the police took my statement, they also contacted Leader 1 for a statement. Initially he agreed to provide a statement, but kept delaying the matter with excuses that he was travelling or busy. Almost eight months later, in October 2017, he decided to inform the police investigators that he would not be providing a witness statement. It is unfortunate that this is the type of trouble and headache our police officers have to put up with, having to manage such bothersome and radical individuals who operate mosques and believe they are above the law. I withdrew my request to file charges, out of respect for police time and money. I however await the perfect day to release the audio file and, on that day, I will be hitting more than just two birds with one stone.

The Price of Reason and Moderation

My sudden and very frequent appearance in international media came as a surprise to many people. For the first time in Australia's history, an Australian Muslim imam had taken a stand to call for reform, while exposing and denouncing Islamic extremists in the country. Throughout my television appearances, I began to reveal the plots of the fundamentalist Muslim community against the interests of Australia.

Some fundamentalist Muslims tried to silence me by targeting the journalists who covered my stories and activism. That attempt to silence me failed because of my large online audience, as I am able to get my message across through social media. Therefore, instead of inviting me on a panel to challenge my message and give me an equal opportunity to speak my mind, they resorted to attempts to assassinate my character.

I have encouraged my tens of thousands of online followers to engage in the debate against extremism, and by contacting their leaders and opinion makers to express concerns about the spread of intolerant Islamism within their areas. I have focused on issues of national security and not on myself, and I believe that it is only fair that you be informed of the difficulties I have endured throughout this time. Here is a brief history of the tactics I have encountered, which you too may expect when you speak out against the infiltration of extremists in the media and government departments.

First, they try to discredit the messenger. In my case, this took the form of being called a "fake shaikh." This tactic lasted only until I had my qualifications independently confirmed. My critics had failed to mention my challenge to any qualified imam to debate me, if I was misrepresenting the words in religious books. I might add that, to this date, no Muslim cleric has accepted the challenge. I leave to you to decide what inferences can be drawn from this failure to debate me.

Secondly, they provided platforms for supposed "moderates" to rail against me, and tried to use them to support the current discredited narrative. They made the mistake of trying to create debates where the narrative would be the centerpiece and not the actual issues I had raised. Among the charges levelled at me was that I was trying to create one world religion. I would not cooperate with these attempts to smother unpleasant truths, and after a couple of failed attempts that tactic was quickly abandoned.

Thirdly, they attacked me at a personal level. While recognizing that defamation could lead to legal action on my part, they passed their accusations behind the security of quotation marks as well as sly inferences about my motivations and dark allusions to my past. As I would not lower myself to engaging with such absurdity, this approach was left to their internet trolls.

Fourth was what is known as the guilt trip. I was told that I was putting moderate Muslims or the broader community at risk. The guilt trip option is mostly used when no rational argument can be raised against your position. My stance is well known, many Muslims are good people, and my advocacy is always against the extremists who hide within the Muslim community.

Fifth, they have used actual force. I have personally been subjected to physical abuse, both in public and private. These include death threats, damage to my car and home, and actual assault. These are the actions of those who have no defense against truth except for intimidation. These attacks on me have come largely from members of the Muslim community. I would say that these actions prove my point that there is indeed a fanatical and violent element within our Muslim community.

Sixth, they have tried blacklisting the messenger. A large media organization made the effort to contact other media outlets, to try to deny me access to any public forum. This of course was reported to me by these other agencies, who were themselves quite surprised by this tactic. The only result was to give my message more credibility.

Seventh, they use outright distortion. This tactic is becoming quite prominent, and it takes two main forms at the moment. Firstly, when the media reports a terror incident, it is reluctant to admit early on that the perpetrator(s) are Muslim when that is in fact the case, and secondarily there is a recent trend of saying that "this person had mental health issues." It seems too hard for the deluded to address the fact that we are dealing with Muslim extremists. One example was when the Australian Broadcasting Corporation (ABC) described me as an extremist, when it is obvious to any reasonable person that I am simply a peace advocate.

These are the kinds of attacks that I have personally experienced; no doubt others will be developed from time to time. All we can do is stay alert to the various twists and turns of our opponents. I say opponents because that is what they are. Our enemies are extremists who want to drag the world into a dark medieval pit of ignorance, bigotry, and death. Our opponents are largely well meaning but deluded folk who think that appeasement will buy them security. They would be wise to heed the old warning: "Those who feed the tiger only gain the privilege of becoming its last meal."

Once the "far left" and Islamic extremists had united to discredit me, I decided to approach the Royal United Services Institute for Defence and Security Studies, the world's oldest think tank on international defense and security, of which Queen Elizabeth II is the patron of the parent branch in England, to conduct an investigation into my credentials and qualifications. RUSI agreed and released the following statement on 20/12/2017, making me the only imam with an examination into his credentials by a royal institute.

Royal United Services Institute for Defence and Security Studies, SA.
Building 160, Keswick Barracks, Keswick, South Australia, 5035
www.rusi.org.au

STATEMENT FOR THE PUBLIC
Re: The Qualifications of Imam Mohammad Tawhidi   20/12/2017

I am able to confirm that Imam Mohammad Tawhidi has been an honored guest of the Royal United Services Institute for Defence and Security Studies, South Australia, where he delivered a most informative address about Muslim extremists who are covertly active in Australia. The Imam's words were well received. Indeed, no-one at that gathering, or since, has questioned his credentials. However, due to the rumors surrounding Imam Tawhidi's qualifications and the unavailability of an independent Shia Muslim Imams Council in Australia, I have conducted an investigation into the authenticity of his credentials as it is an important matter for both RUSI and the general Australian public.

On Friday the 15th of December 2017, a meeting was held within The City of Adelaide to investigate the qualifications, credentials and the Islamic religious position of Imam Tawhidi. This procedure was held in the presence of accredited and official NAATI translator: Dr Ahmad Hashemi-Sakhtsari. The offices of the Grand Islamic Jurisdictions of The Holy Cities of Qum (Iran) and Karbala (Iraq) were both contacted – in two separate phone calls – and after a detailed enquiry from their officials: Sayid Mohammad Mahdi Tabatabai and Shaikh Mahdi Ma'ash, who spoke in Persian (Farsi), it has been confirmed to me that Imam Tawhidi is:

(1) An Islamic Scholar known to the Grand Islamic Authorities and was ordained and pronounced as a Muslim Imam by the Supreme Grand Ayatollah Sayid Sadiq Shirazi, during a public ceremony in Qum, Iran. (2) It has also been confirmed that Imam Tawhidi is indeed qualified to represent Islam and the Muslim community, and that his current credentials which he was presented with by the Supreme Islamic Authorities, (available on his website (www.ImamTawhidi.com) along with the images of his crowning ceremony in 2010), are in fact authentic and true. (3) Furthermore, both Grand Islamic Jurisdictions of Iran and Iraq have rejected the allegations suggesting that Imam Tawhidi is not a qualified or recognized Muslim Imam, and labelled him as an "eminent and erudite Islamic scholar" that had graduated from their Educational Seminaries; in addition to having delivered lessons in Islamic studies and had engaged in advanced theological research with high-ranking Islamic authorities for numerous years. – End

Imam Tawhidi maintains views which may differ to the opinions of his former teachers as he does not claim to be their deputy or representative in any way. Consequently, he has been invited to again address our Institute, since it is fundamental to the principles of our Institute for members to understand and appreciate his insight into the manner in which certain misguided Muslims, living in Australia, intend to disrupt the traditional way of life in this country.

Yours respectfully,

Ron Bannon
Vice-President,
Royal United Services Institute for
Defence and Security Studies, SA.

I certify that the above is true, and that the translation of the investigation provided in the third paragraph is correct, exact and accurate in context and wording.

Dr. Ahmad Hashemi-Sakhtsari
Professional and Licensed NAATI Translator (#13705)

Revealing the Hidden Realities

I wasn't born a reformist, and the thought of liberating Muslim communities from the corruption that has been introduced by Islamist clerics didn't strike me until 2014. Before then, I was a typical Islamist cleric who preached violent Sharia Law, even though I never implemented it. My sermons were infested by corrupt ideas and teachings such as wife beating, as it was part of my educational programming which had prepared me to pursue a career as an apologist missionary for the governing Islamic body in Iran.

The Iranian regime had sent me on trips to western countries to preach the ideology of its Islamic revolution as well as to invite Muslim youth to study within their seminaries. In 2017, I submitted a full report to the governments and intelligence agencies of these countries, exposing Iranian regime affiliates and informing them of everything they needed to know.

Within the Islamic seminaries of Iran, students and aspiring scholars are taught concepts which influence their identities and characters. Being a victim of these corrupt teachings, I found myself living a backward life, drowning in a morally bankrupt ideology. Most Islamic students' lines of thinking are extremely narrow, as there is very little room for dialogue regarding the essential matters of faith. I knew that I had to be careful about what questions I asked, to avoid giving my extremist teachers the impression that my faith and level of belief were inferior to theirs, or that I might be doubting some of the Islamic rulings. We were taught useless knowledge as though it was beneficial science – and we had to accept it because "it came from God."

An important question people ask me regularly is: If you speak about the corruption and extremism that has infested the Islamic religion, why can't every other imam and Islamic scholar do the same? In reality, during previous years, I was concealing the truth; and the majority of Muslim scholars today are also concealing the truth about certain aspects of Islam. This has been taking place since the early centuries of Islam, and it is passed on to generations of Islamic scholars through their educational programming.

As imams, we were commanded to stay silent, to manipulate the truth and even trained to escape questions which corner us, through deception and convenient answers. These subjects are known as "Lessons in Eloquence," which revolve around literature but also taught us terminologies and phrases that would help us escape or divert certain questions that could expose the reality of Islamic extremism.

Another agenda alongside this reality is that the books which contain dark truths are never translated into English, and usually only a limited number of copies are published. They are written and published for grand muftis and imams alone, not for the average Muslim. These books are referred to as "special copies". We need brave and honest imams to act to spread these teachings by scans or electronic copies.

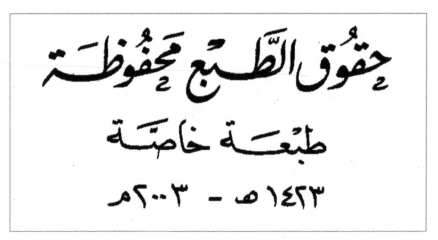

An Arabic label, that reads "Special Print", placed on private books written for Muslim clergymen alone.

Grand Islamic authorities have defended the terrorist companions and fathers-in-law of Prophet Mohammad. They constantly defend those who invaded continents while raping, massacring, and butchering their people.

Ibn Qudamah* said:

The companions of Prophet Mohammad have done a great favor for the Muslim nation, as they brought victory to Allah, his Messenger Mohammad and conducted jihad in the path of Allah,

---

* Ibn Qudamah (1147–1223) was a highly regarded Islamic authority, scholar, traditionalist, historian, and theologian.

utilising both their money and their lives. They protected the religion of Allah and his book. Mohammad's companions have rights upon us, and we must love them with all our hearts and praise them with our tongues. We must not mention their wrongdoings, because the many virtues they have will exceed and hide their mistakes and atone them.[1]

Ibn Fawzan**said: "We must respect the companions of Prophet Mohammad, and not speak against them. It is not permissible to search for their mistakes and show them to the people."[2]

Al-Dhahabi*** said:

If it was proven that the words of the companions were based on hate and anger, then it is not to be taken into consideration. In fact, it should be folded and not narrated, the same way it has been decided to refrain from mentioning the clashes and killings between the companions [of Mohammad]; may Allah be pleased with all of them. However, we still find similar writings in the collections and books and volumes, ... Therefore, they must be folded and hidden. They must be eradicated, so that the hearts will be clean and gathered over the love of the companions and be pleased with them. Hide these writings, mainly from the general public and particular scholars. However, it may be permitted for some scholars to read such reports in private.[3]

After having gone through such a journey and witnessed the corruption and immorality that took place in the name of God and religion, I chose to violate the commands of our Islamic authorities and demand change by speaking out, on behalf of myself and the many moderate Muslims who feel the same way as I do; and who are also victims of Islamic extremism or attempts at radicalization.

The religion of Islam revolves around one God known as "Allah" and the message of Mohammad found in the Quran and books of

---

** Ibn Fawzan is an Islamic authority and currently serves as a member of the Council of Senior Scholars. He is a member of the Permanent Committee for Islamic Research and Issuing Fatwas.

*** Al-Dhahabi (1274–1348) was a prominent Islamic historian and scholar of jurisprudence and Islamic scripture. He was the teacher of many prominent Islamic scholars and jurists, such as Ibn Katheer.

hadith. The hadith are compiled prophetic teachings and traditions. The family and wives of Prophet Mohammad played a vital role in the growth of Islam, by narrating detailed reports of Mohammad's teachings and practices, both during his life and after his death. However, not all of what was written or orally transmitted is true. Some of the teachings contradict logic, common sense, and basic human ethics.

It can be safely said that most Muslims are extremely sensitive about this subject, and extremists are known to react violently whenever the corruptions in Muslim ideology and customs are exposed. Hence, we were trained within the Islamic seminaries and educational institutions to hide the truth and to always be prepared with answers to evade intelligent debate regarding shameful facts within Islam's history.

If the Muslim world is happy with the current state of their religion and ideology, then there should be absolutely no problem with revealing what lies within the Islamic books of theology and history to the rest of humanity.

Cartoon by: Paul Zanetti (www.zanetti.net.au)

Dear Reader

The previous pages contained what I believe is very important for you to know, as they present the journey and events that made me whom I am today.

What we Muslims claim to believe is not what our books teach, and most Muslims are in fact ignorant of what Islam's theological and doctrinal books contain.

The following chapters are a gradual and intellectual exposé of the difficulties within Islamic thought, in all of its aspects and denominations; while pointing out the urgent need for reform. You will come to discover the true beliefs of the majority of Muslims regarding Allah and Mohammad, along with surrounding aspects of the religion such as the Quran and the family of Mohammad.

These disastrous beliefs are enough reason for Islam's current governing bodies to review their teachings, and to amend their main sources of theology, philosophy, and doctrine.

As someone who lives and operates within Muslim societies, I am aware of the safety concerns that come along with writing about these topics. I have taken my safety as well as that of those around me into consideration, especially when writing the third chapter.

CHAPTER 2

Difficulties in the Foundation of Islam: Allah, Mohammad, and his Wives in Islamic Scripture

Allah: *Characteristics and Descriptions*

Monotheistic religions invite people to worship a supreme being, described as the creator of the heavens and the earth: God. In Islam, the characteristics of God are derived from the logical expectations of a God, that God is all-being, all-seeing, all-wise, all-knowledgeable, the most gracious and most merciful. All positive qualities are attributed to the supreme God and all negative qualities are disassociated from God. Islam teaches that there is nothing like God, and that God cannot possibly be described.

Most Islamic denominations claim to believe that God cannot have a material form, because material forms have shapes, and shapes have limits, and limits are negative qualities. This is briefly why Muslims reject the idea that Jesus is God, as God cannot be comprised of human flesh. That being said, therein lies a great contradiction between what most Islamic denominations consider to be God's specifications, qualities, and characteristics and, surprisingly, what most Muslims believe.

Allah: *'A Donkey-Riding Obese Boy Wearing a Golden Burqa'*

Grand Islamic scholar Ibn Taymiyah, referred to by the majority of Muslims as "Shaikh-ul Islam" meaning "the senior cleric of Islam," reported that Prophet Mohammad saw Allah as a young lad, dressed in pearls, and sitting in a green garden.[5] Al-Haythami, a highly distinguished scholar of Islamic scripture, insisted that "Allah was a young lad, who wore a golden Burqa on his face and had two golden sandal shoes on his feet."[6] Other prominent Islamic scholars such as al-Hakim al-Nishapuri, the leading hadith specialist of his age, stated that Allah was a young lad who sat on a throne in the skies. He also believed that Allah was obese, because "the throne would squeak whenever God sits on it."[7]

Imam Bukhari and Imam Muslim also believed that Allah laughs,[8] and that Allah descends from his throne every night to visit Earth, while spending one third of the night accepting the prayers of Muslims.[9] In other reports, Allah descends on a donkey, to the extent that Muslims in Baghdad would place hay and straw on their rooftops for God's donkey to eat, while God accepts the prayers of Muslims.[10]

Four of the most important Islamic scholars in the fields of theology and jurisprudence* have ruled based on Islamic scripture that "Sitting with one leg above the other is an act performed by God, and that it should not be done by human beings."[11]

On the other hand, the grand Islamic scholar Ibn Asakir was extremely offended by the descriptions of Allah being taught in mosques during his era. He wrote:

> They have insisted on their ignorance, declaring that God has arms, legs, teeth, nails *and descends onto the earth while riding a donkey*, with the appearance of a young lad whose hair is as soft as cat fur, wearing a golden Burqa and two golden sandals.[12]

The irony here is that the present-day Islamic scholars who revere and follow the path of all of the aforementioned scholars have issued fatwas (verdicts) ordering the killing and beheading of Christians by describing them as polytheists who believe in a *material* God, Jesus. This set the precedent for the culture that later formed the ideology of Al-Qaeda and ISIS.

A living example is the fundamentalist Grand Imam Saleh Al-

---

* Al-Tabrani, Al-Tabari, Al-Haytami, and Al-Bayhaqi.

Fawzan, who issued a fatwa in an Arabic sermon, declaring:

Islam does not permit freedom of religion. Islam came to ban polytheism and fight the polytheists. If Islam came to permit freedom of religion, there would be no need for the concept of jihad. Those who refuse to worship Allah alone must be fought, and they must never be left alone. They must either believe in Allah, or be killed. Islam did not emerge to give freedom to polytheist and "kaffir"** religions. God has ruled punishments for the polytheists in order to protect people from their wrong ideologies and corrupt opinions, because they are his creations and they must worship him alone without any partners to God. We have been ordered to perform jihad against the polytheists and disbelievers.[13]

While not all Muslims follow the Islamic leadership of Imam Saleh Al-Fawzan, he ranks as one of the most prominent Islamist scholars of the twenty-first century. He is an appointed member of the Permanent Committee for Islamic Research and Issuing Fatwas, and he is only one of the hundreds of Islamic scholars who have issued similar fatwas throughout history.

Allah is "a Dog and a Pig"

The belief that God exists in all places has fundamental roots within the theology of Islam. However, its implementation and interpretation can be extremely disturbing. Grand Islamic authorities have stated: "God has occupied the existence. He has indeed appeared in the black and white [i.e. in everything], and in Christians among Jews, and in pigs among monkeys."[14]

Imam al-Bitaar, who is celebrated as a saint, a mystic, and a spiritual Islamic jurist, writes in his book: "Some of those who have been filled with [divine] inspiration, from among the people of inspiration, say: The dog and the pig are nothing but our God, and Allah is nothing but

** "Kaffir" is the Arabic Islamic terminology to describe a disbeliever in Allah and/or the Islamic religion.

a cleric/priest in a synagogue/church."[15] All of these things are condemned in the Quran.

Regarding Christians and Jews, the Quran states:

> The Jews say, "Ezra is the son of Allah"; and the Christians say, "The Messiah is the son of Allah." That is their statement from their mouths; they imitate the saying of those who disbelieved [before them]. May Allah destroy them; how are they deluded?[16]

It also includes the following warning to Muslims:

> Oh, you who have believed, do not take the Jews and the Christians as allies. They are [in fact] allies of one another. And whoever is an ally to them among you – then indeed, he is [one] of them. Indeed, Allah guides not the wrongdoing people.[17]

Regarding Jews, pigs and monkeys, the Quran states:

> Say (O Muhammad SAW to the people of the Scripture): "Shall I inform you of something worse than that, regarding the recompense from Allah: those (Jews) who incurred the Curse of Allah and His Wrath, those of whom (some) He transformed into monkeys and swine, those who worshipped false deities; such are worse in rank (on the Day of Resurrection in the Hell fire), and far more astray from the Right Path (in the life of this world)."[18]

The Quran also refers to dogs in a metaphor:

> And if We had willed, we could have elevated him thereby, but he adhered [instead] to the earth and followed his own desire. So his example is like that of the dog: if you chase him, he pants, or if you leave him, he [still] pants. That is the example of the people who

denied Our signs. So relate the stories that perhaps they will give thought.[19]

Either top Islamic scholars have little knowledge about their own God, Allah, or they simply enjoy issuing statements which contradict God's holy book. Thus, I ask, how is it possible that God is embodied through His own creation and then condemned within his own holy book? And can such a contradiction be accepted? The obvious answer to me is no.

Insulting the Quran

On July 12, 2010, Pastor Terry Jones of the Dove World Outreach Center, Florida, and President of the political group *Stand Up America Now* announced his plans to burn the Quran. After this announcement, a series of dangerous events took place throughout Muslim countries, including protests in Yemen, Tunisia, and Libya. In Cairo, Egypt, protesters breached the wall of the US Embassy and burned the American flag. Following this incident, the US consulate in Benghazi, Libya, was burnt and looted, leading to the murder of Ambassador J. Christopher Stevens and three other American citizens. Two US soldiers were shot and killed by an Afghan policeman in an attack that was attributed to his anger. The protests led to the murders of individuals from other European nationalities who were mistaken for Americans.

The matter caught the attention of many nations and their leaders, resulting in further action taken against Jones. Governments called for the arrest of Terry Jones, while numerous fatwas were issued, promising millions of dollars to whoever assassinated him. On March 22, 2011, Pakistan's banned Islamic organization Jama'at-ud-Da'wah promised to reward $2.2 million to whoever killed Jones.[20] The FBI then revealed that Lebanese Shia militant group Hizbullah had offered a higher reward of $2.4 million for the head of Jones,[21] while Al-Qaeda featured Jones on a "Wanted Dead" poster in its tenth edition of *Inspire Magazine* in March 2013.[22] Terry Jones was then sentenced to death by an Egyptian court,[23] and the US government strongly condemned Terry Jones, calling the burning of the Quran an act of "extreme intolerance and bigotry."

I too condemned Terry Jones for his actions, not only because burning a book is an unethical and uncivilized practice particularly in the twenty-first century, and could lead to others burning the Bible and Torah, but because the Quran includes figures revered by other religions, including Abraham and Moses, and also contains the story of Mary and the miraculous birth of Jesus Christ. Though I can personally understand the pastor's frustration after the tragic event of September 11, my approach in tackling the ideology of hardline Islam would have been very different.

Personally speaking, I failed to comprehend the level of outrage within the Muslim world after Jones insulted the Quran, leading to the deaths of many innocent people. The reason for that is simply because we Muslims believe in "sacred" books, but we frequently behave in ways that are insulting to the Quran. According to Islamic jurisprudence, blood and urine that exit the human body are considered impure. Islam has incredibly specific rules regarding handling the Quran, and God states in the Quran: "None touch it except the purified [through ablution]."[24] Not all Muslims follow these rulings; in fact, they do the exact opposite. Yes, fundamentalist Islamic jurisprudence insults the Quran.

Prominent Islamic scholar and jurist Ibn Abidin delivered a "healing" verdict, saying:

> One can write The First Chapter of the Quran with blood on his forehead and on his nose, it is allowed for healing purposes, and also with urine too. If it is for a healing purpose, then there is no problem in it.[25]

Other Islamic rulings include: "If someone bleeds and his bleeding does not stop, and they want to write something from the Qur'an with blood on their forehead: It is allowed." He was asked, "If he writes it with urine?" He said, "If it is for the healing purpose then there is no problem in it."[26]

How anyone can consider writing words of their own holy book with what they consider to be impure blood and urine is incomprehensible. Nevertheless, the statements of these scholars inspired many Muslims to write the Quran with their own impurities. The "Blood Quran" was written in the late 1990s with the blood of Iraq's former tyrant, Saddam Hussain. In 1997, on his sixtieth birthday, the Blood Quran was displayed in public.[27] There has been no record of any Islamic scholars condemning Saddam Hussain's action.

From here, the matter only becomes more appalling. The "moderates" of minor Islamic schools of thought actually believe that urinating on the Quran is a moral act. In one incident, a person came weeping to Shah Abdul Aziz, a prominent Islamic scholar of the eighteenth century, saying, "I have seen such a dream that I now suspect my faith has been destroyed." Aziz responded, "Tell me your dream." The man said, "I saw myself urinating upon the Holy Qur'an." To which Aziz said, "This is indeed a very good dream."[28]

Look at a Vagina, but Not the Quran

Grand Islamic jurists not only allowed for the Quran to be written with impurities such as blood and urine, but they went to another level of indecency. Ibn Nujaim, one of the greatest Islamic jurists in the sixteenth century, ruled: "If an individual, during prayer, looks at a copy of the Quran and reads from it, the prayer becomes void. But not if he looks at the vagina of a woman with lust."[29]

The ideological corruption within the Islamic seminaries of Egypt (Al-Azhar) has allowed local Islamic jurists to issue such verdicts. Although the Quran forbids a man from looking at the genitals of a woman he is not married to, they have allowed such indecencies to take place during the offering of prayers which is the most sacred times of the day, the human connection with God. The Quran itself states: *"Tell the believing men to lower their gaze and be mindful of their chastity;* this will be most conducive to their purity."[30]

Clearly, some Muslim jurists have little regard for the Quran and its teachings. They contradict and disrespect the Quran, even though they teach the upcoming generations jihad against those who insult the Quran. This does not make sense to any logical, reasonable, and rational human being. As much as I would like to inform you that the matter of our Islamic scholars and jurists insulting the Quran ends here, I am afraid it does not. Islamic jurists have gone to the extent of protecting each other's status by claiming infallibility of knowledge for each other, and that the scholars of Islam are more sacred and important than the Holy Qur'an and Prophet Mohammad that were both sent by God!

The Grand Islamic Jurist and then Mufti of Iraq, Abul Hassan Al-Karkhi, issued two rulings in his book *The Foundations of Al Kharkhi* (اصول الكرخي) setting a law for Muslims from the tenth century onwards: "Every verse that opposes the statement [ruling] of our scholars, it will be said: This verse of the Holy Qur'aan has been abrogated."[31] Therefore, their loyalty is not with the Quran as they claim. Rather, it lies with their privilege of changing the meaning of the Quran to fit their own agendas; and in many instances their own political interests or affiliations.

While a minority of Muslims do believe the Quran to be an infallible book, most Muslims do not, simply because they believe it is incomplete. They dispute the completion of the Holy Quran not because God has not completed his message, but because God's completed message was consumed by a sheep! Yes, growing up, we were in fact taught that a sheep ate the remaining chapters of the Quran. Aisha, the wife of Prophet Mohammad, said:

> The verse of stoning was revealed, and it was written on a leaf that was kept beneath a bed in my house. When Mohammad became ill, we were preoccupied with his situation, and a little animal of ours, a sheep, came in and ate it.[32]

Indeed, this is what we were taught in the Islamic seminaries of Islam's holiest cities, and I used to tell myself that if Aisha, the wife of Mohammad, had any regard for the Quran, its holy verses would not have been kept on the floor in the first place.

The majority of Muslims along with their scholars are the main insulters of the Quran. They claim to love the Quran, but are deceived, because they are permitted to write it with their blood and urine, and permitted to look at female genitals instead of looking at the words of God, while leaving it to be consumed by sheep. Those who do not commit such practices that insult the Quran but still follow scholars and books that promote vile teachings are simply misinformed or deeply confused.

Do Muslims Love Prophet Mohammad?

The above heading may appear to be a ridiculous question; however, the coming paragraphs will prove that it is nothing less than essential. Muslims are angered whenever Prophet Mohammad is negatively portrayed in a cartoon or insulted, which makes one wonder how our Prophet is treated amongst ourselves. Do we really love him? The following are eight examples that will leave you outraged.

Example One: Black Magic and Satanic Inspiration

Allah states in the Quran: "(O people!) your companion [Mohammad] is not possessed; And Mohammad is not a withholder of [knowledge of] the unseen. Nor is it the word of an evil and accursed Satan."[33] Therefore, according to Islam, the word of Mohammad is the word of God alone. However, while many Muslims may believe this, a large majority of Muslims do not. In fact, they believe the exact opposite.

Grand Islamic Scholar Imam Mohammad al-Bukhari, in his book *Sahih al-Bukhari*, which Muslims view as the most trusted collection of prophetic practices, history, and teachings, and the most authentic book after the Quran, reported that "Magic was worked on the Prophet so that he began to fancy that he was doing a thing which he wasn't actually doing."[34] In another report, he stated that "Magic was worked on Allah's Apostle so that he used to think that he had sexual relations with his wives while he actually had not."[35]

Prominent Muslim scholars, jurists, and historians Ibn Ishaq, Al-Zamakhshari, and Al-Suyuti have all reported that Satan whispered to Prophet Mohammad and put words in his mouth, while Mohammad considered that a fulfilment of his wish and preached Satan's message to the people! They all stated: "The annulment of what Satan had put upon the prophet's tongue came from God" and "Satan substituted something in accordance with the wish which Mohammad had requested, that is, Satan whispered something to him which would enable the messenger to announce his wish."[36]

Therefore, how is it possible for Muslim scholars to praise the Prophet and claim that his message is from God, when they believe Satan (the Devil and enemy of God) whispers in the ears of Mohammad and places words in his mouth?

Example Two: Romantic Ramadans

According to all Islamic denominations, it is jurisprudentially prohibited for a man to engage in any intimacy with his wife during the hours of fasting, and doing so would break his fast and would be considered a sin that angers God. It is also an Islamic ruling that both the husband and wife perform an obligatory ghusl (washing ritual) after intimacy. This wash purifies the body and, without it, one's prayers and fasting are not accepted.

However, Imam Bukhari reported: "At times, Allah's Apostle used to wake up in the morning in a state of impurity from sexual intercourse, not from a wet dream, and then he would fast that day."[37] There was no mention of purification or performing the obligatory Islamic washing ritual before fasting, rendering Mohammad's fast invalid.

Clearly, this is an indication that Mohammad was an impure person and a sinner, a matter which contradicts basic ethics. How could a Muslim who claims to love Prophet Mohammad believe such a history, which was reported two centuries after the death of Mohammad? How these reports are considered "sacred scripture" is beyond the comprehension of any rational person studying Islam.

Example Three: Disrespecting Prophet Mohammad

We Muslims are raised to love the Prophet Mohammad, his companions and fathers-in-law even though Mohammad's companions and fathers-in-law didn't respect him at all.

The Quran contains verses that describe a situation that would often take place at gatherings with Mohammad, namely his companions yelling and shouting in his presence. The Quran states:

> O You who believe! *Do not place yourselves forward* before Allah and His Messenger; ... O you *who have believed, do not raise your voices above the voice of the Prophet or be loud to him in speech* like the loudness of some of you to others ... Those who *shout out to you* (O Mohammad) from without the inner apartments – most of them lack understanding.[38]

From these verses, we understand that those surrounding Mohammad, their Prophet, would put themselves before him when making decisions and disrespect him by yelling and raising their voices near him. They were not kings or chiefs; they were Muslims who believed in his message. *Sahih al-Bukhari*, the second most sacred book after the Quran, reports that two of those arguing and yelling in front of Mohammad were his two fathers-in-law, Abu Bakr and Omar, saying: "The two righteous persons were about to be ruined (by God). They were Abu Bakr and Omar who raised their voices, arguing with each other in the presence of the Prophet."[39]

It is somewhat difficult to imagine that two respected figures would enter a courtroom and begin to make judgments on behalf of the judge they love and revere, let alone begin to yell mindless words and shame each other in the presence of this esteemed judge. This is simply because there is a level of respect that should be afforded to a judge; we rise when they enter the courtroom and remain silent when they speak, because they personify the law. Imagine a Prophet, representing God's law, being in the middle of a loud argument between his companions and fathers-in-law over a decision that only he has authority to make. Where is the regard and respect for the Prophet and his prophecy in all of that?

The question worth asking in this regard is, why did they not listen to the opinion of the Prophet before suggesting their own opinions? Is it because they believed Mohammad speaks nonsense?

Example Four: Prophet Mohammad Speaks Nonsense?

The same revered Islamic scholar who reported the previous scenario, Imam Mohammad al-Bukhari, also reported in the sacred *Sahih al-Bukhari*:

> On Thursday, the illness of Allah's Messenger, Mohammad, was aggravated, and he [the Prophet] said, "Fetch me writing materials so that I may have something written for you in order that you will never go astray after me." The people [present there] differed in this matter and they said, "Allah's Messenger is talking nonsense."[40]

Imam Bukhari continued to testify that Omar, Prophet Mohammad's father-in-law, had said: "The illness has defeated the Prophet, and we have got Allah's Book with us and that is sufficient for us."[41] In other words, what Mohammad was saying was nonsense influenced by illness, and the words of God (the Quran) were sufficient.

On that, Mohammad said to them: "Go away! It is not right that you should quarrel in front of me."[42] Mohammad's cousin, Ibn Abbas, came out of the building saying: "It was a great loss, indeed a great loss, that the Messenger of God couldn't write the document for them because of their disagreement and loud disputes."[43]

I must also mention that not all Muslims believe Mohammad was illiterate, and there is in fact strong evidence suggesting that he wasn't. I plan to write about this in the foreseeable future.

After these four scenarios, it has become somewhat clear that the majority of the Muslims who in fact consider such scripture to be sacred suffer from contradictions in their beliefs. The greatest insult to Mohammad are the Islamic scriptures, and the Muslim nation itself. The coming chapters of this book will emphasize this further.

Example Five: The Impure and Unclean Prophet?

Islamic scriptures revered by most Muslims clearly state that Prophet Mohammad would pray without *ablution* – the mandatory washing and purification ritual before prayer – and that Mohammad's own cousin, Ibn Abbas, testified to the laziness and lack of purity of Mohammad, by saying "The Prophet slept till he snored. Later on, the call-maker for the prayer came to him and informed him that it was time for prayer. The Prophet went with him for the prayer without performing ablution."[44]

Not only is this an insult to the Prophet, but it also means that, according to the Islamic jurisprudence Prophet Mohammad taught, his own prayers were void as he was not pure when offering them. *Sahih al-Bukhari* takes further steps to insult the Prophet by claiming: "Allah's Apostle was seen answering the call of nature [defecating in public] facing with his back towards the house of God in Mecca."[45] It also reports that "Prophet Mohammad went out to urinate while standing."[46]

Yet today, we hear Islamic preachers claiming that it is the law of Allah to urinate while *sitting* down and *behind closed doors*, and that "people who refused to follow Allah would be punished in the grave for indiscretions, like spreading 'evil rumors' and exposing themselves at a public urinal."[47] Throughout their sermons, they complain that "Every male public toilet now has urinals where they just stand up like animals and urinate in front of one another," and "what's worse is we even have Muslims using these urinals."[48] This ignores the fact that urinating in public while standing was actually the documented practice of their Prophet, Mohammad, whom the majority of Muslims believe in.

The version and perception of Prophet Mohammad presented and revered by Bukhari and the majority of Muslims either had a medical condition or an unethical habit of urinating and defecating in public. Islam has strict rulings regarding purity and cleanliness, and so does Arab culture. Bukhari's tale has contradicted both religion and Arab culture, yet most Arabic Muslims consider his tales to be second in sacredness after the Holy Quran.

Example Six: Sexual Power of Thirty Men

Even though Bukhari lived nearly 200 years after Prophet Mohammad, he testified: "The Prophet used to visit all of his wives [for sexual engagement], during the day and night, they were eleven in number, and the Prophet was given the strength of thirty men."[49] Upon reading such nonsense that contradicts reality and the obvious ability and sexual desire of men, one cannot help but wonder what Prophet Mohammad's diet was; because I as a man of Arab origin know very well that no Arab man has the ability to literally satisfy eleven women within the course of one day.

However, the fundamentalist Islamic scholars do come forward and say that they believe Prophet Mohammad was not just any regular man and that he was given the divine power and ability that allowed him to satisfy the sexual needs and desires of all his eleven wives in the duration of one day, so, yes, he must have exceeded the ability of a regular person.

If Prophet Mohammad spent one hour with each of his eleven wives a day, along with the time required to transition from one wife to another, as Islam demands a purity washing ritual after every sexual engagement, that would mean that Prophet Mohammad spent many hours a day engaging in sexual activity, and not preaching the message of Allah. Keeping in mind that the Prophet had to lead the five congregational prayers, which on average would last for at least 15 minutes each. Hence, the five prayers a day led by Prophet Mohammad would exceed one hour a day. Additionally, there were also the special prayers which have not been taken into consideration while making such bizarre claims of the Prophet's sexual activity. These prayers were assigned specifically for the Prophets of God, which the Islamic scriptures state would last for hours.

It can be concluded that it is ludicrous and impossible to accept that Prophet Mohammad had enough time to spread the religion of Islam while having such heavy sexual and worship commitments each day. The fact that Islam spread vastly and rapidly throughout Arabia within just over a decade shows that Prophet Mohammad was in fact engaged in spreading Islam, and at times in exile. A "sacred scripture" such as *Sahih al-Bukhari* cannot be considered a reasonable book, let alone authentic and sacred. In fact, we could conclude that the author of this ancient book was a sly individual who fabricated texts as a political tactic to add to the corrupt and violent material already being preached in his era, as a strategy of rulers to keep the citizens of their nations craving worldly sexual desires. In the twenty-first century, this is simply called false advertising.

Example Seven: Mohammad has Doubts about Allah

In order to create an atmosphere that would allow our senior scholars to fabricate Islamic scripture, they introduced the concept of "Prophetic Doubts in Scripture," which revolved around Prophet Mohammad doubting the very message he preached! The only way to promote this idea was to consider it part of "Quranic interpretation." To give life to this fabricated concept, they chose the Quranic verse that emphasized Abraham's doubts about God giving life to the dead: "Abraham said, 'My Lord, show me how You give life to the dead.' [Allah] said, 'Have you not believed?' He said, 'Yes, but [I ask] only that my heart may be satisfied.'"[50]

Bukhari interpreted this verse in a very strategic way and coated it with virtue by saying that "Prophet Mohammad is worthier of doubting God's words than Abraham,"[51]

Example Eight: The Terrorist Doctor?

The "Most Authentic Sahih Bukhari" reported:

> Some people of the Arabian tribe of Ukl came to Medina and its climate did not suit them. So, the Prophet ordered them to go to the herd of [milk] camels and to drink their milk and urine as a medicine. So they went as directed and after they became healthy, they killed the shepherd and drove away all the camels. The news reached the Prophet early in the morning and he then sent men in their pursuit and they were captured and brought at noon. He then ordered their hands and feet to be cut off, and it was done, and their eyes were branded with heated pieces of iron, they were put in a hot cabin and when they asked for water, no water was given to them.[52]

This is not a depiction of a prophet of peace, mercy, or love. It is a description of an unforgiving bloodthirsty murderer, which prompts the question that, if this incident was indeed true, why did Islam's grand scholar Bukhari remain a Muslim and a follower of Mohammad?

What the Minority Believe about Mohammad

We Muslims have not agreed upon the character of Mohammad until this very day and, as a Muslim reformist, the two questions I am asked frequently, if not daily, are "Do you follow Mohammad?" and "What do you think of him?" While previous pages as well as coming chapters will shed light on the Mohammad perceived by the majority of Muslims, the forthcoming paragraphs clarify what a minority of Muslims believe about Mohammad.

Prophet Mohammad is probably history's most controversial figure. He is both hated and loved by millions, with hundreds of thousands prepared to blow themselves into pieces in his defense. As an intellectual, I have always found it important to look at any historic character strictly through a historic lens, disregarding any reported miracles and divine virtues. Muslims generally do not accept discussion regarding the character of the Prophet of Islam. His character is a red line that cannot be crossed, and the penalty for crossing this red line is, in most cases, death.

Academic study of any historic character is not always accurate, and academics tend to oppose each other on many important issues within the fields of doctrine, theology, jurisprudence, and philosophy. The subject of history is no different, and because we were not present at the time to witness what really took place, all we have to guide us to the truth are historic texts, generally written by people who never saw Mohammad, and were born centuries after him, not forgetting the books that have been destroyed or have vanished throughout the centuries, as well as those that claim Mohammad did not even exist.

I could never deny the fact that the books written about Mohammad were written and presented by scholars from various Islamic sects. With over seventy schools of thought within Islam, all perceiving Mohammad differently, it is impossible to reach a correct and perfect conclusion, but what we can achieve is an idea of how the minority of Muslims perceive their Prophet.

Minority Islamic schools of thought focus on making clear that the development of Islam as a religion, and Mohammad being the Prophet of that religion, are *two separate subjects of discussion.* This is because Islam's development included many caliphs, governments, and thousands of leaders who claimed authority over the religion, all in different parts of the globe, and all of them introduced new concepts, while adding to and removing from the religion. I agree that a fair and non-biased study does not involve holding Prophet Mohammad responsible for the actions of others, otherwise everybody would be guilty of actions they did not commit. However, I will never deny that most Muslims truly believe in scriptures such as *Sahih al-Bukhari*, that depict Mohammad as a pedophile and a terrorist.

The minor Islamic sects believe Prophet Mohammad was a peaceful and humble man. They also believe he was a great leader and a sophisticated politician. I was interested to know where their evidence came from, as it had clearly influenced the works and research of great

western historians and thinkers such as Gandhi, Annie Besant, and
others such as William Montgomery Watt.

They believe in a completely different Mohammad, and their faith
revolves around a man who, they trust, set the best example of
forgiveness, and made everyone understand that Islam strives for the
best for everyone, for its devotees and its enemies alike. This minority
believes that Islam is not a religion which bears a grudge against
anyone and that it stems from a spirit of establishing peace and mercy.

Their books relate plenty of events that reflect the peacefulness of
Mohammad. Briefly, they report that Mecca was a city whose citizens
were famously known for their stubbornness and bigoted tribalism,
and that they were people of mischief and oppression, and people of
cruelty and ruthlessness. They killed for no reason, and inflicted all
manner of torture on migrants entering their city. The Meccan people
forced Mohammad out of Mecca, his birthplace and the land of his
forefathers, and massacred his companions, supporters, and relatives.
They plotted to kill him on a number of occasions, with all of them
ending in failure. They used all manner of iniquity and brutality in their
dealings with Mohammad, and when he returned powerfully to Mecca,
in an incident known as "the Conquest of Mecca," his companion Sa'd
ibn 'Obadah carried the army's banner and began to walk around the
streets of Mecca, waving it as he called out: "Today is the day of
slaughter. Today the women will be taken as slaves."

Sa'd intended to kill so many Meccans that the corpses and flesh of
those he murdered would pile up one on top of the other, and beside
each other; and to take the women as enemies and unbeliever slaves.
The Meccans expected such actions by the army of Mohammad after
they had tortured him and his followers for many years, and taken
Muslim women as slaves and hostages from the first month of the
emergence of Islam.

However, Mohammad ordered Sa'd his companion to return, and
ordered his cousin Ali to carry the banner of the army and to call out
tenderly and courteously to the Meccans the exact opposite of the call
made by Sa'd. Ali then called out repeatedly in the streets of Mecca:
"Today is the day of mercy. Today women will be protected."

Mohammad then gathered the Meccans and repeated the words of Prophet Joseph, saying: "No blame will there be upon you today. God will forgive you; and He is the most merciful." He then addressed them, saying, "Go forth. You are free."[53]

Minority denominations within Islam also report an incident that took place between the great Tamim tribe of Arabia and Prophet Mohammad regarding a number of prisoners held by his army. The historic report states:

> The Tamim Delegation came to Mohammad as intermediaries to secure the release of their prisoners, they entered Medina and came behind the Prophet's house while he was at home. They were more than eighty men from the heads of Tamim and they cried out, "O Muhammad! Come out and face us." He approached them with calmness, showed them generosity and respect, returned their prisoners to them and gave them presents after entertaining them as guests. This resulted in the Tamim tribe gradually embracing Islam, making them one of the largest Islamic tribes and families till this very day.[54]

What the minority of Muslims believe about Mohammad has deeply influenced the works of non-Muslim figures. Many intellectuals outside of the religion of Islam have had a lot to say about Mohammad, and provided some evidence for their claims.

In a statement published in *Young India* in 1924, Mahatma Gandhi stated:

> I wanted to know the best of the life of one who holds today an undisputed sway over the hearts of millions of mankind ... I became more than ever convinced that it was not the sword that won a place for Islam in those days in the scheme of life. It was the rigid simplicity, the utter self-effacement of the Prophet, the scrupulous regard for pledges, his intense devotion to his friends and followers, his intrepidity, his fearlessness, his absolute trust in

God and in his own mission. These and not the sword carried everything before them and surmounted every obstacle. When I closed the second volume [of the Prophet's biography], I was sorry there was not more for me to read of that great life.

We are certain that Gandhi was an anti-war activist and a preacher of peace; therefore, in no way would he make such a public and historic statement regarding a terrorist. Even though it sounds ridiculous, it appeared to me that Gandhi was more of a Muslim than many Islamic scholars, but could only reach such a conclusion if he had convincing evidence for his declarations about Mohammad.

After reviewing examples from each end of the spectrum, my original belief turned out to be correct: there is in fact more than one version of Mohammad.

The political, historical, social, ethical, and jurisprudential books that cover aspects of the life of Mohammad were written by scholars from many sects. They vary and contradict each other due to the different perceptions of Mohammad within all 73 Islamic schools of thought. I encourage my co-religionists to review and evaluate their historical texts. Perhaps that could lead to them following a peaceful version of Mohammad.

Mohammad's Wife, Aisha

Aisha is a sacred historical figure for Sunni Muslims and many Shia Muslims around the globe. In the following journey through Islamic scripture, I have tried to avoid exacerbating sectarian divisions by discussing Aisha both as a historical figure and also as the wife of my own Prophet, Mohammad. I have tried to produce a balanced account of Aisha, rather than merely repeating the beliefs of one denomination.

Mohammad's Marriage to Aisha

There is a massive time gap in the life of Aisha that is rarely addressed. Many things are unclear and unknown, and what raises suspicion is the fact that Muslim scholars and preachers alike do not wish to discuss certain aspects of Aisha's life. She is given the title "Mother of the Believers," and is expected to be offered the utmost respect.

Most Muslims, including prominent Shia Muslim figures such as Ali Khamenei, wish the world to view Aisha as the beautiful girl who was married to Mohammad at the age of six and lived with him until his death. They defend this belief and impose it throughout Muslim societies across the globe. They then present arguments to justify this act of pedophilia and child abuse by claiming that Aisha's marriage to Mohammad at such a young age served a political purpose, and that it had a political connotation[55] or, as the aforementioned historian William Montgomery Watt suggested, that Mohammad married Aisha because he hoped to strengthen his ties with her father Abu Bakr, who later became the first caliph after Mohammad's death.[56]

Such a suggestion implicitly gives approval to a violation of a woman's basic human right: not to be used for political purposes. I recognize that it is important for scholars today to highlight that many girls in history (including English queens) were married off for political purposes. But from a religious perspective, using women for political purposes in the name of God should be considered a serious crime. That being said, I do realize that the politics of that era had some influence on Mohammad's marriage to Aisha, in the sense that Arab culture did not allow the killing of family members or members of allied tribes; and since Abu Bakr was a prominent figure within Arabia, his sons-in-law would not be assassinated by the tribes of Arabia.

However, to claim that Mohammad married a six-year-old girl to prevent his own assassination, while her father Abu Bakr – a non-Muslim at the time – knew of this common tribal and political tactic, is an argument that is extremely hard to sell. The question is, what did Mohammad, a shepherd at the time, and who ranked first on Mecca's Most Wanted list, have to offer Abu Bakr in return for such a favor?

Nothing significant. Therefore, what is the reality that Muslim scholars have attempted to bury by using fabricated tales and weak arguments?

To begin uncovering the truth, an examination of Aisha's age upon marriage to Mohammad is vital. Islam's greatest scholars have argued about Aisha's age when she became the wife of Prophet Mohammad, with some scholars completely rejecting the common belief that she was six.[57]

Muslim scholars do not dispute the obvious permissibility of underage brides in Islam, and their argument strictly revolves around the age of Aisha when Mohammad married her. It is undeniable that most Muslims and Muslim scholars believe Aisha was six or seven at the time of her marriage to Mohammad, with the marriage not being consummated until she had reached puberty at the age of nine or ten years old. A careful examination of Aisha's age at marriage shows the poor quality of the evidence Muslim scholars have leaned upon, or possibly even fabricated for political purposes.

Grand Imam Ibn Hisham is said to have written in "his" *Biography of Muhammad* that Aisha may have been ten years old at the consummation, meaning that the marriage would have occurred at a younger age.[58] One problem with such a claim is that the aforementioned biography of Mohammad was not written by Grand Imam Ibn Hisham himself: it was actually written by Imam Ibn Ishaq, and only edited by Imam Ibn Hisham.[59] The authenticity of such a claim is in doubt, not only because it was not written by Grand Imam Ibn Ishaq, but because no copies of the original book *Biography of Muhammad* currently exist. There are claims that Ibn Ishaq's *Biography of Muhammad* is lost, and that Grand Islamic Scholars Ibn Hisham and Al-Tabari both edited and reviewed it in the eighth century,[60] almost a century after it was published by Ibn Ishaq. Also, Ibn Hisham admitted in the preface to his current edited *Biography of Muhammad*, supposedly belonging to Ibn Ishaq, that he omitted matters from Ibn Ishaq's biography that "would distress certain people."[61] A book that does not exist or only exists in an edited version, and whose editor clearly admits overlooking and subtracting passages from it, is clearly not a reliable source of historical evidence.

The strongest evidence at hand that confirms that Aisha was six years old when she married Mohammad is mentioned by Imam Bukhari in *Sahih al-Bukhari*, as he stated that "Aisha narrated that the Prophet married her when she was six years old and he consummated his marriage when she was nine years old, and then she remained with him for nine years" (i.e., until his death). [62]

Aside from the fact that Imam Bukhari is not an honest reporter of history, there are three grave problems with this report:

1. Aisha made this claim herself, and throughout the entire history and life of Mohammad mentioned in *Sahih al-Bukhari*, neither Mohammad nor Aisha's father Abu Bakr were reported to have said anything regarding Aisha being six when she was married off to Mohammad.

2. The marriage of Aisha and Mohammad acts as the bond between Mohammad and Abu Bakr, and the link between Prophecy and the future Islamic caliphate. A matter of such honor and importance would have been on Imam Bukhari's first-to-mention list.

3. Why were Prophet Mohammad's statements regarding his marriage to Aisha not reported in *Sahih al-Bukhari*, even though his statements regarding his marriages to other women were all reported?

Imam Bukhari, as I shall explain, clearly had something to hide, and it was worthwhile for him to betray history for its sake. Many academics, including Sadakat Kadri, have pointed out that, although *Sahih al-Bukhari* is considered authentic, Aisha's age at marriage was only recorded a couple of centuries after Mohammad's death.[63] This indeed is the reality of this matter.

The Truth About Aisha's Age

The claim that Aisha was six at the time of her marriage to Mohammad is a weak claim, introduced by Islamic scholars to hide a greater reality.

As mentioned earlier, Ibn Ishaq's original *Biography of Mohammad* does not exist and Bukhari's claims cannot be backed by reliable Islamic sources. It would truly be a tragic case if Bukhari (870 CE) had taken the idea from Ibn Ishaq (761 CE), and didn't quote him simply because his book does not exist.

As sophisticated as Islamic history may seem, there are always channels and networks that can indicate the truth. One figure who has been absent from this entire debate about Mohammad marrying Aisha is Aisha's sister, Asma. Asma was eighteen years older than Aisha, and lived for one hundred years, dying 14 years after the death of Aisha. Asma therefore witnessed her sister Aisha's birth and death. Asma was one of the companions of Prophet Mohammad, and she was also his sister-in-law. Therefore, historical records about such a character should be included in this discussion.

Pakistani-American author Asma Barlas PhD, who specializes in Islam and Quranic interpretation, states:

> On the other hand, however, Muslims who calculate Aisha's age based on details of her sister Asma's age, about whom more is known, as well as on details of the Hijra [the Prophet's migration from Mecca to Medina], *maintain that she was over thirteen and perhaps between seventeen and nineteen when she got married.* Such views cohere with those Hadiths that claim that at her marriage Aisha had "good knowledge of Ancient Arabic poetry and genealogy" and "pronounced the fundamental rules of Arabic Islamic ethics." [64]

While Asma Barlas is a Sunni Muslim, the Shia Islamic scholar and historian Muhammad Niknam Arabshahi conducted extensive research into the life of Prophet Mohammad and came to this conclusion on Aisha's marriage to Mohammad:

> According to these sources, we can conclude that Aisha was much older than what is claimed and narrated in some hadith, she was

nineteen years old when she got engaged to Mohammad and she would have been twenty or twenty-two when married.[65]

The debate about Aisha's age merely acts as a distraction from a reality dishonest scholars such as Imam Bukhari tried to bury within the dark pages of history. <u>Only skilled researchers can uncover **the hidden secret** that cannot be seen throughout this entire discussion. The secret that Muslim scholars during the very early years of Islam planned on hiding was that **Aisha was not a virgin** when she married Mohammad. They therefore agreed to lower her age to six when reporting her marriage to Mohammad.</u>

This matter was also noticed by the scholar of Islamic history and American historian Denise Spellberg when she reviewed Islamic literature on Aisha's virginity, age at marriage, and age when the marriage was consummated. Spellbergbelieves that Aisha's youth might have been exaggerated to exclude any doubt about her virginity, and that "these specific references to the bride's age reinforce Aisha's premenarcheal status and, implicitly, her virginity. They also suggest the variability of Aisha's age in the historical record."[66]

Aisha's supposed virginity was championed by Arabia's early Muslim scholars who promoted the idea that Aisha, the only suitable bride for Mohammad, was a virgin who was divinely intended for him. This issue of her virginity was of great political importance to those who supported Aisha's position in the debate on Mohammad's succession, supporting her father Abu Bakr in opposition to Ali, Mohammad's cousin. Supporters of Abu Bakr had been programmed to believe that a virgin had been divinely selected as a wife for their Prophet Mohammad, and to oppose those who differed on this, making the entire discussion regarding her age nothing more than a political discussion.

Although this strengthens the argument that Aisha was in her late teenage years and possibly her twenties when she married Mohammad, *this does not mean that she was not married at a younger age before Mohammad*, especially given the tactic applied by Islamic scholars to present her as a virgin. If she was indeed a virgin, then why is there a 1200-year-old ongoing argument amongst Muslim scholars? She could have been a divinely appointed virgin wife for Mohammad at the age of nineteen or twenty, not necessarily six. The fact that there have been countless attempts to hide a reality about Aisha's life before she married Mohammad *shows there are matters Muslim hierarchies do not want known.*

A valid argument in this regard is that Mohammad had many wives and some of them, such as Khadija, were divorcees. Therefore, why have the likes of Bukhari not altered Khadija's age and presented her as a virgin? The answer to this question is that Khadija did not play a political role, and there was no need to present her as a divinely appointed wife of Mohammad. Aisha on the other hand is the wife of Mohammad and daughter of Islam's first caliph Abu Bakr, making her the link between prophecy and succession. Aisha was also a political figure who led multiple wars, and her decisions shaped the structure of Islam after Mohammad only because Muslims were told she was the divinely appointed wife of Mohammad.

During the early years of Islam, the majority of births and deaths were not officially registered as they are today, and were recorded based on estimations or based on noteworthy events. Basic calculations of significant events have led many Sunni and Shia Islamic schools of thought to believe that Aisha was much older than Bukhari reported.

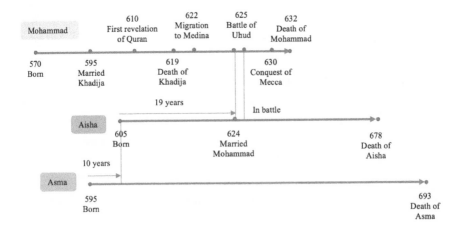

Aisha's Age at Marriage

Dr. Resit Haylamaz, a Sunni Muslim expert on the life of the Prophet and his leading companions, reflects on Aisha's life based on reliable reports. In his book *Aisha: The Wife, the Companion, the Scholar*, he writes:

> For it is known that Aisha's sister, Asma, who was born in 595, was 15 when she became Muslim. This indicates the year 610, when the Prophet started to receive the revelation, and this shows that Aisha was at least 5, 6, or 7 that day, and that she was at least 17 or 18 when she married the Prophet in Medina. Asma was born 27 years before Hijra, the Prophet's emigration to Medina ...

Here there is another critical piece of information. The age difference between Aisha and her sister Asma was 10 years. According to this, Aisha's year of birth was 605 (595+10=605) and her age at the time of Hijra (migration of Mohammad to Medina) was 17 (27−10=17). Since her marriage took place six, seven or eight months after Hijra, or just after Badr, this means Aisha was 17–18 years old at that time ...

Reports regarding Aisha's death can also help to illuminate the issue. The year in which she died is listed as the 55th, 56th, 57th, 58th or 59th year after Hijra, and her age at that time is 65, 66, 67 or 74. Just as there is no agreement regarding her date of birth, there is no agreement regarding her date of death.

Reports to the effect that she died in the 58th year after Hijra and that she was 74 when she died give the impression that they are sounder than others because they give detailed information – such as the day she died being Wednesday, that it corresponded to the 17th of Ramadan, that upon her request she was buried at night after the *Witr* Prayer in the Jannat al-Baqi Cemetery, that again upon her last request the Funeral Prayer was led by Abu Hurayra, and that she was lowered into the grave by persons like her sister Asma's two sons, Abdullah and Urwa, her brother Muhammad's two sons, Qasim and Abdullah and her brother Abdurrahman's son, Abdullah.

Therefore, when calculations are made according to this date, we see she lived 48 years after the Prophet's death (48+10=58+13=71+3=74). This means she was born three years before his Prophethood and, in view of this information, she was 17 when she married (74–48=26–9=17).[67]

Aisha's age at her marriage to Mohammad was reduced to six years old only to hide the fact that she was a non-virgin adult when she married Mohammad, with numerous relationships before him. She later admitted to this, saying: "I had a beautiful slave, and I took her out to show the public, hoping to 'catch with her' the young men of Quraysh" (a mercantile tribe in Mecca).[68]

When all of these calculations, authentic historic reports and self-confessions about Aisha are put together, the evidence that she was 18–21 when she married Mohammad is too strong to be ignored or discarded.

The "Modest" Lives of Mohammad's Wives

During the life of Mohammad, Muslims believed that he would be assassinated. Aside from all the battles he had engaged in, there were countless attempts to kill Mohammad, conducted by both apostate Muslims and the idol worshipers of Arabia. Some of those who embraced Islam and became Mohammad's companions had also plotted to kill him before they became Muslim; two of those were his future fathers-in-law, Abu Bakr and Omar ibn al-Khattab. The Quran includes a verse that stresses the probability of Mohammad's assassination: "Mohammad is nothing but a messenger. [Other] messengers have passed away before him. So, if he was to die *or be killed*, would you turn back on your heels [to disbelief]?"[69]

When Mohammad died, his wife Aisha accused the Jewish people of Khaybar of poisoning Mohammad "by sending him a cooked poisoned sheep after the battle of Khaybar in the year 628."[70] Aisha then claimed that Prophet Mohammad said, while on his deathbed: "I still feel the pain caused by the food I ate at Khaibar, and at this time, I feel as if my aorta is being cut as a result of that poison."[71] These claims by Aisha must have been fabricated as Mohammad died in the year 632, four years after the battle of Khaybar; and neither Mohammad nor the sheep would have lasted four years after consuming the poison.

After realizing the massive error she had made, Aisha began to claim that "Mohammad died as a result of pleurisy,"[72] an inflammation of the membranes that surround the lungs and line the chest cavity, even though Islamic history has not once reported that Mohammad suffered from inflamed lungs during his lifetime. The question is, why did Aisha fabricate this nonsensical story that contradicts other evidence? Grand Islamic jurists such as Al-Dhahabi have denounced her claim, saying "This is false." [73]

The truth is that, after the death and burial of Mohammad, those accused of assassinating him were his two wives, Aisha and Hafsa, daughter of Omar ibn al-Khattab, the "divinely appointed virgin wives of Mohammad" and "Mothers of the Believers," as they are labelled by most Muslims. The facts reported by all Muslim schools of thought regarding Mohammad's murder point the finger at Aisha and Hafsa, not the "poisoned" sheep or "inflamed lungs."

Ibrāhim al-Qummi, a tenth-century Islamic authority, jurist, and student of Hassan al-Askari, the ninth great-grandson of Prophet Mohammad, reported in his exegesis on the Quran (*Tafsir al Qummi*), which is based on testimonies of Mohammad's family members and grandsons:

> Prophet Mohammad informed his wife Hafsa the daughter of Omar Bin Al-Khattab of a secret, and told her that [he foresaw that] Abu Bakr will become the first Caliph after him, then your father Omar. Hafsa asked him "Who informed you of this?" Mohammad said, "The most knowledgeable God." Hafsa then raced to inform Aisha, and Aisha informed her father Abu Bakr. Abu Bakr then arrived at the house of Omar and said to him "Aisha informed me of a matter she heard from Hafsa your daughter whom I do not trust! Thus, you ask your daughter." Omar then approached his daughter Hafsa and asked her "What is Aisha narrating from you?" Hafsa then denied saying anything of such to

Aisha. Omar then said to Hafsa "If it's true, tell me, in order that we hasten it." Hafsa then admitted, saying "Yes, the Prophet informed me of that." Then, all of them gathered to poison Prophet Mohammad.[74]

It is more than clear that the wives and fathers-in-law of Mohammad plotted to assassinate him using poison. Prophet Mohammad had clearly ordered his family and companions not to place anything inside his mouth should he fall ill or unconscious.[75] Despite this, Grand Imams Bukhari and Muslim both reported Aisha's confession that she along with Hafsa had poisoned Mohammad by means of "Ladd." Ladd is an Arabic verb which means "the action of placing something strange into the mouth." The sacred Sahih al-Bukhari reports:

> We poured "medicine" in one side of the Prophet's mouth during his illness and he started pointing to us, meaning to say, "Don't pour medicine in my mouth." We said, "(He says so) because a patient dislikes medicines." When he improved and felt a little better, he said, "Didn't I forbid you to pour medicine in my mouth?" We said, "(We thought it was because of) the dislike patients have for medicines." He said, "Let everyone present in the house be given medicine by pouring it in their mouths by force while I am looking at them."[76]

In another historic report regarding this incident, after regaining consciousness Mohammad questioned them about who had placed a strange substance inside his mouth while he was unconscious, and Aisha and her entourage informed him that it was his uncle Al Abbas and not them. To this he replied: "It was in fact by Satan,"[77] implying that their actions were demonic.

One cannot help but wonder, if it was really medicine that would benefit him, why would Prophet Mohammad order them not to place it in his mouth? And why the lack of trust towards his wives, ordering that everyone present in the house should be forced to consume the same "medicine" they placed into his mouth? Clearly, it was something that Mohammad knew was harmful for him, hence he tried to prevent them from placing it inside his mouth. All of those present during this incident continued to live after Prophet Mohammad's death, which means that they did not agree to consume what Aisha had placed in his mouth. The fact that they denied feeding him this substance during his life, and accused his uncle of it instead, reveals that it was not medicine Aisha placed inside Mohammad's mouth. This is supported by the fact that he died shortly after swallowing it.

After Mohammad's poisoning and death, Aisha ordered that news of his death must not spread until her father Abu Bakr returned to Medina to take power. To appease her wishes, Omar and Uthman, the second and third fathers-in-law of Mohammad, informed the Muslims that their Prophet wasn't dead. In a public gathering, Omar said, "If I hear anyone claim that Mohammad has died, I shall strike them with my sword." He added: "Mohammad hasn't died, rather his soul has ascended to the heavens like Moses, and he shall descend and return to his body on earth."[78] He sent Salim bin Ubaid as a messenger to the city of Sanh (حنسلا) outside of Medina to inform Abu Bakr of Mohammad's death.[79] During this time, Uthman spread news that "Mohammad had been elevated to the heavens, just like Jesus the son of Mary."[80] When Abu Bakr arrived in Medina and saw the body of Mohammad, he confirmed that Mohammad had in fact passed away, and assumed the caliphate shortly after. [81]

Throughout time, prominent Islamic scholars have always known this reality, as it exists in our most sacred Islamic sources. However, the clerical institutions always strive to maintain a noble image for the wives and relatives of Prophet Mohammad for the "greater purpose" of upholding the positive reputation of the religion and its messenger.

Aisha After Mohammad

In the Holy Quran, there is a crystal-clear verse directed from Allah to Mohammad that compares his wife Aisha with the wives of the prophets Noah and Lot. The verse states:

Allah sets forth an example for those who disbelieve, the wife of Noah and the wife of Lot. They were under two of our righteous servants, but they both betrayed them [their husbands]. Nothing could protect them from the wrath of God, and it was said to them: "Enter the Fire along with those who enter!"[82]

Muslims believe that God threw the wives of Noah and Lot into hell because of their infidelity. However, even though the Quranic verse states that God had already set an example for Mohammad regarding his wife Aisha's betrayal, Muslim scholars insist on diverting attention from the context of this verse by claiming that Aisha betrayed the doctrine and message of Mohammad, not her relationship with him. Either way, Aisha would still be deserving of the death sentence under Sharia Law, whether it be for infidelity or apostasy. How Muslim scholars continue to preach that Aisha is "the pure Mother of the Believers" after the revelation of such a Quranic verse is beyond my comprehension. The Islamic texts condemn the woman Aisha developed into but, for political reasons, Muslim scholars have elevated her to the status of a saint.

Both Shia and Sunni Islamic denominations believe that the wives of Mohammad are like mothers for all Muslims, in the jurisprudential sense that nobody is allowed to marry their own mother. This means that marriage was illegal for the wives of Mohammad after his death. This ruling is deduced from the following Quranic verse: "The Prophet is worthier of the believers than themselves, and his wives are [in the position of] their mothers."[83]

Allah revealed the above verse to Mohammad because Talha bin Ubaidullah, the cousin of Aisha, had yelled loudly amongst a Muslim congregation, "Should Mohammad die, I shall penetrate Aisha."[84] This statement was considered a serious insult in Arab culture, hence the aforementioned verse was revealed to secure the honor of Mohammad. Upon her decision to engage in the Battle of the Camel in Basra, Iraq, her cousin Talha approached her and objected that she travelled without a Mahram (male guardian), saying, "It is not Halal for you to

* Another way of saying "vagina".

travel without a Mahram!" Therefore, she became intimate with him.[85]

Before this had even taken place, Malik al-Ashtar, who was the general of the Islamic Army and loyal supporter of Prophet Mohammad had received reports in Medina that Aisha was roaming around the tents of the soldiers in Mecca in a suspicious manner. Therefore, he wrote a letter to her saying:

> Dear Aisha, you are the widow of the Messenger of Allah [Mohammad], and He had ordered for you to remain in your home. If you do so, then that is good for you, and if you decide to continue in your audacity and stripping your body from its coverings, while showing people your pubic hairs,* I shall fight you until you return to your house.[86]

Aisha responded in a letter, saying, "I have received your letter, and I understood everything in it. However, God is there to protect me from you and people like you."[87] This is the family and companions of Prophet Mohammad testifying against the wife of their beloved Prophet Mohammad.

One could argue that Aisha should have been free to get married after the death of Mohammad; however, she was also accused of having numerous affairs even during the life of Mohammad. Four prominent figures within Islam and Arabia testified that Aisha had committed adultery with Safwan ibn al-Mu'attal, a nomad, a member of Mohammad's army and a commander in the Muslim conquests. The four testimonies came from Abd-Allah ibn Ubayy, Hassan ibn Thabit, a companion of Mohammad best known for his poems in defense of Mohammad, Mistah ibn Uthatha, and Hammanah bint Jahsh, sister-in-law and first cousin of Mohammad who fought alongside him in the battle of Uhud.

Islamic scriptures state that Aisha did not receive the death penalty for adultery, which was required under Sharia Law, because God immediately interfered and sent the Angel Gabriel to the crowd with "divine revelations" which declared Aisha's innocence.[88]

When this was taught to me in Islamic studies lessons, I had two options:

1. To believe that God immediately interfered and declared Aisha innocent, saving her from execution, because she is the wife of Mohammad. This overlooks the thousands of Muslim females who were and still are being stoned, beheaded, and murdered due to false allegations.

2. To believe that the Sharia Law penalty was not carried out against Aisha not because she was innocent, but because out of the four witnesses required for such a sentencing to take place, one of them was a woman (Hammanah bint Jahsh), which meant that her testimony was half that of a man and could not be used in an Islamic trial. This means that Aisha wasn't as modest as Islamic scripture claims, but simply lucky.

Although a few non-Muslim historians have dismissed this incident, claiming that it is a mere rumor, it is however obvious that such figures, both loyal followers and family members of Mohammad, would not find it in their interest to lie about Aisha, especially while knowing that falsely accusing her of immodest acts would damage their Prophet's reputation. But they were honest people who had the best interests of their Prophet at heart, while many events demonstrate that Aisha the wife of Mohammad was indeed a promiscuous woman.

Prophet Mohammad exited the house of Aisha, informing his companions that "The Horns of Satan would appear from here,"[89] i.e. this area. He then called his companions and requested their advice on how to handle the recurring rumors of Aisha's sexual affairs. Therefore Ali, Mohammad's cousin and future successor, investigated the issue and delivered the strongest opinion that advised Mohammad to divorce Aisha.[90] Mohammad however didn't divorce Aisha, probably because he did not want Muslims to consider divorce a solution to all problems. He knew that Muslims emulated his decisions and applied them to their daily lives.

Months later, Aisha began speaking about Mohammad beating her. She said, "The Prophet gave me a painful strike to my chest."[91]

The most sacred books of Islamic hadith report several incidents which raise questions about Aisha's modesty as well as adding to the solid evidence of her multiple affairs. Numerous prominent early Islamic scholars and experts in scripture have recorded that Aisha's friend Abdullah al-Khaulani said that he had slept as a guest in her house. In the morning, Aisha saw him washing his clothes and inquired why he was washing them. He informed her that he had ejaculated on them, and that he was also scraping any dry semen from the clothes of Prophet Mohammad.[92] This was not a lone incident. Another friend of Aisha, Hammam bin al-Harith, also said that he spent a night at Aisha's house, and was spotted by her slave while "rubbing off the semen from the clothe of Mohammad."[93]

While washing their clothes first thing in the morning might sound normal to a non-Muslim reader, it sounds extremely serious for a Muslim because, according to many Islamic jurisprudential rulings, semen is considered impure and it needs to be washed or removed from clothes before they can be worn for prayers; as prayers may only be performed with pure clothes. Therefore, in order for Aisha's male friends to be able to offer their dawn prayers, they woke up early in the morning and washed their clothes. The questions which arise concerning these two incidents are:

1. What were two male friends doing in the house of Aisha, both waking up washing semen from their clothes?

2. If one of the men had experienced a wet dream, what are the chances of her second friend also experiencing a wet dream?

3. Why were they scraping and rubbing their semen from the clothing of Mohammad? Was Mohammad away that night and were they wearing their Prophet's garments as sleeping clothes?

4. Or were Mohammad's garments used as sheets beneath both men and Aisha? Islamic history makes it very clear that Mohammad and Aisha owned very little in their very small house.

5. Why would two prominent Arabian men narrate such incidents to
    other Muslims knowing that it would offend them and affect the
    reputation of Mohammad's family? One can only assume that the
    two men spoke of these incidents to emphasize their nearness and
    closeness to the wife of Mohammad, which in turn would bring
    great honor to them.

Mohammad al-Baqir, the third grandson of Prophet Mohammad, who
is revered by Shia Muslims for his religious leadership and respected by
Sunni Muslims for his knowledge and Islamic scholarship as a jurist in
Medina, stated: "Everything Allah prohibited had been committed and
performed after the death of Mohammad. They even penetrated his
wives."[94]

In addition to Aisha's previous confession where she said, "I had a
beautiful slave, and I took her out to show the public, hoping to 'catch
with her' the young men of Quraysh,"[95] Islam's greatest historians and
grand scholars have confirmed that it was Aisha's will that she be
buried a distance from Mohammad and not beside him, because she
confessed that:

> I coupled behind the Apostle of Allah, and I do not know what my
> situation is going to be with Mohammad. Therefore, do not bury
> me beside him, for I would hate to be his neighbor in the grave
> without knowing what my situation would be like. Bury me beside
> his wives instead, and place his shirt above me, for it may save me
> from the punishment of the hereafter.[96]

The most troubling issue here is that even her own allies did not hold
back from mentioning her actions, as though it was a matter of
common knowledge. Muawiyah, Prophet Mohammad's brother-in-law
and the fifth caliph of Islam was Aisha's close ally. Aisha also testified
that Muawiyah was the only one recording divine messages as they
descended to Mohammad from heaven.[97] Therefore, he was a member
of Prophet Mohammad's family, an ally and a person trusted by God

and the Muslims. Yet when Aisha visited Muawiyah one afternoon, he said to his aide: "I do not have the energy to talk with this adulteress."[98] Ali, the cousin of Mohammad said, "Her obscenity was boundless."[99]

I personally am <u>not concerned</u> by how many sexual relationships Aisha had during her life, but <u>what bothers me</u> as a researcher is to read that hundreds of people were murdered by Aisha's father Abu Bakr because they engaged in sexual activities "outside the laws of Sharia," while his beloved daughter Aisha received exceptional rulings and special treatment. The point here, is that the companions of Mohammad applied Sharia Law to everyone but themselves and their loved ones.

I am not God so I will not judge Aisha and her actions. However, I will not be forced by the Islamic religious institutions and clerical hierarchies to revere her, even if she was the wife of my Prophet.

Aisha's Breastfeeding Fatwa

Aisha's sexual desires were not hidden from the Muslims of Arabia. All Muslim denominations agree that, after the death of Mohammad, his widowed wife Aisha implemented the practice of "breastfeeding the adult" or "adult suckling" (رضاع الكبير) as a form of making men related to her. This meant that men who were not her relatives would become related by her suckling them and that also there would be no need for any restrictions on those suckled men who wanted to visit her.

In an authentic Islamic report (hadith), Grand Imam Ahmad bin Hanbal stated:

> A'isha took that as a precedent for whatever men she wanted to be able to come to see her. She ordered daughters of her sisters and brothers to give milk to whichever men she wanted to be able to come in to see her. The rest of the wives of the Prophet refused to let anyone come in to them by such nursing.[100]

In a modern commentary on *Sahih Muslim*, Islamic scholar Dr. Musa

Shahin Lashin reports that "Aisha opined that adult breastfeeding makes an individual Mahram [halal related], and she practically breastfed a young man, and he would enter upon her, but the remainder wives of Mohammad rejected it [adult suckling]."[101]

Based on Aisha's verdict, Dr. Izzat Atiyya, a prominent Islamic scholar, teacher and Head of the Al-Azhar Hadith Department within Al-Azhar University – Islam's most prestigious university – issued a fatwa in 2007 stating that the Islamic rules of gender segregation and veiling can be circumvented if a woman suckles a man. Alternatively, a man can also be breastfed by the sister or mother of the woman.[102]

After this matter received global attention, it was investigated and articles were published by Al Arabiya News and the BBC. Al-Azhar University then suspended Dr. Atiyya because he provided the public with information and scriptures that must be kept hidden among scholars, as exposing them tarnishes the image of Aisha, Mohammad's wife. Dr. Atiyya fired back at Al-Azhar University by explaining his fatwa in an interview given to *Al-Watani Al-Yawm*, a weekly newspaper published by Egypt's ruling National Democratic Front. Dr. Atiyya repeatedly asserted that the sources he cited belonged to Islam's most sacred texts and had the highest possible authority. In his research, he proved that no less than 90,000 contemporary scholars confirmed that the hadith he referred to is authentic. He provided religious evidence for his "adult suckling" verdict. These are two of the numerous authentic reports he cited:

1. *Sahih Muslim*, a hadith compilation considered the second most authentic after *Sahih al-Bukhari*, reports: "Aisha said that Mohammad said to the daughter of Suhail: Suckle Abu Hudhaifa and you would become unlawful for him, and [the rankling] which Abu Hudhaifa feels in his heart [sexual desires] will disappear."[103]

2. Sunan ibn Majah, one of the six major hadith collections, reports: "Aisha said: 'The Verse of stoning and of breastfeeding an adult ten times was revealed, and the paper was with me under my pillow. When Mohammad died, we were preoccupied with his death, and a

tame sheep came in and ate it.'"[104]

After defending his position and insisting that adult suckling was legitimate in Islam based on the actions of Aisha, "the Mother of the Believers," Dr. Atiyya received waves of pressure from the Muslim world. He then apologized and withdrew his verdict. However, this does not invalidate the evidence that proves Aisha suckled adult men.

The Middle East Media Research Institute conducted intensive research on this subject, revealing that "Egyptian Minister of Religious Endowments Dr. Muhammad Hamdi Zaqzouq likewise criticized the fatwa, saying: 'Fatwas like these harm Islam and serve our enemies.'"[105] Indeed, Islamic universities and institutes are extremely sensitive about which scriptures are leaked to the public. The original Islamic sources are in Arabic, and both original sources and their translations can only be published with the license of Al-Azhar University. Before issuing the license, they inspect the book, making sure that only what people should know is published.

Interestingly, the fatwa of breastfeeding later spread to other states in the Middle East and also sparked outrage in Saudi Arabia, where women were not allowed to drive. The fatwa implied that, in order to be alone with a male driver in a taxi, they would need to breastfeed the driver. Gulf News published an article titled "Saudi Women Use Fatwa in Driving Bid," reporting:

> Saudi women plan to turn a controversial fatwa (religious ruling) to their advantage and launch a campaign to achieve their long-standing demand to drive in this conservative kingdom. If the demand is not met, the women threatened to follow through the fatwa which allows them to breastfeed their drivers and turn them into their sons. The campaign will be launched under the slogan: "We either be allowed to drive or breastfeed foreigners."[106]

However, this is not the only incident that the governing Islamic body should be ashamed of. Our most sacred books have reported that

Aisha, the wife of our Prophet Mohammad, openly talked about her sexual experiences with Mohammad. Aisha had no children with Mohammad, and it is my opinion that Aisha was suffering from jealously of Mohammad's other wives; this could explain the fabrication of dozens of quotations regarding him, and many intimate stories, such as:

- "At times, Allah's Apostle used to get up in the morning in the state of 'impurity' after having sexual relations with his wives. He would then take a bath and fast."[107]

- "The Prophet used to kiss and sexually embrace [his wives] while he was fasting, while he had more power to control his desires than any of you."[108]

Most Muslims consider Aisha's fabrications as sacred scriptures, and these scriptures form the basis of Islamic laws. The above cited narrations by Aisha contradict the rulings about fasting, namely, that there should be no sexual intimacy, as the entire religious philosophy of fasting is to refrain from any worldly desires as well as food and drink. The Fatwa Institute (Markaz al-Fatwa), administered by the Qatari Ministry of Endowments and Islamic Affairs, issued a fatwa in 2003 stating:

> It is permissible for the husband to engage in foreplay with his wife and entertain himself with her body in whatever way he wishes, except for anal and vaginal sex, during her menstrual period and fasting times. The evidence for the permissibility of the husband to "suck" the tongue of his wife is based on the narration in *Bukhari*. And what has been reported from Aisha, that Prophet Mohammad used to kiss her and suck her tongue when he was fasting.[109]

These deliberate fabrications from Aisha serve nothing but her agenda. A modest woman would never speak of the sexual experiences between herself and her husband, especially when knowing that it will be recorded throughout history. A respectful wife would be expected to honor the privacy of her husband, let alone of an apostle of God.

Aisha also went to the extent to teach Muslim men how to bathe and perform their Islamic washing rituals, when other men could have explained this to them. Shockingly, she did not just explain it to them verbally, but she went as far as demonstrating the entire washing ritual in front of them. "Aisha was asked about the bath of the Prophet. She brought a pot containing water and took a bath and poured it over her head and at that time there was a screen between her and us."[110] If she was teaching them how to shower, the screen would have had to be transparent, as there would be little benefit to teaching people who could not see her.

Aisha certainly did not lead a modest lifestyle, in contrast to what is usually taught to Muslims, and her life provides a sharp contrast to the level of strictness and oppression against Muslim women and their sexuality in modern times. I find this unacceptable. It does not make sense to me that, in the twenty-first century, Muslim women are not allowed to drive on the same land that Aisha, the wife of Mohammad, rode her camel on. If female driving is an immodest act, then how would Islam describe the infidelity of Aisha?

There are several reasons why Mohammad would marry a woman like Aisha and not divorce her even after she had cheated on him. Although many scholars believe Mohammad's original intention was a political strategy, I believe that he married Aisha to prove to the anti-feminist society of Arabia that it is not a shameful act to marry a divorced woman; and he remained with her to set an example to his nation that divorce is not a solution encouraged by God, and that one should always remain patient and consider such problems as a test from God. That would be the typical thinking and attitude of every Prophet of God.

Another matter that is rather clear in the life of Mohammad is that he did not discriminate between his wives. Even though the Muslims had an ongoing war with the Jewish nation, he married Safiyyah, daughter of Huyayy ibn Akhtab, the chief of the Jewish tribe Banu Nadir. This tribe had challenged Mohammad as the leader of

Medina,[111] and planned along with allied nomads to attack Mohammad.[112] Despite this, Mohammad said to Safiyyah, "If my other women insult you for your Jewish heritage, inform them that Aaron is my father, Moses my uncle, and Mohammad my husband."[113]

CHAPTER 3

Islam During Mohammad's Era

The speed at which Islam and the first Muslim nation developed and spread after the murder of Mohammad raises many questions. One of them is how an emerging religion with a relatively small number of adherents was able to invade and take control of continents within a matter of a few years. Misunderstandings about the history of this period have led to the majority of Muslims being misled by later extremists and prominent authors with worldly agendas. To begin with, we must inquire about the Muslim population at the time and gather information regarding their fighting skills. During the life of Prophet Mohammad, it is clear that Muslims focused primarily on Mohammad's directives as the messenger of Allah, and therefore it is essential to explore the situation of the Muslim nation throughout that period.

In his time, Prophet Mohammad never technically had a government. Governments are based on two branches: an economic system and a military branch. Neither of these existed during the time of Mohammad. The Muslim nation had a public treasury known as Bayt al-mal (House of Money), which acted as a department that dealt with the revenues and all other economic matters of the state. This public treasury was not a permanent department, as Mohammad immediately distributed all the money and revenues he received. There were no salaries paid, and there was no state expenditure. Hence there was no need for a public treasury. [11]

As for the military branch, there was no standing Muslim army. The Muslim citizens of Mecca and Medina were all volunteers during battles, because jihad was part of their faith, and they defended their lands and beliefs when they came under armed attack. There was also no need for military barracks or training centers to prepare them for jihad as just about every Arab trained their sons to ride horses and handle swords from a very young age. Therefore, what is referred to as "Mohammad's government" was in reality a nation of Muslims governed by the Quran and its laws. There was no actual government or parliament. Mohammad only spoke of God's kingdom and law, never his own. The philosophy behind this is that religions are sent to guide people, not to rule over them. This means that all "Islamic governments" are illegitimate, as Islamic law is not suitable to be used as the law of a government that is imposed upon non-Muslim citizens. Citizens of any nation should be allowed to democratically elect their leaders and vote on the formation of laws. Governing people by "God's sword" is not godly.

A question worth asking in this regard is: what was the Muslim population at the time doing to try to take over the world? Mohammad announced his prophecy in Mecca, and spent thirteen years preaching within Mecca. Islamic historians have reported that throughout these thirteen years, he only managed to gain tens of followers, including family members.[115] Mohammad's exile to Medina took place on 28 June 622 CE. The Battle of Badr, the first battle in Islamic history, took place on 13 March 624 CE against the Meccans, with *only 313 Muslim soldiers*. The Meccan army had 950 soldiers and was defeated by the Muslims. However, the Meccans killed 15 of Mohammad's soldiers, making the Muslim adult male population approximately 300.

On Saturday March 23, 625 CE, Prophet Mohammad lost his second military encounter to the Meccans due to a breach of his orders by the Muslim archers, who left their assigned posts to despoil the Meccan camp. They were surprised by an attack from the Meccan cavalry which appeared from behind a mountain and surrounded them. Out of the 800 Muslim soldiers, 75 were killed, and Prophet Mohammad himself was severely injured.

The last of Mohammad's war engagements came only five years later, with the Expedition to Tabouk, Arabia, in October 630 CE, when as many as 30,000 Arab soldiers set off to prevent a Byzantine invasion. However, the problem was that there was no sign of the Byzantine army and the battle did not take place. Also, the Muslims were not interested in confronting the Romans, and most of them made excuses not to participate. Mohammad had to provide gifts and other incentives to the many Arab soldiers to encourage them to join his army,[116] while others simply volunteered for political reasons.[117]

Before his death, Mohammad ordered Muslims to join the army of Usama ibn Zaid, whom he appointed as a commander to an expeditionary force to avenge the murder of Usama's father, Zaid ibn Harithah, his close companion who was murdered by the Kingdom of Moab and Byzantine-held Darum. Mohammad insisted that all Muslims join in this battle, saying, "May Allah curse whoever does not join the army of Usama." Usama learnt of Mohammad's death the next day, and cancelled his journey by returning to Medina. Caliph Abu Bakr insisted that Usama complete the journey and increased his army to 3000 Muslim soldiers.

Upon reviewing this chapter of Islam's history, we discover that not only were Muslim soldiers a minority, they were also disobedient to the orders of their own Prophet, which resulted in several severe defeats in battle. Also, the 30,000 Arab soldiers Mohammad provided with incentives and gifts to persuade them to join his army were not all Muslims. Most of them were Arab allies and tribes led by local chiefs, as it was part of the region's politics to lend power to each other when in need.

Therefore, our Prophet Mohammad led a disobedient army that didn't exceed 3000 soldiers. It would have been impossible for him to invade countries and continents. Out of the 100 conflicts Muslims engaged in during his lifetime, Mohammad and his key companions took part in 20 battles, simply because most of the battles during his time were minor skirmishers, such as the Nakhlah expedition, led by Abdullah bin Jahsh, involving only eight Muslim soldiers. The last thing such an incompetent Muslim army would think of doing would be to try to take over a world ruled by enormous empires and dominant armies.

When examining this episode of Islam's history, there are two things which I feel a researcher must always keep in mind: the historical facts for which there is evidence, and the exaggerations added onto the facts in order to present Muslims as an invincible minority during and after the life of Mohammad. These exaggerations in the recorded history served as motivational "facts" for Muslims and aimed to plant fear in the hearts of people from other religions; they were tactical and strategic propaganda.

CHAPTER 4

Islamic Leadership: Murder, Invasions and Terrorism

During the early centuries of Islam, a culture of war and violence existed amongst the Arabic nations as a form of conflict resolution, a show of strength, and in many cases self-defense. Alongside these three uses of violence, the politics of the Arabs in general depended upon the sword and their economic stability depended upon alliances with senior chiefs within the region for the transportation of goods. When studying such uses of violence between nations, we find that their wars operated upon on an agreed code of ethics and laws.

Prophet Mohammad engaged in 28 expeditions during his lifetime. That is an undeniable fact as there is a substantial body of evidence to support it. On one occasion, as mentioned previously, Mohammad led an army to Taboukin October 630 CE, in present-day north-western Saudi Arabia, on a mission to face the Byzantine army. The Byzantines did not attend this battle and ignored the Muslim army. After twenty long days of camping in Tabouk, Mohammad and his army returned to Medina. It is worth mentioning that the rulers of that era, Heraclius of the Byzantine Empire, Armah the king of Ethiopia, Munzir the governor of Bahrain, Khosrow II the great king of Persia, and the Muqawqis of Egypt, did not unite to defeat the army of Mohammad. This was because these well-established empires and dominant armies knew and obeyed the contemporary customs of the battlefield. At the same time, Mohammad knew his military limits and that he was leading disobedient, lazy, and unfit soldiers; therefore, he made sure that his battles and expeditions all fell within the accepted customs of war.

Islamic soldiers were religiously forbidden from acts of terrorism such as attacking children and women, and even forbidden to harm trees or pollute rivers with blood. When two forces faced each other in an agreed-upon battle, after travelling days to meet their opponents, it was not terrorism. It was considered a planned war. The point I am trying to make is that many later acts of Islamic terrorism have been justified as planned wars conducted according to the accepted customs of battle, when this was clearly not the case. There were customs of battles and wars in those days, and they played a major role in conflicts. However, terrorism is a different matter. This is why when Mohammad's terrorist successors broke the accepted customs of the battlefield and began their invasions, the surrounding empires united against them. In the year 636, Emperor Yazdegerd III of Persia united with his Byzantine counterpart, Emperor Heraclius, against Islam's second caliph, Omar, who was their common enemy. Heraclius then married his granddaughter to Yazdegerd III. This was an old Roman tradition to seal an alliance. Both emperors then started their preparations for a massive organized retaliation on their respective fronts to crush the threat of the Islamic caliph's army once and for all.

The Appointment of Caliphs

From the very beginning of Islamic caliphates, Muslim caliphs were appointed in the most absurd and uncivilized manner. There was no agreed-upon law or method for appointing caliphs to be rulers over the Muslim nation. In most cases, the leading figures of the Islamic religion fought over the caliphate. After Mohammad was murdered in the year 632, Muslims divided into two groups: those in favor of Ali, Mohammad's cousin, being the caliph and successor, and those who favored Mohammad's father in law, Abu Bakr.

Eventually, Abu Bakr was announced caliph of the Muslims in Saqifah, a roofed building belonging to a Jewish tribe called Banu Sa'idah. It was used as a meeting point for the gathering, which was a crucial turning point in the history of Islam. In the gathering of Mecca's chiefs in Saqifah, many shocking matters occurred. The close blood relatives of Prophet Mohammad were opposed to the appointment of Abu Bakr as caliph over the Muslims, and did not attend this gathering. The key figures of Islam and closest companions of Mohammad such as Ali ibn Abi Taleb, Salman al-Farisi, Abu Dhar al-Ghifari, Miqdad ibn Aswad, and Ammar Bin Yasir did not attend this appointment. The appointment of Abu Bakr was conducted by Abu Bakr himself, Omar ibn al-Khattab and Abu Ubaidah. Since Abu Bakr and Omar were the fathers-in-law of Prophet Mohammad, and key figures in Arabia before and after Islam, they managed to gather the support of eighty other Muslims. What I find so amusing amidst the political clashes and battle for worldly positions is the reaction of Ali, Mohammad's cousin, in that when the Muslims approached him and demanded that he become caliph over them, Ali said, "I put a curtain against* the caliphate and kept myself detached from it." He added: "To me, this world leadership of yours is not worth the mouth-fart of a goat."[119]

Behind the scenes of Islamic history, other matters took place which Muslim scholars do not wish to discuss. To begin with, why was Omar appointed as the second caliph after Abu Bakr? Why not the first? Islamic history shows that Abu Bakr and Omar battled over the caliphate in Saqifah. Omar said:

When I was walking towards Saqifah, I fabricated a statement regarding myself [by Prophet Mohammad], and when we reached the gathering location I wished to speak, but Abu Bakr told me to shut up. He then praised and glorified the lord, and stated regarding himself what I had fabricated to say regarding myself, and I felt as though he was reading my mind. I then extended my hand to him and pledged allegiance to him.[120]

Abu Bakr still had to find a way to placate Omar ibn al-Khattab, who ranked equally with him as both a companion and father-in-law of Prophet Mohammad. It was also clear that throughout the entire caliphate of Abu Bakr, Omar was not pleased with him, even after Abu

* This means to put a barrier between myself and the caliphate.

Bakr had promised Omar the Islamic caliphate after him. When Abu Bakr died, Omar made a public statement saying, "The pledge of allegiance to Abu Bakr was a mistake that has ended, and Allah (God) has protected the Muslims from its evil!"[121]

One may ask, didn't Mohammad appoint a successor in order to avoid this conflict amongst his family and companions? Shia Muslims believe the rightful successor of Mohammad is his cousin Ali, whom he appointed in Ghadir, saying, "Whomever considers me his master, Ali is his master." This statement was followed by congratulations from both Abu Bakr and Omar.

However, both major Islamic denominations, Sunni and Shia, agree that when Mohammad was on his deathbed, he called for a paper and pen, but Omar ibn al-Khattab objected to bringing a paper and pen to the Prophet and said, "The pain of illness has overcome him. The man is talking nonsense." Yes indeed, the future second caliph of Islam said that his beloved Prophet of God was talking nonsense!

Imam Bukhari reported:

> Prophet Mohammad said, "Fetch me writing materials so that I may have something written for you, which you will never go astray after." The people [present there] differed in this matter and people should not differ before a Prophet. They said, "Allah's Messenger is talking nonsense." The Prophet said, "Leave me alone."[122]

Not only did the companions insult their "beloved Prophet," they were too busy fighting over the caliphate to even prepare his funeral! Prominent Islamic scholar Professor Shibli Noman testified:

> It is true that Omar [and Abu Bakr] went off to Saqifah leaving the Prophet's dead body unburied; it is also true that on arriving at the Saqifah, Omar disputed over the Caliphate with the other companions and continued in his efforts to overthrow their cause in a manner as if no calamity had befallen him; and it is also true

that they [Omar and Abu Bakr] forced not only the companions but Ali and Bani Hashim as well to acknowledge the election of Abu Bakr as Caliph– though the latter did not do so readily.[123]

Eleventh-century judge, compiler of hadith, and Islamic scholar Ibn Abd al-Barr testified that it was Ali, Mohammad's cousin, who prepared his burial. He reported that Aisha the wife of Mohammad had said: "We did not know about Allah's Messenger's burial except when we heard the voice of shovels on Wednesday night. Ali, Abbas, and the tribe of Bani Hashim prayed over him."[124]

How could it be that Muslim presidents and kings today receive an honorable funeral after their deaths, but the Prophet of Islam, Mohammad, was buried without significant funeral rites? It was because his companions raced to fight over the leadership. We Muslims will never be able to prove the legitimacy of our Prophet's successors because their caliphates were silent revolutions that transformed prophetic succession into kingship.

The First Caliph of Islam: Abu Bakr

In my opinion, the culture of terrorism in Islam was officially introduced by Abu Bakr, our first caliph and father-in-law of Prophet Mohammad. He legalized it and gave it a religious coating by using violent verses of the Quran, which he interpreted to his own benefit. As he was a caliph, a ruler, this introduced a new Islamic code of conduct to be followed by future generations of Muslims.

Aside from the fact that our Caliph Abu Bakr had plotted to assassinate Prophet Mohammad before embracing Islam, there are two main acts of terrorism he introduced after becoming the companion, father-in-law, and successor of Mohammad: beheading his opponents and burning his opponents alive. The crimes of ISIS are not merely a result of personal desires or political tactics aiming to bring fear to surrounding governments; they are in fact revivals of practices committed by Islam's first caliph as sentencing for opponents of Islam.

The Beheadings

Since many Muslims, including the entire family of Prophet Mohammad, didn't pledge allegiance to Abu Bakr, he resorted to the use of force to protect his government and throne. More importantly, he formed healthy relations with surrounding kingdoms to prevent any revenge attacks from wars during the time of Prophet Mohammad, wherein he was also a participant, since he knew very well that he was not left with much of an army. Abu Bakr then focused on the economic aspect of his kingdom, disguising it as a caliphate.* He revived the Islamic finance system of *zakat*, and ordered all Muslims to pay Islamic taxes to his caliphate.

When Abu Bakr didn't receive the response he desired from the Muslims, he requested that Malik ibn Nuwayrah start collecting the Islamic taxes, and was prepared to kill whoever didn't pay him *zakat* (charity tax)[125]. Malik was a close and trustworthy companion to Prophet Mohammad, and Mohammad had appointed him as an officer whose main responsibility was collecting taxes and dispatching them to Medina. Aside from this, Malik was a chief of some distinction, a famous warrior known for his generosity, hospitality, competence with his use of weapons, courage, eloquent poetry, and his striking charm. He was married to Layla bint al-Minhal who was considered one of the most beautiful women in Arabia. Malik possessed all the qualities which Arabs looked for in the perfect male. However, Abu Bakr's decision to make Malik the collector of Islamic taxes didn't have a successful outcome because Malik was an opponent of Abu Bakr and his caliphate. When news of Mohammad's death reached Malik, he had just collected a large amount of Islamic tax money but had not yet dispatched it to Medina. He refused to submit the funds to Abu Bakr and instead returned them to the taxpayers, announcing to them "your wealth is now yours."[126] Abu Bakr desperately needed Malik to begin collecting taxes from the Muslims, as the far and distant tribes knew Malik from the time of Prophet Mohammad, and had trusted him with their Islamic taxes. When Malik refused to do so, Abu Bakr ordered Khalid ibn al-Waleed to pressure Malik into it.

---

* The difference between a kingdom and a caliphate in this sense is that a religious kingdom governs the affairs of a group of citizens and their religious affairs in a specific location, whereas a caliphate considers itself a successor of God's messenger Mohammad which is administering God's actual government on Earth. Although caliphates may exist in certain parts of the world, their ideology pushes them to govern the entire globe.

The tragedy of Malik has been reported in numerous Islamic sources.[127] An exceptionally accurate account of the event was written by Sir John Bagot Glubb:

> Abu Bakr sent Khalid Ibn al-Waleed to Malik's tribe with 4000 men. Malik was a chief of some distinction, a warrior, noted for his generosity and a famous poet. Bravery, generosity and poetry were the three qualities most admired among the Arabs. Unwilling perhaps to demean himself by bowing to Khalid, he ordered his followers to scatter and he himself moved away across the desert alone with his family. Abu Bakr had given orders that the test to be applied to suspected rebels was that they be asked to repeat the Muslim formula and that they answer the call to prayer. Khalid, however, preferred more aggressive methods and sent out parties of horsemen to round up the fugitives and plunder their property. One such party seized Malik ibn Nuweira and his family and brought them in to Khalid, although they claimed to be Muslims. The men of Medina who were with the army protested vigorously against Khalid's ruthlessness, but without avail. The prisoners were placed under guard but, during the night, Malik ibn Nuweira and his supporters were killed in cold blood. Within 24 hours Khalid had married the widow of his victim.[128]

Many Muslims defend Khalid and have nicknamed him the "Sword of Allah," while claiming that his sexual interaction with Layla was through a legitimate marriage. This claim cannot be true as Islamic jurisprudence does not allow marriage during the 'waiting period' after a woman is divorced or widowed (around 4 months and 10 days).

Sir Glubb went on to state that "Khalid's marriage to the beautiful Layla gave rise to the suspicion that Malik had been killed with the object of making her available to the conqueror."[129] There is a consensus among Muslim scholars on this matter, and prominent Islamic poets have written about this tragedy.[130] Countless Islamic sources testify that Khalid also cooked Malik's head in a saucepan and ate from it after he had beheaded him. He did that to place more fear in the hearts of the Arab tribes.[131]

When Abu Qatada, a companion of Mohammad, hastened to Medina to complain to Abu Bakr about what Khalid had done to Malik and his wife, Khalid was summoned to answer the accusation. Khalid exclaimed, "I will not sheathe a sword which God has drawn for His service." Abu Bakr accepted Khalid's excuse and set him free.[132]

Omar objected to Khalid's actions and said to him: "You enemy of Allah! You killed a Muslim man and then leapt upon his wife. By Allah, I will stone you."[133] However, Omar did not stone Khalid due to Khalid's prominence within Arabia and, surprisingly, Omar appointed Khalid the leader of the Islamic armies during his caliphate!

Regarding this horrific killing and beheading of Malik, eating his head and raping his wife, Muhammad al-Tijani, a prominent Tunisian Muslim scholar, academic, and theologian, said: "It is a case in which Islamic history does not want to go too deep, for the sake of the Companion's [Khalid's] honour."[134]

A moment's research on this matter will reveal that this monstrous and horrific culture was instituted by the caliphate of Abu Bakr. While one could argue that beheadings had in fact existed during the time of Mohammad, the difference is that Mohammad clashed with his enemies during wars and on battlefields, which gave his enemies an equal opportunity to respond, such as in the battle of Uhud, where Muslims were slayed by the Meccans. Abu Bakr, on the other hand, invaded cities and villages without warning, and took his victims by surprise.

Today, ISIS commits the very same crime by beheading its opponents and eating the heads of its victims after cooking them in pots. The Caliph of ISIS adopted the name "Abu Bakr al Baghdadi," that is, "Abu Bakr of Baghdad," instead of his real name Ibrahim Awad Ibrahim al-Badri, in order to revive the method of violent governance initiated by Abu Bakr, the first caliph of Islam.

Burning People Alive

When the world saw ISIS militants placing their victims in cages and burning them alive, they wondered where this culture had emerged from. Islamic jurists rule that it is forbidden to kill with fire, because of a report by Imam Bukhari that states: "No one should punish with fire except Allah [God]."[135] This however is not what most Muslims believe, because *Sahih al-Bukhari* was compiled 214 years after the death of Mohammad, and because it contradicts the verdicts and rulings of the first caliph of Islam, Abu Bakr, who used to punish with fire. Abu Bakr wielded the divine authority of Allah over all Muslims, including Imam Bukhari. Thus, any opinions different from those of the Islamic caliph are deemed irrelevant in Islamic jurisprudence.

In a period of just two years, our Caliph Abu Bakr burnt hundreds of people alive. Banu Sulaym were an Arab tribe that in the pre-Islamic era had dominated part of the Hejaz, a region in the west of present-day Saudi Arabia. They maintained close ties with Mecca and Medina, and fought in a number of battles against Prophet Mohammad before ultimately converting to Islam before his demise in 632 CE. Most of the Banu Sulaym tribe apostatized from Islam during the rule of Abu Bakr, after witnessing the corruption of his caliphate. Abu Bakr classified them all as apostates and waged war against them. He assigned Khalid ibn al-Waleed, who had recently beheaded, cooked, and eaten the head of Mohammad's companion, Malik ibn Nuwayrah, before raping his wife, as his main adviser and architect of strategic planning of the wars on apostates. Abu Bakr gave him the command over the strongest Muslim army and directed him towards central Arabia.[136] He then sent him a letter saying:

> If Allah allows you to grab hold of Banu Hanifa, don't waste too much time with them. Head towards Banu Sulaym, and pressure them mercilessly, as there is no Arab tribe that I am annoyed with more than them. Thus, If Allah allows you to grab hold of them, I will not blame you if you were to burn them with fire, kill and butcher them as their punishment.[137]

When the Banu Sulaym tribe heard that Abu Bakr had sent Khalid to murder them all, they formed an army led by Abu Shajarah, an ex-Muslim and Arabian warrior. "Caliph Abu Bakr's army reached the army of Banu Sulaym the next morning. Khalid ordered them to prepare their weapons and arranged their position and his army began to butcher the apostates."[138] An army general's usual duty is to give orders and monitor the battle; however, to satisfy Caliph Abu Bakr,

Khalid stepped down to the battlefield and began killing many of them, he then launched an attack on the remaining apostates and they fled. He captured many of them and took them hostage. Khalid then gathered them in a building and burnt them alive.[139]

Prominent Islamic jurists Ibn Kathir, Ibn Al-Athir, and Al-Tabari have all testified that our Caliph Abu Bakr burnt people alive as a form of punishment. One of these incidents involved a man by the name of Fuja'ah al-Sulami who approached Caliph Abu Bakr announcing that he was a Muslim and wanted to fight the apostates. Abu Bakr then prepared him with weapons, including swords and spears, and archers and supported his mission. Fuja'ah was accused of killing Muslims instead of apostates, and therefore Abu Bakr ordered him to be arrested. Abu Bakr burnt Fuja'ah alive by preparing a massive fire and throwing him into it with his hands and legs tied together.[140]

On his deathbed, Abu Bakr allegedly regretted killing Fuja'ah in such a way.[141] Even if we were to assume that our Caliph Abu Bakr had sincerely regretted burning Fuja'ah alive, he is still accountable for the hundreds of other people he and Khalid burnt alive, stoned, and threw off high buildings and off mountain tops while alive, for the "crime" of not believing in his leadership.[142]

Islamic authorities today do not wish the actions of their caliphs and successors of Mohammad to look like they contradict Islamic teachings. Therefore, they have resorted to creating excuses for these acts of terrorism, making it permissible to burn with fire by way of retaliatory punishment, stating: "Whoever burns others is to be burnt."[143] Abu Bakr also said that homosexuals are to be burned alive. However, the people Caliph Abu Bakr burnt alive were innocent people, even according to his own standards. They had not burned anyone alive and neither were they known to be homosexual.

It should not be surprising that Islamic governments are terrorist governments, simply because they are founded upon terrorist formulas that lead them to be the most active sponsors of terrorism. For example, the Islamic Republic of Pakistan has long been accused by its neighbors, as well as the United States and the United Kingdom, of being responsible for sponsoring, supporting, and tolerating terrorist activities. The United States Defense Secretary has described Pakistan's tribal regions as havens for terrorists.[144] After reading about the crimes committed by Abu Bakr and his general Khalid ibn al-Waleed, it is no longer shocking nor unexpected when individuals such as Agha Ali Ibrahim Akram, Muslim historian and Lieutenant-General of Pakistan's army and its Ambassador to Spain, shamelessly describes Khalid ibn al-Waleed as one of the finest military generals in history.[145]

Muslims, Islamic governments, and caliphates will never be able to escape this bloody and violent history. It is ours, forever engraved. It is part of our being and existence. The only way forward is to turn around and condemn the violence and terrorism that was committed in our name by the Islamic caliphs.

Massacre after Massacre

In May 632, as previously mentioned, Prophet Mohammad appointed Usama ibn Zaid as the commander of an army to respond to the Romans in an agreed-upon battle within Palestine. The next day Usama set out for his expedition, but he then learnt that Mohammad had died and therefore he returned to Medina. Abu Bakr then ordered Usama to increase his army to 3000 men, and to attack the inhabitants of the Kingdom of Moab and Byzantine-held Darum, to kill or capture as many as he could, and Usama did so.[146]

The strange thing about this situation is that the Romans of the Byzantine wanted to engage in war with Prophet Mohammad; hence Usama returned to Medina as it would be meaningless for an army general to engage in a battle on behalf of a deceased Prophet. It would also not benefit the Byzantine Empire to announce victory over an army whose Prophet had passed away. They would prefer the leader, Mohammad, to be alive to witness or hear of the outcome of the battle. When the Romans heard of Mohammad's death, they returned from Moab and Darum to where they had set out from. However, Abu Bakr didn't want a just and fair battle with the Romans; therefore, he ordered Usama to take advantage of the army's absence and massacre the citizens.

From studying the life and political tactics of Caliph Abu Bakr, I believe he sent Usama even after Mohammad had died and increased his army to 3000 soldiers for an important reason, namely to get as many influential Muslim figures and warriors out of Medina as possible in order to ensure a smooth transition to the throne, without any obstacles or objections in his path. It is also possible that he sent those he was intimidated by, hoping they would be killed by the Romans should they be surprised by an army upon their arrival, or possibly die on the way back to Medina from injuries.

Caliph Abu Bakr exhorted maximum effort to censor written reports that would reveal his true actions to surrounding regions and future generations. Writing and oral transmission of reports were the only forms of media at the time. Therefore, with the distances between regions, it wasn't difficult for a ruler to prevent news reaching a wide audience. Recording events was a source of income for many, and the more accurate a journalist was, the more valuable their reporting. Abu Bakr's own daughter, Aisha the wife of Mohammad, testified: "One morning my father said 'Oh my daughter! Bring me all the Hadiths that are with you'. I gave them to him and he burnt them."[147]

Attempting to Burn Mohammad's Ex-Wife

Prophet Mohammad had married a woman named Qutaylah one month before his death. She lived in another location and therefore they did not meet often due to his illness. Historians have also testified that there was no intimacy between her and Mohammad. During his severe illness before his death, Mohammad gave Qutaylah the option of choosing to wear the veil, as a married woman, or divorcing him and marrying another man. She chose divorce, left Islam and went to marry a man by the name of Ikrimah ibn Abi Jahl. When Caliph Abu Bakr was informed of this news, he stated, "I was urged to burn the house over them," but Omar convinced him otherwise, saying "She is not a mother for the believers (wife of Mohammad), Mohammad did not enter her or make her wear the veil." Whereupon Abu Bakr remained silent.[148]

Qutaylah would have been killed if she and Mohammad had a complete husband and wife relationship. How this makes sense to Muslim authorities today is beyond me. Clearly, Omar was portraying himself as a religious and pious individual in this sole instance, because when his caliphate began he burnt many homes and villages.

The Fabrication of Religion

Caliph Abu Bakr admitted to fabricating parts of the religion, and making statements that were not the teachings of the Prophet. In other words, he used his caliphate to hijack Islam and introduce his own religious system; and when he was appointed caliph, he testified to engineering parts of the religion. Grand Islamic jurist Ibn Kathir has reported that Abu Bakr sat on the pulpit of Mohammad and said: "Oh, people! Yesterday I said things which I did not find in the Book of Allah nor did the Prophet entrust them to me." He then continued to address the Muslim congregation by ordering them to pledge allegiance to him, saying: "Allah has placed your affairs in the hands of the best one among you [himself], the Companion of the Prophet, so get up and pay allegiance."[149]

Appointing Omar as the Second Caliph

On his death bed, Caliph Abu Bakr verbally announced that Omar would succeed him as caliph. The Muslim nation wasn't pleased with Omar due to his murderous history, evil reputation, and corrupt nature, and this was well known to Caliph Abu Bakr. The people publicly objected to Abu Bakr's decision and said, "He has appointed

Omar as though there was no other man to appoint, and we have experienced Omar's treatment before he becomes Caliph, therefore how will he treat us if he had authority over our necks!?" They raised their voices at Abu Bakr saying, "Once you meet your Lord, what will you answer him after you appoint Omar as Caliph after you!?" Abu Bakr then proved his blasphemous disbelief by saying: "Are you trying to scare me with my Lord? I will tell God that I appointed the best of your creation as Caliph over them."[150]

During his life, Abu Bakr insisted that the tyrant Omar would succeed him. However, as humans get closer to death, we begin to reflect upon our choices in life and the decisions we have made. The time came when Abu Bakr was severely affected by illness, and commanded Uthman bin Affan to write his will. Abu Bakr then began to pronounce his will while Uthman recorded it on paper, and when he reached the following words: "I have appointed as a successor" Abu Bakr requested Uthman to leave a space and not to write anyone's name. Abu Bakr became unconscious before mentioning the name of his appointee, but Uthman took the document and filled in the space with Omar's name. Abu Bakr then regained consciousness and said to Uthman: "Show me the document!" When he read the document, he saw that Omar's name was written as the appointed successor. Abu Bakr said, "Who did this!?" Uthman replied, "I did." Abu Bakr then said, "You would have been more fitting for it [the caliphate] had you written your own name instead."[151]

When Abu Bakr died, Omar accepted the caliphate based on this will and earlier promises made to him by Abu Bakr. However, it is interesting that Omar prevented his own Prophet from writing a document due to him being ill, while accusing him of "talking nonsense," but had no problem accepting a document written by Uthman, on behalf of the unconscious Abu Bakr, only because it was to his benefit. Our caliphs – who are the fathers-in-law of Prophet Mohammad – were nothing more than hypocrites hungry for the seat of leadership. **Therefore, I reject their authority, even though this is seen as a form of apostasy by the majority of Muslims.**

Our Caliph Abu Bakr committed many crimes during his rule as caliph, but appointing Omar as a caliph after him, while knowing his nature, was the worst. Abu Bakr had now paved the way for the crimes, murders, massacres, wars, and invasions of Caliph Omar.

The Second Caliph: Omar ibn al-Khattab

Terrorism was the mastered art of our second caliph, Omar ibn al-Khattab, who just like Abu Bakr, was also the father-in-law of Prophet Mohammad and his companion. He embraced Islam in the year 616 CE, at the age of 32, and reigned from August 23, 634 to November 3, 644. During his entire time in Mecca, before and after embracing Islam, Arabia had never witnessed or heard of terrorism worse than the terrorism introduced by Omar during both caliphates, Abu Bakr's and his. He is presented by most Muslim historians as a charming warrior and a perfect role model for all of humanity. However, the reality is that he was far from charming, both before and after embracing Islam. The following examples from his life are historical facts we Muslims can never deny; they are engraved in our history and identity, but have never been translated for the outside world to read.

Murdering His Daughter

One of the crimes committed by our Caliph Omar was the murder of his own daughter, as he was ashamed that his wife had given birth to a girl. His wife hid the newborn daughter in the house of her brother, who lived in a different area, and informed Omar that his daughter had passed away while he was travelling. Once the baby had grown into a young girl, her mother brought her home, truly believing that Omar's heart would become merciful once he saw his daughter, and that she would have passed the age when newborn girls could be buried alive out of shame. When he saw his daughter for the first time, he remained silent. A few days passed, then he took her to the desert and began to dig a grave for her. As he was digging her grave, the young girl cleaned the sand from his beard. When he had finished, he climbed out of the grave and told his young daughter to look inside the hole. He then pushed her into the hole and buried her alive.[152]

Omar had seven wives, Zaynab, Qurayba, Jamila, Atiqa, Um Hakim, Um Kulthum daughter of Jarwal, and Um Kulthum daughter of Caliph Abu Bakr. Because Omar had multiple wives in one building, Muslim historians do not know the name of the daughter he murdered and who her mother was. However, Caliph Omar himself confessed to this crime.

Dr. Muhammad Shinqiti, an Islamic jurist and interpreter of the Quran, who was a former member of the Council of Senior Scholars, Saudi Arabia and a teacher within the two sanctuaries of Mecca and Medina, reported:

Omar ibn Al-Khattab said, "There were two things in the pre-Islamic era, one of them makes me cry and the other one makes me laugh. The one that makes me cry; I had taken a daughter of mine to bury her alive and I was digging the hole for her while she was dusting my beard off without knowing what I am planning for her, when I remember that, I cry. And the other one is that I used to make a God of dates that I put over my head to guard me during the night, then when I woke up I would eat it, and whenever I remember that I laugh at myself." [153]

Prominent Islamic jurists and influential scholars have also testified to this incident within their publications. They explain:

Arabs used to dig a hole under the pregnant woman whenever she experienced labor, in order that the child will be placed into it when delivered. If he was a boy they would take him out of it and if she was a girl then they would leave it and they would dump soil over her body till she dies, and that Omar Ibn Al-Khattab testified to the Prophet Mohammad, saying" O Messenger of Allah, I have committed female infanticide during the pre-Islamic era." [154]

A Torturer of Women

Omar earned a reputation for being violent towards women even before he embraced Islam, whether they were related to him or not. Aside from the fact that he buried his own daughter alive, violence and torture were his preferred options when dealing with females.

He wasn't "courageous" enough to kidnap and torture men who were converting to Islam at the time. He kidnapped a slave woman called Labina[155] who had become Muslim before him, and "kept on beating her until his arms grew tired and the whip fell from his hand, then he stopped to rest."[156] On another occasion, as reported by grand Islamic scholar Ibn Hisham, editor of *The Biography of Mohammad* and master of Arabic philology, Omar kidnapped another slave woman called Zennaira from the Arabic tribe of Bani Adi: "He beat her until he was tired, then he said to her: 'I apologise to you that I had to stop hitting you, that is only because I got tired!'"[157]

Eminent Islamic historians and biographers Al-Baladhuri and Al-Waqidi both reported that Omar kidnapped both Labina and Zennaira, and was torturing them on the same occasion. Mohammad's close companion Hasan ibn Thabit testified against Caliph Omar, saying:

> I went to Mecca as a Pilgrim, and while Prophet Mohammad was inviting people to his faith, I saw Omar Ibn al Khattab busy suffocating slave-girl Labina until she relaxed in his hands, whereupon I yelled, "She is dead!" [when she was still alive]. Then he left Labina and bounced over to Zennaira to do the same to her.

Hassan couldn't defend the women because he feared "being tortured and persecuted." Omar's actions were so extreme that "Abu Bakr passed by and saw how the slave women were being tortured, so he bought them from him and set them free."[158] Although Abu Bakr was himself also a terrorist, he did, at times, show mercy towards women.

Violence and Intolerance

Our Caliph Omar ibn al-Khattab "disciplined" people using violent methods. Muslim scholar and prominent author Ali Muhammad al-Sallabi documented that Omar was famous for carrying his stick with which he struck people. He struck some of the governors because of some deeds that they committed. During Omar's visit to Syria, he entered the house of one of his governors and found they had too many possessions and assets. Omar got angry and started hitting them with his stick. During Umar's visit to Syria, some of the governors came to meet him. The first ones who met him were Yazeed the son of Abu Sufyan and Abu Ubaydah, then Khalid, who came riding his horse and wearing fine garments that did not befit the Jihadists. Omar dismounted his horse, picked up some stones and started stoning them, and said, "How quickly you have changed your ways! Are you welcoming me in this manner?"[159]

What is more interesting than the way they welcomed him was the way he greeted them – by stoning them!

Wife Beater

As a Muslim, I have to admit that our Caliph Omar ibn al-Khattab, the father-in-law of Prophet Mohammad, was a misogynist. His attitude didn't change when he embraced Islam, because he still believed women should receive the worst treatment possible. Many grand jurists of Islam have testified to this, including the eminent Al-Hakim Al-Nishapuri, a prominent intellectual and leading historian of Islamic scriptures, He reported:

> Al-Ash'ath ibn Qays [a Muslim chief] said: "I was a guest at the home of Omar one night, and in the middle of the night he went and hit his wife, then he called onto me and said: 'O Ash'ath, learn from me something that I heard from Prophet Mohammad saying, A man should not be asked why he beats his wife.'"[160]

On another occasion, Caliph Omar's wife Jamila asked him for money and was physically assaulted in return. During their divorce case, Omar testified to Prophet Mohammad, saying, "I slapped her with a blow that floored her, because she asked me for what I did not have."[161]

Beating Another Man's Wife

When examining the life of Caliph Omar in depth, we find that his violence towards women had no limits. In one incident:

> A woman came to Omar and said: My husband is very bad and is not good. Omar said to her, "Who is your husband?" She said, "Abu Salamah." Omar knew him, for he was a companion of the Prophet. Omar said to her, "We only know good about your husband." Then he asked a man who was near him, "What do you say?" He said, "We do not know anything but that he is good." Omar sent for her husband and told her to sit behind him [Omar]. A man soon came back with her husband and Caliph Omar asked him, "Do you know this woman?" He said, "Who is she O Caliph?" [because she was wearing a burqa] He said, "She is your wife!" He asked, "What is she saying?" He said, "She claims you are very bad and not good." He said, "What a bad thing she has said, by God, she is the best clothed woman and has the most comfortable home, but her husband is impotent." Omar then said to her, "What do you say?" She said, "He is telling the truth." Omar took his stick and started hitting her, saying, "O enemy of yourself, you have taken his youth, consumed his wealth and now you're saying things that are not right about him." She said, "O Caliph, let me off this time, and by God you will not see me do this again."[162]

Such a matter could have been resolved in a more just and appropriate way. If she had indeed been exposed as a liar, there was absolutely no need to beat her with a stick in front of the entire gathering. Omar's swift resort to violence reveals a lot about his character.

Go and Beat Your Wife!

In Islam, if a woman suckles two unrelated children, they become related to each other in the sense that they are not allowed to marry each other when they grow up. Imam Malik ibn Anas* reported in his book *Muwatta*, the earliest authentic written collection of Islamic reports, that Abdullah the son of Omar ibn al-Khattab said:

> A man came to my father Omarand said, "I have a slave-girl and I used to engage in sexual intercourse with her. My wife went to her and suckled her. When I went to the girl, my wife told me to watch out, because she had suckled her!" Therefore, Omar ordered the man to beat his wife and to go to his slave-girl [to enjoy her company] because kinship by suckling was only by the suckling of the young.[163]

This of course stems from Caliph Omar's ruling that slaves are property, and can be fornicated with under any circumstances. In this case, he ordered a man to cheat on his wife once he had finished beating her.

The Rapist Caliph

It was on August 3, 2010 when I discovered that our second Caliph Omar, father-in-law of Prophet Mohammad, was a rapist. I had purchased an Arabic encyclopaedia titled *The book of the Major Classes* (*Kitab-ut-Tabaqaat-il-Kubraa*), a compendium of biographical information regarding the lives of recognized Islamic figures, authored by Ibn Sa'd, a prominent Islamic scholar and Arabian biographer of the eighth and ninth century. The last two volumes of this encyclopedia contain detailed reports regarding women in the early years of Islam.

Islamic history doesn't mention how Caliph Omar and his wife Atiqa bint Zayd came to be married. However, within this encyclopedia lies a testimony regarding Atiqa which most Muslim scholars have kept secret. Atiqa's own brother, Ali bin Zayd, said:

---

* Malik ibn Anas was an Arab Muslim jurist, theologian, hadith expert, founder of the Maliki Islamic denomination, and the premier scholar of prophetic traditions.

Atiqa was married to Abdullah the son of Abu Bakr, he died leaving her with a kind request that she marries no one after him. She agreed to his request and did not get married, rejecting many proposals. Caliph Omar proposed to her and she rejected him, he then approached her religious guardian and ordered him to marry Atiqa off to him, and he did. Omar then approached her, entered her home, wrestled with her till he won, and then coupled with her. When he finished, he said "uf, uf, uf"* – he then left her house and did not return to her. Atiqa sent her slave woman to inform Omar that she is prepared to be his wife.

She said this because of the earlier Islamic marriage process conducted by her guardian.[164] Atiqa was a victim of forced marriage to Omar, consummated by rape. What makes this incident even more shocking is the fact that Atiqa and Omar were cousins, with Nufayl being their common grandfather.

Caliph Omar: Female Slaves Should Not Be Modest

Three of the most significant authors and specialists in the field of Islamic scripture* have authenticated a report that "Omar saw a slave-girl wearing Hijab [headscarf], he then beat her and said: 'Do not make yourself look like free/liberated women!'"[165] Another report states:

A slave girl came to Omar wearing a complete body veil, he said to her: "Have you been freed?" She said: "No." He said: "Take it off your head. The veil is for the freed women only." She hesitated, so he got up to her with the whip and hit her on the head, until she threw it.[166]

Ibn Hajar reported two versions of this incident, with a second report testifying that "Omar began his sentence stating: 'Take off your veil, you stinky! Are you resembling yourself to free women?'"[167] Grand Imam Al-Albani commented on this report, saying: "This is an

* An Arabic expression of surprise or amazement, similar to the word "wow" in English.

* Grand Islamic Jurists Abi Shaybah, Al-Albani, and Ibn Hajar al-'Asqalani, all of whom are scholars of Islam who represent the majority of the Islamic world in the field of Islamic reports (hadith).

authentic report."[168]

Exploiting His Female Slaves

I thought that I had heard about all the forms of oppression and humiliation that women endured at the hands of our Caliph Omar. Then I had to think again. I was disgusted and offended to read a report classified "authentic" in the books of two aforementioned prominent Islamic scholars, Al-Bayhaqi and Al-Albani, that stated: "The slave-girls of Omar were made to serve us with uncovered hair and their breasts were shaking."[169]

After reading the previous examples, this should not have surprised me. Clearly, our "modest" Caliph Omar considered slave women as property who were not entitled to cover themselves, and he believed that they should reveal their beauty to his perverted and strange guests, thus shaming the women. How we were raised to label such a man "Prince of Believers" is beyond me!

It's Illegal to Cry

Prophet Mohammad's cousin, Ibn Abbas, narrated an incident that occurred before his eyes:

> When Zainab the eldest daughter of Mohammad died, he [the Prophet] said: "Join my pious friends and companions [in paradise]," whereupon the women began to cry. Omar then started to beat them with his whip, so the Mohammad took his hand and said: "Leave them O Omar!" Omar then said to the women: "Do cry, but be careful not to whoop like Satan!"

More than ten grand Islamic historians and jurists have reported this barbaric and violent incident and classified it as "authentic."[170]

Caliph Omar also prohibited crying over the death of Caliph Abu Bakr, the very caliph who appointed him. He went on to beat his daughter Aisha, the widow of Prophet Mohammad, for mourning the death of her father. Grand Islamic jurists Ibn Hajar Asqalani, Ibn Sa'd and Al-Tabari all reported:

> When Abu Bakr died, A'isha held a gathering in which eulogies had been recited for him. Omar was informed of it, so he forbad them from doing so and ordered Hisham Ibn Al-Walid to "Bring the sister of Caliph Abu Bakr (Um Farwa) out for me!" He then lashed her. When the news reached the mourners, they escaped out of the building, and "He brought the women one by one and beat them with his whip."[171]

Torturing Questioners

Islam had never been ruled by a savage tyrant like our Caliph Omar. Prominent scholars and interpreters of the Quran* have reported a tragic incident whereby a loyal and devout Muslim by the name of Sabeegh bin Asal al-Tamimi (Arabic: صبيغ بن عسل التميمي) travelled to Medina with the intention of understanding and interpreting the Quran. Prophet Mohammad had died and therefore he approached the gathering wherein Caliph Omar was present. He greeted the gathering and informed Caliph Omar that he had arrived in order to learn from his knowledge. The man asked Caliph Omar about the "decisive and allegorical" verses of the Quran.**

However, Caliph Omar did not know the answer and was embarrassed before the gathering. Thus, he beat Sabeegh with a tree branch until his back was completely wounded and bleeding. Omar then left Sabeegh to regain his breath, and then commenced beating him again, and repeated this three times. Sabeegh then said to Omar, "If you wish to kill me, then kill me once and for all, and if you wish to punish me, by now, I have forgotten the questions I dared to ask you [due to the severity of the punishment]." Caliph Omar then freed him, and wrote to the Muslims to shun Sabeegh and not to allow him into

* Grand Islamic jurists Al-Darimi, Al-Asbahani, and Ibn Asakir.
** Known in Arabic as "Muhkam and Mutashabih."

their gatherings.[172]

Such an episode could only occur due to the caliph's lack of knowledge. Many Muslim children have memorized the entire Quran by the age of 10, yet Islam's greatest figure at the time was ignorant about the most basic laws of Islam. Caliph Omar did not know that the Quran contained a verse about the certainty of human death: "(Oh, Mohammad,) Indeed, you are to die, and indeed, they are to die." He said: "By God, it seems like I have never heard of this verse until today!"[173]

During the pre-Islamic era and throughout the early years of Islam, Arabian society looked down upon women, and officially considered them uneducated creatures existing to serve men. To them, a woman's intellect is half that of a man. However, they made an exception in this case, as it was said that "Everybody has more knowledge than Omar, even women!"[174]

Yet the Muslim world ignores the ignorance of our caliphs and continues to glorify them. Abdullah ibn Masud, the personal servant of Prophet Mohammad, used to say: "If the knowledge of Omar was put on a scale, and that of all the people of the world on the other side of that scale, Omar's side would win."[175]

The companions and fathers-in-law of Prophet Mohammad were delusional people who reigned over the Islamic nation while lacking knowledge in the basics of the religion. The Muslims who glorify them and consider them to be infallible figures are even more deluded.

Quick to Behead People

When I examined the caliphate of Caliph Abu Bakr earlier in this chapter, it became clear to me how and when the culture of Islamic beheadings began, and that ISIS, with all of its crimes, was simply reviving practices established by the caliphates. Caliph Omar is no different, not only when he reigned, but even during the time of Prophet Mohammad. Imam Muslim reported that two companions of Mohammad had an altercation whereby one kicked the other on his buttocks. They both yelled for help. Prophet Mohammad heard their calls and came to inquire about the situation. He told them to leave the matter and to consider it a detestable thing.

Abdullah bin Ubay heard of this altercation and threatened to settle the matter on his own once he reached Medina. When Prophet Mohammad was informed of Abdullah's threat to take matters in his own hands, Omar stood and said: "O Messenger of Allah [Mohammad], allow me to chop off the head of this hypocrite [Abdullah]! Mohammad objected saying 'Leave him, let not the people say that Mohammad kills his companions.'" [176]

Muslims do not shy away from this reality. In June 2018, Mohammed Al Awadi, a prominent "moderate" Islamic preacher from Kuwait and affiliate of the Muslim World League, appeared on television to discuss matters concerning Islam. He proudly said:

> Prophet Mohammad would make sure to send suitable ambassadors to other nations, and would never appoint Omar as an ambassador, because if someone was to make a mistake around him, Omar – May God Be Pleased with Him – would destroy his house and chop his head off. [177]

Burning His Son's Home

It was well known within Arabia that Caliph Omar treated his own sons in an unacceptable manner. He was aggressive, violent, and would threaten them with death. The life of Omar before and after he embraced Islam remained the same. Religion failed to improve his lifestyle, even though he imposed the religion on the lands he invaded to "improve the lifestyles and faith of the nations."

Imam Bukhari reported that Abdullah, the son of Omar, used to sleep in the mosque of the Prophet Mohammad when he was young and unmarried. [178] Abdullah clearly had a family, a prominent Meccan family. But why was Abdullah sleeping in the mosque? Omar not only killed his young daughter, as mentioned earlier, but he also sought to burn down the houses of his own sons, and they slept in a mosque because Omar couldn't burn it down as they slept!

Prophet Mohammad stated that walls should not be covered with cloth. The early Muslim scholar of Islamic scripture, Ibn Abi Shaybah, conveyed an authentic report that "Omar was informed that one of his sons has covered the walls of his house with cloth. Omar then said, 'By Allah, if that is true, I will burn his house.'"[179] Such an unhinged approach towards members of his own family reflects what lay in the hearts of the fathers-in-law of our Prophet Mohammad. They deserve condemnation, not admiration.

Burning an Innocent Man's House

Burning with fire was a common practice for our Caliph Omar, and I have always asserted that he was a terrorist. Our caliphs were in fact the ancestors of Al-Qaeda and ISIS, and remain their role models until this very day.

Abd Al-Razzaq as-San'ani, an eighth-century Islamic scholar of Islamic scriptures (hadith), reported:

> Caliph Omar discovered alcohol in the house of a man from [the tribe of] Thaqif. He had already been lashed for alcohol consumption in the past. Therefore, he [Omar] burnt his house, and asked, "What is your name?" He replied, "Ruwayshid." He [Omar] retorted, "Rather, you are 'Fuwaysiq' [an abusive word meaning immoral person]."[180]

Here we have the caliph of Islam, who is considered the representative of God, burning the house of a man whose name he does not even know. This proves that there were no professional methods of investigation or questioning, just pure barbarism and instant sentencing with the most brutal punishments imaginable.

The Never-Ending Hypocrisy

Other Muslim scholars have defended Omar's decision, claiming that the person whose house was burnt as a result of possessing alcohol was not a Muslim. Not only does this not justify Omar's case, but it in fact makes it worse. Firstly, the majority of non-Muslims are allowed to drink alcohol in their respective religions, therefore a Muslim caliph has no right to impose Islamic Sharia Law onto a non-Muslim. Secondly, if the man was in fact a Muslim, this only reveals the true nature of our caliphs. Omar himself was an alcoholic, before and after embracing Islam. Therefore, in either case, punishing someone for drinking alcohol would be a hypocritical and horrendous crime!

Although, even before Islam, the consumption of alcohol was frowned upon by the chiefs of Arabia,[181] and then it was prohibited by Islam, Caliph Omar presented excuses to continue consuming it. Numerous prominent Islamic scholars from various centuries have testified to the fact that Caliph Omar was an alcoholic throughout his entire life. On one occasion, Omar drank wine and said, "We drink wine in order that it may help digest the camel's meat, and to stop it from harming our bodies."[182] According to another report, when the wine was too strong, Omar would mix it with water, drink, and advise those around him to do the same.[183]

Caliph Omar then attempted to counter his reputation as an alcoholic by punishing those who drank alcohol. Al-Nasa'i, a notable scholar of Islamic scripture reported: "Omar sensed alcohol from a man and inquired about what he had consumed. He said, if it was an intoxicating drink, I will whip him. He then whipped him with the complete number of whips [80 lashes under Sharia Law]."[184]

In another historical report by Ibn Abi Shaybah,

Omar Ibn al-Khattab was accompanied by a man during a trip. The man was fasting, and when he ended his fast, he reached out to Omar's bota bag [canteen] that was hanging from his camel and drank from it. Omar then punished him under Sharia Law [80 lashes]. The man said, "I drank from your bota bag!" Omar responded saying "I whipped you for your drunkenness."[185]

By now, Caliph Omar had enacted his own laws that allowed a Muslim to drink on the condition that they don't become drunk.

During his last days, and after he was stabbed with a knife in his stomach, the doctor asked Omar what his favorite drink was. Omar said "wine!" They brought him wine and it began to pour out of his stomach wounds as he drank it.[186] Omar was drinking alcohol up until his death, after it had been prohibited by Prophet Mohammad, if there was anyone deserving of the eighty whips of Sharia Law, it was our Caliph Omar.

Humble Caliphs or Ostentatious Kings?

The crimes committed by our Caliph Omar have led historians to inquire whether he believed himself to be a king or a humble successor of a prophet. The attitude of Caliph Omar demonstrates ethics which are similar to those of tyrants who oppress their nations while using the country's riches for their own benefit. While hunger and poverty were affecting the very Muslim nation that considered him their caliph, Omar enjoyed the luxury of boundless jewelry, to the extent that Omar's family gained a reputation for dressing their servants in gold!

Omar's outcast and homeless son Abdullah, who used to sleep in Prophet Mohammad's mosque during his father's life, as mentioned earlier, acquired an enormous amount of wealth during his father's caliphate. Historians note that "Abdullah the son of Omar used to dress his daughters and female servants in gold,"[187] even though Caliph Omar was strict on the dress code of female servants, making sure that they did not attempt to dress similarly to free women. On one occasion, "Caliph Omar saw the female servant of his son Abdullah dressed in the dress of a free woman."[188] This was not accepted by the society of the time, because the dress code of a free woman was more expensive, and dressing female servants in gold was an act common only amongst extravagant kings. Omar of course gained great wealth from serial invasions of other nations, as I will discuss in later chapters of this book.

Disturbing Ethics

During my 2014 trip to Al-Azhar University, Cairo, I spent an entire week within its main library. Historical Islamic reports and scriptures that have not yet been translated for the outside world to read have narrated appalling and deplorable information about the characters of our caliphs, the fathers-in-law of Prophet Mohammad. Indeed, our ethics reflect the type of people we are. I shall mention only two historical reports from the many that I read, for which I also managed to find a legitimate online reference.

Daily prayers are an important obligation in the daily life of an adult Muslim. Ibn Qayyim al-Jawziyya, an important medieval Islamic jurist, theologian, and spiritual writer who was considered "one of the most important thinkers" of Islam, testified in his Arabic book that "Omar would not pray for a month until he had a bath,"[189] i.e. the Islamic washing ritual to regain purity.

As for answering the call of nature, our Caliph Omar displayed the most vulgar conduct one could imagine. We all know that many animals bury and hide their waste. However, the famous jurist and expert in Islamic scripture Al-Bayhaqi reported:

> Omar's servant Yasaar said "When Caliph Omar used to urinate, he used to say, 'give me something to clean myself with' and I would give him something, or that he would wipe himself [his penis] on the wall or floor, and he never used to wash it."[190]

This sickening action was a regular public performance by our Caliph Omar. He would urinate in public and wipe his penis on the walls. Sixteenth-century Islamic scholar of scripture and jurist, Al-Muttaqi al-Hindi, reported that Prophet Mohammad's cousin "Ibn Abbas, said that he saw Omar ibn al Khattab urinate and wipe himself [his penis] on the wall and then wipe both his hands together."[191] And in a second historical report Omar exited the rest room and ate without washing his hands.[192] Yet he preached that "Cleanliness is half of one's faith".[193]

Satan Fears Caliph Omar

In Chapter 2, I examined how most Muslims believe in the scripture which teaches that Satan placed words into the mouth of Prophet Mohammad. Not only is this offensive, but it also shows that Satan is not afraid of Mohammad, the Messenger of God. However, what we do find is that Satan is supposedly somehow extremely frightened of Caliph Omar.

Although Prophet Mohammad was born in the sixth century and died in the seventh, Imam Bukhari came along in the ninth century with an interesting testimony, claiming that "Prophet Mohammad said: 'O' Omar! By God in Whose Hands my life is, whenever Satan sees you taking one way, he follows a way other than yours!'"[194]

It seems that one scholar lied to regular Muslims, then other scholars believed his lie and built upon it! After Imam Bukhari's fabrication, other prominent Islamic scholars* reported that "The Messenger of Allah said: 'Indeed Satan is afraid of you O Omar!'"[195] It is unclear whether our greatest scholars blindly trusted each other's works without any investigation or whether they were foolish enough to believe such a ridiculous tale. Nevertheless, this fabrication and addition to Islamic scripture to paint a brave picture of Caliph Omar did manage to reach the western world. It made me tremendously happy to find out that the following non-Muslim British scholar saw the reality of this hidden agenda and nonsensical tale.

Dr. David Samuel Margoliouth was a British orientalist, scholar, and a Laudian Professor of Arabic at the University of Oxford. After authoring his book *Mohammed and the Rise of Islam* (1905), *Encyclopædia Britannica* (15th edition), described him as "brilliant as an editor and translator of Arabic works." In this book, he quoted the above lie, "'If Satan were to meet Omar,' said Mohammed, 'he would get out of Omar's way,'" and commented:

* Such as Grand Imam Al-Tirmidhi.

Yet we have <u>no record</u> of any occasion on which Omar displayed remarkable courage, though many examples are at hand of <u>his cruelty and bloodthirstiness</u>; at the Battle of Hunain <u>he ran away</u> and on another occasion owed his life to the good nature of an enemy.

Probably the above story is in the main true. Novelists sometimes employ similar motives; an impetuous but chivalrous man finds that he has rushed into an ungentlemanly act, and in his extreme desire to atone loses command of his will. The shock which Omar experienced at having wounded his sister made him anxious to do anything which would atone for it; the most obvious course being to express admiration for the Koran and become a Muslim, he hastens to adopt that; he is admitted into the society, and becomes its most fanatical member. Moreover, to this sister he appears to have been fondly attached; when, as children, they looked after their mother's camel in the desert, Omar used when it grew hot to throw his garment over his sister and tend the beast, exposed without any coverage to the sunshine. This explains the difficulty that Omar's conduct on other occasions displays no trace of chivalry. He was a wife-beater; he went to the length of scourging some women for weeping over the death of one of Mohammed's daughters.[196]

If Islam's second Caliph Omar was present in a particular area, there would be no need for Satan. He did Satan's work and more, so it would be natural for Satan to move out of the way. Satan is known in Abrahamic literature for opposing the message and will of God, and not as a criminal who committed atrocities and mass murders as our Caliph Omar did.

The Death of Caliph Omar

In Chapter 7 of this book, I will focus on the "Islamic conquests" conducted by Caliph Omar during his reign. I wish to conclude this section by examining the death of Caliph Omar and the transition of the Islamic caliphate to Caliph Uthman, the third caliph of Islam.

The death of Omar ibn al-Khattab has been presented by Islamic scripture and historical reports in a very suspicious and ambiguous manner. Early Islamic scholars and narrators of Islamic history have hidden many realities surrounding the murder of Islam's second caliph. There have been many fabrications regarding this incident, and many of them have been translated and used as supposedly authoritative research material.

The man who assassinated our Caliph Omar was Piruz Nahavandi, referred to as Abu Lulu'a.* He was a Persian Muslim living in Persia who rose against the invasion of Caliph Omar and joined the opposing Sasanian Army. Piruz was captured in the Battle of al-Qadisiyyah, then sold as a slave to Al-Mughirah, a companion of Prophet Mohammad.

From the very beginning of the Islamic religion, it has always been considered shameful for a Muslim to be killed by another Muslim, but being killed by a non-Muslim is seen as a level of martyrdom. Because Piruz was Persian, it was easy to accuse him of disbelief and associate him with Zoroastrianism. Eighth century grand Islamic jurist, Al-Haythami, reported:

> When Abu Lulu'a stabbed Omar, he stabbed him twice. Omar was thinking that maybe he had done injustice to someone amongst the people – so he [Omar] called Ibn Abbas [Mohammad's cousin] who loved, adored and listened to him, and asked him "Who stabbed me?" Ibn Abbas said: "Abu Lulu'a the Zoroastrian slave." Ibn Abbas said: "I saw happiness in the face of Omar." On that Omar said: "Praise be to Allah Who did not make my decree of death to be at the hands of a man who claimed Islam."[197]

Prominent Islamic jurist and scholar Ibn Taymiyyah said:

> AbuLulu'a is a Kafir [disbeliever] according to the consensus of the people of Islam, he was a Zoroastrian of the worshippers of the

* Arabic for "father of Lulu'a," his daughter.

fire. He killed Omar due to his grudge for Islam and its people and due to his love for Zoroastrians. It was done in revenge for all the disbelievers, this is because Omar was the one [the head of state] who conquered their lands [for Islam] and killed their heads of state and who distributed their wealth.[198]

After being sold to Al-Mughirah, one of the companions of Mohammad in Medina, Piruz visited Caliph Omar and requested a decent salary for his exhausting and strenuous labor. Omar rejected his request, and sent Piruz back to his master Al-Mughirah. This angered Piruz because he was a talented and skilled craftsman who had lived an honorable life before Omar's invasion. While pondering all the crimes Omar had committed, including the personal oppression he had endured and the tragedies poured onto his homeland and family, he decided to take revenge by assassinating Omar. Prominent hadith specialist and Islamic scholar Ibn Hibban reported:

Abu Lulu'a waited for Omar, he came to him at dawn prayers and stood behind him ... He hit him in his shoulder and hit him in his side, then Omar fell down and he hit by his dagger thirteen men. Among them seven were killed and Omar was carried and taken to his house.[199]

Islamic historians have not agreed on how Piruz died. Nevertheless, his tomb is located on the road to Kashan, Iran. Ever since the building of the tomb in the eleventh century, his grave has sparked controversy within the Islamic world. Most Muslims believe that the tomb should be demolished because Piruz assassinated Mohammad's second successor.[200] A minority of Muslims champion Piruz till this very day and consider him a genuine Muslim and defender of the religion of Islam.[201] Many prominent Islamic scholars in Iran have investigated the origins of Piruz in Persian history along with his residence in Medina, Arabia. Shaikh Ali Namazi, an Islamic scholar and professor of Islamic scripture and history, stated that "Piruz was of the great Muslims." I

personally wouldn't depend on this testimony alone because Ali
Namazi was a somewhat biased Shia Muslim. In fact, Zoroastrians
were oppressed by Caliph Omar's invasions, and oppressed even more
after they accused Piruz of being Zoroastrian. But the undeniable fact is
that Piruz was Muslim and not Zoroastrian. We can be sure of this
because he stood in the first row of congregational prayers, knew how
to offer Islamic prayers, and was allowed to stand directly behind the
caliph of Islam, Omar. It is not easy to stand and pray directly behind
the leader of the Islamic caliphate, as his security and assistants were
very protective of him. However, the fact that Piruz was given that
space to pray directly behind Omar as he led the prayers shows that he
was a Muslim and well known to the mosque.

While Caliph Omar was suffering from the wounds that were to
lead to his death, he speedily gathered the chief Muslims and Uthman
bin Affan was appointed as the third caliph of Islam. Meanwhile Omar's
son Abdullah raced to behead the young daughter of Piruz, Lulu'a, as
revenge for his father's assassination. He also murdered Hormuzan, a
Persian governor held captive by Omar's army, who had already
converted to Islam.[202]

Caliph Uthman then excused Abdullah for killing them, Piruz's
daughter and Hormuzan, in revenge for his father's death, because
Uthman did not want to sentence Abdullah to death, and cause two
funerals to take place in the house of his good friend Omar. The value
of this friendship didn't last long, as Caliph Uthman allowed Amr ibn
al-As, the companion of Mohammad, to stand in his pulpit and ridicule
Omar, saying "The left-handed cross-eyed son of Hantima has gone!"
Mentioning the mother of an Arabian man in such a context is
considered a great insult.

★★★

It is part of our Islamic culture to honor and glorify figures who are not
worthy of glorification. When narrating reports of Islam's battles, our
scholars never fail to inflate and exaggerate facts and stimulate their
imaginations. For example, they spend hours lecturing us in mosques

and schools about how Caliph Omar would kill one thousand soldiers in one battle, and that the ground would shake if he entered battlefields. These fabrications are extremely minor compared to the much greater lies that have now become entrenched doctrine and, unfortunately, believed in by most Muslims.

If Caliph Omar was a bloodthirsty, child-killing and woman-murdering individual, why did our ancestors allow him to reign over them? Why did they not revolt and rise against his tyranny? The Muslim population was still small in comparison with surrounding nations, and Muslims of that era could have easily regained control and elected a more reasonable leader. Our ancestors are partly responsible for remaining silent throughout the many centuries of corrupt Islamic leadership.

The Third Caliph of Islam: Uthman bin Affan

The caliphate of Uthman bin Affan played a vital role in the evolution of Islamic leadership from prophetic succession to kingship. He too was a father-in-law and companion of Prophet Mohammad. Although signs of this transformation could be seen throughout the first two caliphates of Islam, it became official during the final years of Uthman's rule.

Born in the year 579 CE, Uthman reigned as the third caliph of Islam following the death of the second Caliph Omar on November 3, 644 CE. The Islamic conquests had all taken place during the reign of his predecessor Caliph Omar, making Uthman's transition into an established position of leadership fairly smooth. His reign lasted for about sixteen years, with many incidents occurring during his reign that shaped the future of Islam.

I have been studying the life of our third Caliph Uthman for the past fifteen years, aiming to understand his character, politics, leadership, and ideology by examining scriptures and historical books published by various Islamic schools of thought, in order to gain a broad spectrum of ideas and come to fair conclusions. However, after what I had come across in my journey of studying the lives of earlier Islamic caliphs, I wasn't going to be surprised if I came across anything outrageous about Uthman. He tried to lead a modest life and to be a moral leader. Whether or not he reached his goals is a different question, but he was not innocent either. Similar to the first and second caliphs of Islam, Uthman's life contained several stomach-turning events.

Murdering His Wife, Ruqayyah

Caliph Uthman was married to Ruqayyah, the daughter of Prophet Mohammad. She was born in the year 601 CE and died at the age of 23. She bore Uthman one child, Abdullah,[203] and travelled with him to several continents. After Ruqayyah fell ill in the year 624, Uthman was excused from the military by Prophet Mohammad to care for her.[204] However, Uthman was furious that Ruqayyah had fallen ill during the Battle of Badr, as he missed out on all the booty and spoils of war after the victory. Therefore, he beat her until she died and then became intimate with her maid that same night.[205]

During her burial, her father Prophet Mohammad wept excessively, and cursed Uthman five times, then said, "May no man couple with the maid of his dead wife."[206] He then ordered that Uthman be banned from approaching Ruqayyah's grave during her funeral.[207]

After Uthman became Caliph, he delivered a sermon in which he said, "Am I not the son-in-law of your Prophet?" to which Aisha the wife of Mohammad responded, "You were a burden upon Mohammad and his daughter, and you know exactly what you did to them!"[208] Islamic historian Al-Ameli commented on this particular event, saying that "Caliph Uthman had committed a very great sin against Ruqayyah, one that Islamic history could not tell us about."[209]

Stoning an Innocent Woman

A married Muslim woman gave birth to a child after six months of pregnancy. Her husband insisted that she had been unfaithful and cheated on him three months prior to the conception because "the period of a female's pregnancy should be nine months." Her husband complained to Caliph Uthman while holding the newborn child as evidence of his wife's adultery. Uthman immediately ordered her to be stoned to death!

Ali, the cousin of Prophet Mohammad, heard of the matter and raced to Caliph Uthman to question him about the verdict that he had issued. Ali then defended the woman, saying that a six-month pregnancy is not impossible, and cited verses of the Quran to prove his point. Uthman was then convinced and ordered the lady to be freed, but she had already been stoned. Before her stoning she told her sister: "Do not be upset with me. I vow that nobody has seen my body except my husband." And the newborn child grew up to look similar to his father.[210]

The caliphs' ignorance of the affairs of their citizens led to the killing of many people. What makes it worse is the absence of any advisors to the caliphs, leaving them to make compulsive decisions at the expense of people's lives. By this action, a life was taken, a child orphaned, and an entire family scarred due to a simple misunderstanding that could have been resolved through consultation.

Theft of the Islamic Nation's Treasury

Uthman wasn't only Islam's third caliph, he was also the father-in-law of Prophet Mohammad. This means that he was expected to have some honesty and transparency when dealing with the Islamic finances entrusted to him. During his caliphate, the Islamic Empire was extremely wealthy, as he had inherited all the treasures and wealth acquired from the serial Islamic invasions conducted by the earlier caliphs. He not only stole Islamic finances, but proceeded to spend the monies for the benefit of his friends, family, and allies, and certainly not for the benefit of the religion. He would stand at the pulpit of Prophet Mohammad and say, "This is the money of Allah, and I will grant it to whomever I desire, and prevent from it whomever I desire."[211]

Caliph Uthman prevented his opposition from accessing any Islamic finances even though they were entitled to them. He promoted and paved the way for the tyrannical Umayyad Dynasty that was to later inherit his rule, starting with Muawiyah. He said, "If the keys of paradise were in my possession, I would have given them to the Umayyads." When Ammar bin Yassir, the companion of Prophet Mohammad, objected to this statement, Uthman began to physically assault him, and the people had to separate him from Uthman.[212] I will shed light on their atrocities in Chapter 7 of this book.

Death of Caliph Uthman

The murder of Uthman is known as Islam's "first fitna,"* and it came after the increasing influence of the Umayyad family over Muslim society. They betrayed him and questioned the policies of his caliphate along with his religious beliefs, and concluded that he wasn't suitable to be the leader of the Muslim nation.[213]

The aforementioned wife of Mohammad, Aisha, was actually the driving force behind Uthman's assassination. She hated Caliph Uthman for many reasons, mainly because he refused to surrender her inheritance from Mohammad. Aisha, believed to be "the Mother of the Believers" and who is mentioned in the Quran, was heard raising her voice amongst the gatherings of Medina ordering the Muslims to "Kill Na'thal** for he has become a disbeliever."[214]

After the Umayyad family had secured the support of Mohammad's wife, Aisha, a large protest was organized around the house of Uthman. The Muslims formed a siege around the house of their own caliph, demanding the appointment of a new caliph. Even after Uthman insisted that he was the "rightly guided Caliph" by God, they set his house alight and entered his house. They found him reciting the Quran, and went on to strike his head and stab him, soaking the Holy Quran with his blood.

Uthman's wife, Na'ila, came to his rescue. When she raised her hand to stop a sword from striking him, her fingers were cut off. When she turned around in pain, the attacker, who was Ibn Hamran, hit her bottom and said, "What big buttocks she has!" Then he landed a strike on Uthman and killed him.[215]

Na'ila, the widowed wife of Caliph Uthman, wrote a letter to

---

* "Fitna" is Arabic for sedition or treason.
** Na'thal is an insulting name for Uthman. It means "hyena."

Muawiyah, the patriarch of the Umayyad family, who was appointed governor of Syria by her husband Uthman, shaming him for not putting enough effort into saving the life of her husband. Muawiyah responded with a letter asking for her hand in marriage. She rejected his proposal and, on his second attempt to propose to her, she broke off a few of her teeth and sent them to him, signaling that she was not as beautiful as she used to be.

These are just a few examples of the crimes committed by our caliphs since the death of Prophet Mohammad. The Muslims had reached a stage where they began to assassinate their own caliphs, demanding reform. We were taught in our Islamic seminaries to hide these facts from the people, to not mention them in our lectures nor translate them from Arabic, and to claim they are distorted reports placed in Muslim books by Jewish people. Al-Tabari, a prominent and influential Islamic scholar and historian, reported on the death of Caliph Uthman, saying, "We have mentioned many of the reasons that his murderers cited as an excuse for killing him, and <u>we have avoided mentioning many others that should not be included</u>."[216] In reality, we see the same scenarios occurring in the twenty-first century, where Muslim nations are overthrowing their corrupt leaders and insisting on reform.

The Caliph of Islam: Ali ibn Abi Taleb

To this day, Muslims argue about whether or not Ali was the first appointed successor of Mohammad. Sunni Muslims believe that the caliph after Mohammad was Abu Bakr, while the minority denomination, Shia Muslims, believe it was Ali. Therefore, this split between the minority of Muslims who believe in the succession of Ali and the majority who pledge their allegiance to Abu Bakr has existed since the early days of Islam. However, it is worth mentioning that all Muslims today love Ali, regardless of their denomination or whether or not he was the actual first caliph. As for the other early caliphs, different Islamic denominations have different beliefs about each of them.

The dispute about whether Ali was worthier of the caliphate than the first three caliphs came to an end after the death of Uthman, when the entire Muslim nation agreed that Ali should be their caliph. Ali, however, did not wish to be involved in the battle for leadership between the Umayyad family and the family of Prophet Mohammad. Eventually, events led to Ali assuming the Islamic leadership. Ali described that moment, saying:

> At that moment, nothing took me by surprise, but the crowd of people rushing to me. It advanced toward me form every side like the mane of the hyena so much so that [my two sons] Hassan and Hussain were getting crushed and both the ends of my shoulder garment were torn.[217]

Ali's reputation was different from the caliphs who reigned before him, simply because he was young during the time of Prophet Mohammad, and had not engaged in any political or military events during the rule of the first three caliphs. However, one cannot deny Ali's engagement in wars alongside his cousin Mohammad. Indeed, he was the flagbearer of Islam and was involved in battles during its early years.

Once Ali had been announced caliph of Islam, the Umayyad family lead by Muawiyah began their political campaign against him, refusing to surrender various districts to his caliphate. This was in response to Ali's efforts to abolish policies introduced by the first three caliphs which he disagreed with. Ali's reign lasted around five years, ending with his assassination. Whoever wishes to examine the condition of the religion of Islam under Ali's rule will realize that the strategies he applied were not only ideas, but policies executed at the right time to give his nation the best results possible. Being adored by the Muslims, other than those who wished to overthrow him, it was fairly easy for Ali to introduce a new economic and political system to the regions he governed. He focused on improving relations with other nations, and was welcomed because he didn't engage in any military expeditions nor invasions after the death of Mohammad.

Sir William Muir, Scottish Foreign Secretary to the Indian government and Lieutenant Governor of the North-Western Provinces, said: "When Ali obtained the rule of half of the Moslem world, it was rather thrust upon him than sought."[218] Today, Ali is known by his famous saying, "People are either your brothers and sisters in faith, or your equals in humanity." His eloquence, wisdom, and knowledge, as displayed in the book *Peak of Eloquence*,[219] gave a new image to Islam and, although he never claimed to be a deity, it is understandable why many began to worship him.

After studying the lives of Islam's caliphs and Mohammad's companions, one can conclude that, out of all the caliphs who governed Islam after Mohammad, Ali was the wisest when he needed to make difficult decisions. One of the famous battles during Ali's rule was the Battle of the Camel. The Muslims had already fought one civil war during the caliphate of Abu Bakr, Aisha's father and Islam's first caliph after Mohammad. Within the same generation, they faced the grim prospect of fighting another. Despite the clear Islamic jurisprudential rulings stressing the obligatory obedience of Muslims towards their caliphs, Aisha could not tolerate Ali being on the throne of the caliphate. Her hatred of Ali was overpowering. If someone other than Ali had become caliph, she might not have embarked upon the cynical adventure in which tens of thousands of Muslims were killed. Her only aim was to make her nephew and adopted son, Abdullah bin Zubayr, the new caliph.

Aisha insisted on Mohammad's other murderous wife, Hafsa, going with her to Basra, Iraq, to take part in a war against Ali. She was willing to go with Aisha, but her brother, Abdullah bin Omar, forbade her to do so as he believed Ali was Islam's most just caliph. Aisha's brother, Mohammad bin Abu Bakr, was also a loyal companion of Ali. However, Aisha claimed that she was engaging in a mission of peace. This was the strangest of all missions of peace, as "Aisha was escorted to Basra, Iraq, by 3000 warriors, bristling with deadly weapons, and thirsting for the blood of innocent Muslims."[220]

On her way from Mecca to Basra, Iraq, where the battle was about to take place, Ali sent her a letter saying:

> In the name of God Who is Most Beneficent and Most Merciful.
> You have left your home in direct contravention of the
> commandments of God and His Messenger, and now you are
> sowing seeds of civil war among the Muslims. Just pause for a
> moment and think about this: What do you have to do with
> armies and wars? Is it your job to fight? And fight against whom?
> Against the Muslims? God has commanded you to stay in your
> home. Therefore, fear Him, and do not disobey Him, and return
> immediately to Medina.[221]

Despite Ali's efforts to prevent the civil battle from taking place, Aisha
had no desire to acknowledge Ali's letters, and proceeded to wage war
among Muslims, leading to 21,000 casualties.[222]

This incident did not come as a surprise to the Muslim world
because, as mentioned, "Prophet Mohammad stood up and delivered a
sermon, and pointed to the house of Aisha, and said: 'Sedition is right
here,' while repeating three times, 'from where the thorns of Satan
come out.'"[223] Such prophetic statements regarding his own wife raise
many reasonable questions. What exactly were Aisha's plots during her
lifetime that allowed Mohammad to predict his wife's political agenda?

Ali's caliphate came to an end in the fifth year after he was brutally
struck with a poisoned sword as he prayed by Abd al-Rahman ibn
Muljam, a man he nurtured and fed. He was struck on the nineteenth
day of Ramadan, corresponding to January 27, 661 CE, while he was
prostrated in dawn prayer. Once wounded, he requested that nobody
seek revenge, and said that if he survived he would pardon Ibn Muljam.
Ibn Muljam was the first political prisoner in the caliphate of Ali, and
that was because he assassinated him. Caliph Ali died two days later on
January 29, 661 CE.

CHAPTER 5

The Murder of Mohammad's Daughter and Her Unborn Child: The Worst Crime of our Caliphs

She was beaten and her right was usurped
And then they let her taste the pain of injuries and wounds
May that hand be cut who hit her
And the hand of those who are content with that ... and follow him
May God not forgive him, and nor
Make him safe of the fear of the Day of Resurrection.[22]

Our early caliphs established a culture of burning people along with their homes if they disagreed with their decisions or politics. History shows that fire was their preferred method of punishment. One of their victims was Lady Fatima, the innocent daughter of their own Prophet Mohammad. The murder of Lady Fatima was a result of a political conflict, as she and her husband Ali, Islam's future Caliph, refused to pledge allegiance to Caliph Abu Bakr. In order to understand the tragedy of Fatima's murder, it is crucial to understand where Fatima stands within the religion of Islam, and most importantly to understand the extent of violations of women's rights by the Islamic caliphs themselves.

Fatima is loved and revered by all Muslims regardless of their denomination, and she was the closest child to her father Mohammad and his only daughter at the time of his death. She was born on July 27, 604, to Khadija, Mohammad's first wife. Fatima supported and cared for her father Mohammad to such a degree that he gave her the title "Mother of Her Own Father," to emphasize the limitless care she had for him. Fatima is considered a vital character in Islam for both men and women. Mohammad emphasized the importance of Lady Fatima further, by informing Muslims that "Fatima is the Mistress of women in paradise."[225]

To Muslims, Fatima ranks among the likes of Mary, the mother of Jesus. Mohammad's descendants today are all from Fatima's lineage. Therefore, Fatima occupies a high status and position in the religion of Islam, which leads me to the question: What does Islam say about those who harm Fatima? Prophet Mohammad said: "Fatimah is a piece of me, whoever upsets her has upset me."[226]

From this brief introduction, it becomes clear that a *true Muslim* considers Lady Fatima to be a sacred figure who deserves the utmost respect. The caliphs of Islam were obliged by Islam to show respect to Fatima, as they saw Mohammad honoring and her in front of the entire Muslim nation. So, what happened to Fatima the only daughter of Mohammad? And why do Islamic authorities hide her story from the world?

Immediately after the death of her father Mohammad, Fatima did not accept the caliphate of Abu Bakr, and believed Ali her husband was worthier of being caliph, as her father Mohammad had already mentioned it. This stance cost her her life, because, according to the ideology of the caliphs of Islam, women are not allowed to have political opinions or interfere in the affairs of men.

The Theft of Fatima's Inheritance

After Mohammad's death, the caliphs of Islam and fathers-in-law of Prophet Mohammad robbed his household and belongings. Prominent and influential Islamic scholar, historian, and exegete of the Quran, Al-Tabari reported:

When Mohammad passed away, Abu Bakr and Omar took the first

two shares, which were the share of the Prophet, and share of his near kin, and they used it in the way of Allah as the charity of the Messenger of Allah.[227]

However, when Caliphs Abu Bakr and Omar passed away, their children inherited their property without any disputes from the succeeding caliph, and their wealth was not used as "ongoing charity for the deceased," simply because wealth left behind is distributed according to the will of the deceased person and his children, not according to the opinions of in-laws. Nevertheless, the wealth of Mohammad was utilized by Islamic caliphs for jihad, massacres, and invasions, in clear opposition to the following Quranic verse:

Whatever Allah has restored to His Messenger, it is for Allah and for the Messenger, and for the near of kin and the orphans and the needy and the way farer, *so that it may not be a thing taken by turns among the rich of you.*[228]

How could an Islamic caliph and successor of Mohammad rob the inheritance of the Prophet of God and oppose the clear instructions in the Quran?

Sahih Muslim, Islam's second most sacred and authentic book after the Quran, reports thatFatima, the daughter of Mohammad, sent an intermediary to Caliph Abu Bakr asking him to give her her share of inheritance from the Prophet. However, he refused to hand over her inheritance, claiming that "Mohammad said, 'our property is not to be inherited, and whatever we leave is charity.'"[229] This was a very mysterious statement from Caliph Abu Bakr, as the will of Mohammad bequeathed his property to his daughter Fatima and other family members, and if it contained anything about his estate being given to charity, she wouldn't have claimed it publicly in the first place. However, it was clear that Abu Bakr refused to give Fatima her share of the inheritance because she opposed his caliphate and did not offer allegiance to him. As time passed and his caliphate became more established, he wrote Fatima a document handing over her inheritance. However, Omar saw her leaving the gathering with Abu Bakr with the document and tore it apart. She then said to Omar: "May God tear your stomach the same way you have torn my document,"[230] which interestingly did end up happening.

Lady Fatima died angry with the caliphs and, according to Mohammad, whoever angers his daughter Fatima has angered him, and whoever angers him has angered God.[231] Therefore, my co-religionists insist on glorifying individuals whom God is – according to their own belief – angry with. A rational and believing Muslim does not adore and praise those who have angered God.

The Murder of Lady Fatima

Lady Fatima's ongoing refusal to pledge allegiance to Abu Bakr caused the internal conflict between the companions and in-laws of Mohammad and his direct family members to escalate. The Muslim nation knew that Fatima, the daughter of Mohammad, was a living piece of their Prophet, and her silent opposition caused instability for the entire fledgling caliphate. Omar, the upcoming caliph, set out to burn the house of Fatima and her husband Ali, who would later become Islam's 'fourth' caliph.

On behalf of Abu Bakr, Omar ordered the soldiers of the Islamic caliphate to gather what Arabs called "jazl"– a type of wood that catches fire quickly and is extremely difficult to put out. On their way to the house of Mohammad, Muslims informed Omar that Fatima was inside the house and that she was pregnant with Mohsin at the time. Omar responded saying "Even if so!"

Ali and his companions were also in the house, refusing to pledge allegiance to Abu Bakr. As a result of this, Abu Bakr ordered Omar to "remove those gathered in the house of Fatima and Ali, and if they refuse to come out, then fight them!"Fatima came out of the house and said, "O Abu Bakr and Omar! Do you want to widow me!? Have you arrived in order to set my home on fire!?"Omar said, "O daughter

Mohammad! I swear by God that we love you, but if your house continues to be a meeting place for conspiracy any longer, I will set fire to it on account of this!"[232] Omar then rushed to the scene to force them to pledge allegiance willingly or unwillingly.[233]

As Omar and his men approached the house, Fatima closed the door, and she believed that they would not enter her house without her permission. Omar set a fire around the house of Prophet Mohammad and entered without permission by kicking the door open. He wanted Ali to pledge allegiance to Abu Bakr.

> He surrounded her house with firewood to then burn it along with whoever was inside. He also hit Fatima until he caused her to miscarry her baby, and proceeded to strike her across the face, causing her to fall and leaving her in agony and total distress.[234]

The pregnant Lady Fatima was brutally beaten, and as a result of this attack she suffered the pain of smashed ribs, a miscarriage, and being impaled by a large nail that was in the door.[235] Fatima began screaming and pleaded for help, and Omar said to the crowd, "We have nothing to do with women and their opinions."[236]

Lady Fatima died a few months after the attack, and was buried in secret by her husband Ali, as she did not want any of her killers to attend her funeral. Until this day, the site of her grave remains unknown. This was not because she didn't want people to visit her grave, but because she wanted to prevent the tyrants from exhuming her body. Knowing the nature of his companions and fathers-in-law, Mohammad predicted this would take place. During his last months, he said:

> I am crying for my progeny, for the crimes that will be committed against them by *the evildoers of my nation* after my death. It is as if I can see my daughter Fatima being oppressed and crying: "O Father!" but no one will come to help her from among my nation.[237]

He was right about that.

The most authentic sources of Islamic history from both the Sunni and Shia denominations have reported and testified to this incident. Other than the references and sources already cited, several high-ranking prominent scholars have testified to this incident. The author of one of Islam's two most sacred books, *Sahih Muslim*, testified:

Fatima was angered by Abu Bakr and quit talking to him till she died; and she lived for six months after the death of the Prophet. When she died, Ali buried her in the night and did not inform Abu Bakr about her death; and he offered funeral prayers himself.[238]

Politically and socially speaking, this is perhaps the worst thing that could have happened to the caliph at the time, that is, the daughter of Prophet Mohammad dying with a written will demanding that the caliph did not offer prayers over her deceased body.

Prominent scholar Hassan Farhan al-Maliki stated that

In the early era of Abu Bakr, their division was due to the attack on the house of Fatima. Some companions who were with Ali did not like pledging allegiance to Abu Bakr; and this is proven with authentic reports.[239]

Scholars from the minor Islamic sects, such as the Shia school of thought, have supported this account. Al-Majlisi, a chief scholar and specialist in Islamic scripture, reported:

Omar tried to forcefully enter Fatima's house, and she refused to allow him in. Therefore, he set the door on fire, squashed Fatima behind the door and caused her to miscarry Mohsin. Omar then beat Fatima with the scabbard of his sword, and ordered his slave, Qunfuz to whip her.[240]

Prominent scholars of the majority Sunni Islamic faith have also supported the minority in their historical reports. Shibli Nomani said: "there is no reason to deny the occurrence of this incident in the light of rationalization. Omar was a man of hot and irrational temper and such an act would not have been inconsistent with his nature."[241]

Islamic Scholars Who Have Covered up the Violence

Just as criminal caliphs and Islamic terrorists are guilty of conducting violent acts that endanger lives, many Islamic scholars are also guilty of covering up and concealing these crimes; or minimizing the crimes of terrorists. These scholars must be exposed, even if they lived centuries ago. They should not be allowed to get away with what they have done, as their methodology has influenced the recording of history throughout the decades.

These extremist Islamist scholars knew that, if Muslims heard about the murder of Fatima, they would no longer respect the caliphs, who were considered the link between Muslims and God. Therefore, they began to raise questions in order to spread doubt about the incident, or even to deny its occurrence.

Although the grand Islamic scholar Ibn Athir was generally honest when reporting on Islam's history, he was understandably biased on this particular issue. He tried to conceal the beating of Fatima that lead to her miscarriage, by saying that "Mohsin passed away young."[242] This distracts the mind of the researcher from the fact that he was killed when in his mother's womb. Yes, we know he died young, but how young? Similar to the Islamic concept of legitimate deception, *Taqiyyah*, this tactic used by authors is known as *Tawriyah*,* or what I call the politics of the pen. Other prominent Islamic scholars such as Al-Tabari were also deceptive, saying that "Mohsin died while he was small,"[243] but they don't tell you how small – so small he wasn't born yet?

Nevertheless, the truth shall shine like the sun, even if clouds cover it. Arthur Buehler, senior lecturer in religious studies at Victoria University wrote: "There are multiple renditions of these events,

---

* Tawriyah is an Islamic concept describing concealing the truth by creative lying, which is not a sin. For example, if someone declares "I don't have a penny in my pocket," most listeners will assume the speaker has no money on him, though he might have dollar bills, just literally no pennies. This is legitimate according to Sharia Law and does not constitute "lying," which is forbidden in Islam.

ranging from Umar threatening to burn Fatima's door down to actual violent entry into their house, bringing about the death of Muhsin and even precipitating Fatima's death."[244] In a more detailed essay, Bridget Blomfield states:

Unfortunately, Mohammad could not change her destiny. Fatimah would experience a life of suffering and the majority of her family would be martyred ... In the story of Fatimah's life, suffering is considered an unavoidable experience of what it means to be human.[245]

Referring to one account of Islamic history, she wrote:

Fatimah hides behind the door of her house because she is home alone and unveiled. Her husband's enemy, Omar, tells his forces to burn down the house. Omar then forces open the door and Fatimah is impaled by a large nail. She is then pulled from behind the door and beaten repeatedly until she miscarries. Fatimah dies hunched over in prayer after giving birth to a stillborn child.[246]

Confessions of the Crime

While Islamist scholars and extremist clerics wish to hide the crimes of the Islamic caliphs, there will always be those that do not believe in *Taqiyyah*, the concept of deception, and will tell the truth. This cannot be prevented because there is no organized governing Islamic body which monitors what is published regarding the religion.Many prominent Islamic scholars have chosen to inform the world of the truth of this incident. The following are only five of the many confessions to this tragic crime from both Islamic denominations, the Shia and the Sunni.

1. Sunni Muslim jurist Ibn al-Mibrad (died 1503), testified that

"Mohsin: He was a miscarriage child, some say he died as a little child, *but the correct opinion is that Fatima had a miscarriage.*"[247]

2. Shia Muslim jurist Ibn Shahar Ashoob (died 1192) testified that the children of Fatima are "Hassan, Hussain and *Mohsin the miscarried baby.*" He continued to say that Prominent Islamic scholar Ibn Qutaybah* also said *"Mohsin was miscarried due to the strike* of Qunfudh Al-Adawi (Omar's servant)."[248]

3. Sunni Muslim Ibn Abd Rabbihsaid: "Abu Bakr sent Omar ibn Al-Khattab with the order, 'that you remove those gathered in the house of Fatima, and if they refuse to come out, then fight them.' Omar brought fire to the house of Fatima, then Fatima met him and said: 'O son of Al-Khattab! Have you arrived in order to set my home on fire?' He (Omar) replied: 'Yes, unless you people give pledge allegiance to Abu Bakr as others have done.'"[249]

4. Shia Muslim Al-Tabari attested to the assault made on the house of Lady Fatima, by testifying: "She passed away on a Tuesday, seventy-five days after the death of her father Mohammad,and the cause of her actual death was Qunfudh, the servant of the man (Omar ibn Khattab), who pounded her with the scabbard of the sword by his command. So, she miscarried Mohsin, and became ill from that with a severe illness.And she did not let anyone from those who had hurt her to enter upon her."[250] He also wrote:"Omar was enthusiastic on burning the house of Fatima."[251]

5. Sunni Muslim Al-Baladhuri (297 AH/892 CE) said: "Abu Bakr sent for Ali so that he can give allegiance but he didn't. So, Omar came [to the house] and Fatima met him at the door. She said: Omar, you want to burn my door down? Omar replied: 'Yes, in order to strengthen the religion your father brought!'"[252]

Islamic scholars may hide as much of the truth as they wish, but what can they say if the killers themselves admitted to this unforgivable and brutal crime?

---

* Ibn Qutaybah was a renowned Islamic scholar of Persian origin. He served as a judge during the Abbasid Caliphate and was also a polymath who presented research on various Islamic subjects such as Quranic exegesis, the science of hadith, theology, philosophy, law and jurisprudence, grammar, philology, history, astronomy, agriculture, and botany.

Regret of the Killers

When death approaches faithful and devout humans, they tend to ponder and contemplate the wrongdoings committed during their lives and the decisions they regret, as well as what they might be held accountable for on the Day of Judgement. As Muslims, we know that our final destination will be either paradise or hellfire. When the time had come for the first caliph of Islam, Abu Bakr, to depart from this world, among his last words to his companions were: "I wish that I would not have opened/trespassed the house of Fatima, and had left it."[253] Caliph Abu Bakr reached such a state of worry that he wished he had never existed, saying: "I wish I was this tree which is eaten and nourished" and "I wish I was grass eaten by livestock."[254]

Caliph Omar was also heard numerous times regretting his actions, saying, "I wish I was like this straw, I wish my mother never bore me, I wish I was nothing, I wish I was completely forgotten."[255] Before his death he said, "If I owned all there is on Earth, I would have sacrificed it to avoid the fear of punishment."[256]

The editorial board that translated forty volumes of *The History of Al-Tabari* have commented on these statements by the caliph, saying that this story seems to refer to the attempt to force Ali and Fatima to swear allegiance to Abu Bakr as caliph. They also suggest that there is something hidden between the lines of these reports, which has been concealed in Islamic history.[257]

The Hidden Grave

It was, and still is, part of Muslim culture in general and Arab culture specifically to request to be buried inside one's own home or in an unknown location if one believes one will die oppressed. In Lady Fatima's case, after she was attacked in the brutal way that led to her murder,[258] she chose to be buried by her husband Ali in an unknown location,[259] never to be revealed until today.[260] Many Islamic scholars have assumed that Fatima's grave is located between the house and pulpit of Prophet Mohammad,[261] but the evidence for that remains extremely weak and unreliable. One of the main reasons why Fatima made this decision was to make a public statement that Caliph Abu Bakr would not lead the funeral prayers of Prophet Mohammad's daughter.[262] This was so concerning for the Muslim nation that they tried to locate the grave of Fatima, and ordered a group of women to exhume her body in order that the caliph could pray over it.[263]

Islamic scholars have reported: "When Fatima passed away, Ali buried her secretly and camouflaged her gravesite" and turned towards the direction of her father's grave, Mohammad, and said "In the sight of God, your daughter is buried secretly, her rights are taken away unjustly, her inheritance is withheld for no valid reason. It all happened just after you left and your memories are still fresh."[264]

Post-burial Conflict

The morning after her burial, a gathering took place in front of Fatima's house, as Caliph Abu Bakr planned to lead the funeral prayers. The crowd discovered that Fatima was already buried. Omar said to Abu Bakr, "Did I not tell you about what they are planning?" The companion of Mohammad, Miqdad, informed Omar and Abu Bakr that the burial had been performed according to the will of Fatima, "and she willed that you two may not attend her funeral." Omar immediately began to strike Miqdad on his face and didn't cease until the crowd interfered to separate them and freed Miqdad from him. When freed, Miqdad stood up in front of Omar and said:

> It is not surprising for you to hit me, you also hit the daughter of the Messenger of Allah with the sword in shield on her ribs, and injured her and made her arms swell as a result of your whips, until she died in that state.

Omar then turned to Ali, Fatima's weeping husband, and said: "You washed the body of the Messenger of Allah without informing us, and then prayed over Fatima and did not let us be present." Ali ignored them as they had plotted the murder of Mohammad and had just killed his wife Fatima. However, Ali's brother, Aqeel, stood and told Omar: "You attacked her and she left this world while her back was covered in blood and she was angry with you two." Omar then held Aqeel to strike him as he had just hit Miqdad, and this is when Ali could no longer be patient with Omar. Therefore, he stood and held Omar by his clothes and said to him: "By God, it seems that you won't stop until I expose what is inside you,"[265] meaning: until I rip your chest open.

Poetry Regarding the Tragedy

Sayyid al-Himyari wrote:

> Beaten, she was, and of her rights deprived,
> And was made to taste, after his demise, of wounds.
> God sever the hands that her did they hit,
> And of that who agreed thereto and followed suit.
> God may never forgive him nor
> Spare him of the horror of leaving the grave ...[266]

***

> They collected firewood to burn the house
> And lit it even though there were children in it.

***

> She was beaten and her right was usurped
> And then they let her taste the pain of injuries and wounds
> May that hand be cut who hit her
> And the hand of those who are content with that and follow him
> May Allah not forgive him and nor
> Make him safe of the fear of the Day of Resurrection.[267]

***

How much value does the family of Prophet Mohammad hold in the eyes of Islam's caliphs? Based on Islam's own history, they have been accorded little value, and we have been trained by our hierarchies and Islamic authorities to hide this reality from other Muslims. This is exactly what Muslims did to Mohammad's family after his demise: their inheritance was stolen, their home was burnt, a child was killed in the womb, a daughter was murdered, and a grave hidden. Yet my co-religionists have the audacity to murder whoever draws a cartoon about Prophet Mohammad!

CHAPTER 6

The Great Crime: The Killing of Hussain

Imam Hussain was the second son of Fatima, the daughter of Prophet Mohammad. He was born on January 10, 626 in Medina, and soon became a voice for hundreds of millions of Muslims around the world.

After the poisoning and murder of Prophet Mohammad in the year 632, Islam witnessed many divisions that led to the formation of 73 denominations, with some Muslims glorifying the family of Prophet Mohammad more than his companions, and vice versa. The leadership battle after Prophet Mohammad's death was indeed influenced by politics, which led to the transformation from prophetic succession to kingship. Hussain had witnessed all the Islamic conquests and invasions conducted by the early caliphs of Islam, and did not join in any of their battles due to his opposition to them.

Hussain preached a message of humanity, peace, and justice. Hussain's sacrifice for the reformation of Islam has inspired all those that hear about his message and story. Hussain's revolution was aimed at saving the people from corruption, humiliation, mortification, and ignorance. However, the price Hussain had to pay for the freedom he sought was not small; it was actually his own life and the lives of his dearest family members.

Who Was Yazid, the Killer of Hussain?

Yazid was the second caliph of the Umayyad Islamic Caliphate and the sixth caliph of Islam. He is also known as "Yazid the Tyrant."[268] His reign lasted for three years, ending with his sudden death. However, the crimes he committed during those three years exceeded all the crimes committed before him. He is annually vilified in Shia Muslim ceremonies, nor is he any more popular among Sunni Muslims. Yazid is reviled for brutally killing Hussain, the grandson of Mohammad, and massacring his family and children while taking his female family members hostage, simply because Hussain refused to pledge allegiance to him.

Yazid was ordained caliph upon his father's death; however, he faced immediate opposition from Muslims who rejected the dynastic principle. Many Arabs who were used to choosing leaders by consultation rather than heredity refused to pledge allegiance to Yazid. Therefore, Yazid sent armies to capture Medina and place Mecca under siege. During the siege, the Kaba (God's House) was damaged after Yazid fired his catapults at the Muslim opposition. They had sought refuge around the Kaba assuming that they would be safe there, since war and conflict are not allowed within mosques, and especially not the Kaba or within its surroundings. Yazid's attacks on the holy Meccan mosque caused anger and rage amongst the Muslim nation at large.

Al-Masudi, an Arab historian and geographer who was the first to combine history and scientific geography,* said: "In the Muslim nation, Yazid was like Pharaoh amongst his people, but Pharaoh was more just to his people." He added: "The injustice, intrepidity and impiety of Yazid also penetrated into the Muslim nation."[269]

Yazid's chief opponent was Imam Hussain, Mohammad's grandson. This was not because Hussain wanted power, but because the Muslim nation had witnessed Yazid's terrorist crimes in previous years, against both Muslims and non-Muslims. Being the prominent and loved grandson of Mohammad, Hussain's refusal to pledge allegiance to the second Umayyad Caliph, Yazid, was seen as a threat to the entire Umayyad Dynasty. Thus, the family and successors of Prophet Mohammad were given two options: either pledge allegiance to the kingdom of the caliph, or face death. Yazid's appointed governor in Medina, Walid, then requested that Hussain come to a meeting.

Hussain had witnessed the brutal murders of his own father and mother, and he suspected that there might be a plan to assassinate him in that very gathering. Therefore, he summoned a group of his loyal

* Al-Masudi is also referred to as the Herodotus of the Arabs.

companions and brothers, and requested that they arm themselves. He said to them:

> Walid has called me just now, and I think that he will propose something which I may not accept. I cannot trust him. You should, therefore, come with me, and when I enter his house you should stay outside beside the door. *As soon as you hear me speaking aloud, enter the house to prevent him from doing me any harm.*[270]

In that gathering, Hussain was ordered to pledge allegiance to Yazid, and he responded by saying, "I will certainly not be contented with taking the oath secretly, and would like to take it in the presence of the people." Walid agreed to this, not realizing that Hussain was delaying having to pledge allegiance to a tyrant such as Yazid. Hussain said: "Then you should wait till tomorrow, so that I may arrive at a decision in the matter." Walid said: "Alright. You may go now and come tomorrow along with the people to take the oath of allegiance."[271]

Marwan, one of Yazid's main men, was also present at the meeting and objected, saying:

> I swear by Allah that if Hussain leaves this place without taking the oath of allegiance to Yazid, it will no longer be possible for you to lay hands on him without bloodshed. You should, therefore, detain him till he takes the oath and in the event of his refusing to do so, you should chop off his head![272]

On hearing the words of Marwan, Hussain stood in his place and raised his voice saying: "You despicable person! Who will kill the grandson of Mohammad, you or Walid?" The group waiting outside then stormed into the meeting and protected Hussain from any harm.

Hussain rejected their demands and said:

> I will never give Yazid my hand, like a man who has been humiliated, nor will I flee like a slave ... I have not risen to spread

evil or to show off ... I only desire to enjoin good values and prevent evil.[273]

He added: "Someone like me does not pledge allegiance to someone like him."[274] Hussain's final decision was: "Death with honor is far better than life in humiliation."[275]

The Massacre of Karbala

Imam Hussain (Peace be Upon Him) sacrificed himself instead of accepting injustice. He was unwavering in his desire for peace and justice. His teachings are as relevant today as they were centuries ago.[276]

Indian Prime Minister Narendra Modi

Karbala is a city in Iraq and a holy place to Muslims as it embraces the body and grave of Imam Hussain after he was massacred along with his family members, less than 50 years after the death of Mohammad. Shia Muslims consider this the greatest tragedy of all time. The many dimensions of the brutal murder of Hussain reflect the enormity of this calamity. The blood that was spilled in Karbala continues to inspire people around the world to raise their voices against cruelty, to live with integrity and to put humanity before politics.

The tragic event began when the Muslim citizens of Iraq sent hundreds of letters to Hussain, demanding that he save them from the tyranny and dictatorship of Yazid. The letters indicated that the people had prepared themselves to welcome Hussain in Kufa, the capital city of Iraq at the time, and were looking forward to his leadership. Upon hearing this news, Imam Hussain decided to send his cousin Ibn Aqeel as an emissary to Iraq, to meet the people and convey the news of his arrival. Hussain then organized a caravan and headed to Iraq to meet the oppressed nation that had pleaded for his arrival and protection.

The caravan kept proceeding toward Iraq; however, many days passed without Hussain hearing a response from his cousin Aqeel.

Yazid's spies and informants learned about Ibn Aqeel's presence in Iraq and the arrival of Hussain. They discovered that Ibn Aqeel was engaging in secret meetings with people who rejected the terrorist Islamic caliphate of Yazid. This matter angered Yazid, causing him to fire the current governor of Kufa, Al-Numan, and replace him with Ibn Ziyad.

When Hussain's caravan reached the outskirts of Kufa, he was surprised to hear of his cousin's murder. Ibn Ziyad had ordered Ibn Aqeel to be arrested, tortured, and beheaded, and his body thrown from the top of the castle to the ground. He was then dragged through the marketplace to send a public message to opponents of the Islamic caliphate.

Muslim scholar Al-Hindi describes the treason and betrayal of the Kufans, who pleaded for help in their letters to Hussain, and then left his messenger to be murdered in such a horrendous manner. He says:

Dragged ... your body was through the markets,
Were they not calling you "Prince," just yesterday? [277]

Hussain, while grieving the murder of his cousin and messenger, turned to his companions who had accompanied him in the caravan and said, "Our followers have deserted us. Those of you who prefer to leave me may do so freely and without guilt." Many of his companions then left him out of fear of being killed. Hussain then continued his journey with his closest companions and fellow family members. Soon enough, he was faced with 1000 soldiers led by a man known as Hurr, ordered by Yazid to block Hussain's path and prevent him from entering the capital city. Hussain informed Hurr that he was responding to the call of the Muslims who had invited him to come to Iraq from Medina, and even showed him the bagful of letters he had received from them, but Hurr said that the letters did not concern him.

Hussain then decided to return to Medina, but Hurr informed

Hussain, the grandson of Mohammad, that he had been ordered to detain him and bring him to the governor. During the journey to the governor, Hurr received an order from the governor's messenger ordering him to "force Hussain to a halt, and make him stop in an open space where there is no vegetation or water." The weather was awfully hot, and the region between the cities of Kufa and Karbala is known to be extremely hot and humid. Hurr knew that Hussain's caravan included children and women, therefore he informed Hussain of the contents of the letter. Hussain defiantly resumed his journey until he saw an army blocking his way from a distance.

Hussain stopped and asked nearby people the name of the area. They informed him that the area was called Nainawa. He said, "Does it have another name?" They said Al-Taff. He said, "Does it have another name?" They said Karbala. Hussain said, "Yes indeed, Karbala. This is where we shall set our camps."

The name Karbala is made up of two words: karb and bala, with *karb* meaning "severe grief" and *bala* meaning "hardship." Muslims believe that the incident was foretold by Prophet Mohammad, and that Hussain knew of the betrayal and corruption that would occur after Prophet Mohammad. He was fully aware that he would have to be the greatest sacrifice in order for the people to regain their freedom.

When Yazid's governor, Ibn Ziyad, received confirmation that his army had succeeded in laying a siege around the camp of Hussain, he sent additional army units to Karbala even though he knew that Hussain's companions did not exceed 72 men. The soldiers all knew who Hussain was, the most beloved one to Prophet Mohammad; therefore, it was easy for them to be convinced that he should be allowed to leave Iraq and return to Mecca. The leader of the later army, Ibn Sa'ad, thought Hussain's proposal to leave Iraq and return home was reasonable. However, when Yazid and his companions heard that Hussain wished to return home without paying allegiance to the Islamic caliphate, they demanded that Hussain be given one option: war.

They ordered the troops to surround Hussain's camp, laying a blockade around the camp to block access to the Euphrates River. This tactic was intended to pressure Hussain to surrender to Yazid, as it was extremely hot, and the children and women slowly began to dehydrate. However, Hussain refused to bow down to the terrorists.

A historical painting displaying the camp of Hussain being surrounded by the armies of Yazid.

One of the main reasons why Yazid sent such a great army in the first place was because he supposed that the entire Muslim nation would rise with Hussain, but Hussain was left alone.

Two days later, Hussain found himself completely surrounded by 100,000 soldiers, not allowing him to return home, and demanding that he pledge allegiance to Yazid. They demanded war, and Hussain, the reformist grandson of Mohammad, refused to surrender. Towards midnight, he called all his companions into his tent and said to them: "The enemy wants my blood, not yours. I permit each and every one of you to go back to your families. Use the darkness of this night as a form of safety for you." The companions refused to leave Hussain, and said, "We will either live with you or die together with you."

To this Hussain said: "I have never seen companions better than mine." This statement referred to the corruption and disloyalty of the companions of his grandfather Prophet Mohammad, which Hussain had witnessed.

The Tragedy

During the dawn of October 10, 680 CE, the swords of jihad were being sharpened, and arrows were being soaked in poison. This time it was jihad against the family of their own Prophet Mohammad.

Hussain's family and companions had not consumed water since they had been placed under siege in the hot Arabian desert. Despite this, they stood alongside Hussain because they believed in his message of reform, peace, and justice; therefore, they did not complain to Hussain or question his mission throughout the entire calamity.

Hussain stepped out of his tent holding his six-month-old son, Abdullah,* and walked towards the army of Yazid to plead for water for the women and children. He raised Abdullah into the sky and said to the army, "If you're here for my blood, then what crime has this child committed?" The army knew Hussain was the most beloved grandson of Mohammad, and many of Yazid's soldiers began to rethink their position, with many agreeing that Hussain deserved water and honorable treatment. Consequently, the general of Yazid's army, Ibn Sa'ad, ordered Hurmula, who was a talented archer, to end the ongoing debate between the soldiers. Hurmula reached for his bow and arrow, and launched a three-headed poisoned arrow into the throat of baby Abdullah, making him the youngest victim of that unfolding massacre.[278]

Hurr, the previous commander of Yazid's army who initially blocked Hussain's road back to Medina, was emotionally broken to see such a tragic scene. Upon realizing the gravity of the situation, he along with his son turned against Yazid's army and rushed toward Hussain to join him. Hurr's defection worried Yazid and his other generals because he was a prominent member of their military, and they feared that other popular and influential figures within their army would follow Hurr and join Hussain; after all, he was the most loved by their own Prophet Mohammad.

* Abdullah is also known as Ali al-Asghar.

As a result of the growing tension within the army, its chief general Ibn Sa'ad launched an arrow into the air, indicating the commencement of what has often been called a battle, but in reality was a massacre. Due to the political clashes and developments during his time, Prophet Mohammad foresaw the martyrdom of his grandson Hussain during his life, and said, "My Hussain will be killed in a manner which nobody has been killed in."[279]

The army generals of the caliphate of Yazid ordered their troops to set fire to the tents of Hussain's camp, and to frighten the females and young children. They began to loot the camp of Hussain, and when Shimr, who would later behead Hussain, reached Hussain's five-year-old daughter Ruqayyah,* he slapped her face and pulled her golden earrings off her ears, causing her ears to bleed. Out of fright, she ran into the battlefield screaming, "Father, where are you?"[280]

Hussain's men began to defend the women. The first was Wahab,** a Christian man who decided to sacrifice himself in defense of Hussain. He bid farewell to his mother and wife, who had accompanied Hussain's caravan, and approached the army of Yazid, saying:

> You evil dark-hearted people, do you know what you are doing? You have blocked the road of the grandson of your own Prophet Mohammad! Has Hussain oppressed you in any way? Or has he taken away any of your rights? Or has he shed any blood, that you need to take revenge for, that you want to kill him!?
> I vow in the name of Jesus! That if you don't leave Hussain alone, you shall never see the light of day, until the day of judgment! Misery and disaster will befall all of you, and you will never receive God's mercy nor his blessings.[281]

Shimr yelled out from Yazid's army, "Stop your unpleasant lecture and tell us who you are!" Wahab continued:

> I am Wahab the Christian man. I swear by God; Jesus Christ is eager and waiting to meet Hussain in paradise. I swear by the

---

* Ruqayyah is also known as Sukayna bint Hussain.
** Full name: Abdullah ibn Omayr Abu Wahab al Kalbi.

creator of the Moon, Sun, Stars, Earth and great Seas; and I vow by God who brings rain, I have come to support the grandson of Mohammad, and to give my life for him.[282]

Shimr mockingly responded, "Is there no Muslim to help Hussain, that he is being helped by Christians? Go away Christian, we do not fight Christians." To which Wahab replied, "May your mouth be destroyed, you cursed individual. You have used your own sword against your own book of God."

Shimr sarcastically replied, "Do you even know the names of the weapons you are carrying?" implying that Wahab was not as good a soldier as them. To prove him wrong, Wahab spent a moment performing stunts on his horse, proving to Yazid's army that he was more than just a talented fighter. Being unable to tolerate this, Shimr ordered the army to "make his mother mourn over him!" After Wahab took down one of their fighters, they surrounded him, filling his body with arrows. Shimr then said, "Crucify him like Christians are crucified!" Wahab was placed on a cross, and dragged along the battlefield. The soldiers were then ordered to "behead him and send his head to his mother." When they carried the head to his mother's tent, they said to Wahab's mother: "This is a gift to you from our commander." Wahab's Christian mother then carried the head of her son back to the battlefield saying, "Where we are from, we do not take back what we have given as a sacrifice for God."[283]

Amidst all of this, Hussain was trying to protect the remaining women and children from the stomping of the horses and the fire that had engulfed his camp. The companions of Hussain began to fall one after the other. To those studying the history of this massacre, Hussain's companions appear to have been brave and sincere men who welcomed martyrdom and did not fear the army of Islamist terrorists.ₒ

By noon that day, Hussain ordered his remaining companions to stop engaging in combat and to prepare themselves for noon prayers.* As Hussain was leading the prayers, a few of his companions were guarding him from oncoming arrows being launched at him from

---

* Muslims pray five times a day: at sunrise, noon, afternoon, evening, and night.

Yazid's army. Once the prayers were finished, one of Hussain's guards fell with 17 poisoned arrows in his back.

Hussain's family members, brothers, and sons were brutally murdered. One incident that deeply affected Hussain was the death of his loyal brother Abbas, who went to tackle the soldiers by the river to collect water for the women and children. He reached the water and, after remembering the thirst of his brother Hussain, he threw the water back into the river and refused to drink. However, he filled his bota bag with water to quench the thirst of the young children, mounted his horse and turned back towards the camp, and discovered he was faced with tens of soldiers. They pierced the bota bag with arrows, and struck his right arm with a sword, chopping it off entirely. He carried the water with his left arm, and that too was chopped off. He was struck with a metal pole on his head, causing him to fall off his horse. He died shortly after.

By the afternoon, all of Hussain's companions had been murdered and beheaded. The two who remained were Hussain and his son Ali, who was ill and unable to fight. Hussain was experiencing severe thirst, dehydration, and exhaustion, and was extremely tired from running from one end of the camp to the other protecting the women and children, while heading to the battlefield to bring back the bodies of his family members, but he wasn't going to surrender. Hussain held his sword in his hand and said, "O Lord, my consolation is the fact that your majesty is witnessing what I am going through." He then turned to the motionless armies and said, "Is there no-one to give me victory? Is there no-one here who will protect the women and children?"[284]

Hussain was surrounded by Yazid's army and he fought till his last breath, until his body was transformed into a bed of arrows. Historians state that the body of Hussain had a wound and injury in every part of it. He was then beheaded, and his head was placed on a spear just like the heads of his family members.

The family of Hussain, consisting of women and children, were all taken hostage from Karbala, Iraq, to Damascus, Syria. They were made to walk barefoot and were physically assaulted continuously throughout the entire journey as they witnessed the heads of their

men, and Hussain, raised on spears. Yazid's army decided to go all the
way to Egypt, in order to publicize and celebrate their victory
throughout the Muslim nation while dragging the family and daughters
of Mohammad, their own prophet, in chains.

When they reached Egypt, they passed by the monastery of a Christian
archbishop. As usual, they raised Hussain's head on a spear and
guarded it while leaning the spear against the wall of the monastery. At
midnight, the archbishop saw the head on the spear and said to them:
"Who are you?" They replied, "We are associates of Ibn Ziyad and
Yazid." He asked, "Whose head is this?" and they replied, "It is of
Hussain, the son of Ali and Lady Fatima, the daughter of the Prophet of
Allah." He asked, "You mean your own Prophet?" and they replied
"Yes." Hearing this he said, "You are among the worst of men. If Jesus

would have had a son, we would have placed him upon our eyes and we would have honored him greatly."

He then asked them, "Could you do me a favor?" They asked what it was, and he replied:

I have ten thousand *dinars* with me.* You may take it and give me the head of Hussain. Let it remain with me until the dawn, and when you proceed further, take it back from me in the morning.

They replied, "We have nothing to lose." Saying this, they handed the head over to him and he gave them the ten thousand dinars in return. The archbishop washed the head of Hussain, perfumed it, and kept it

* The dinar was the currency of the time.

upon his thigh. He wept profusely until dawn.[285] The "Mosque of Hussain" shrine exists in Cairo today, marking the location of this incident, and the rock on which the head of Hussain rested.[286]

When they finally reached Yazid's castle in Syria, they placed Hussain's head in a bucket. Yazid began to strike the head with a stick. Little Ruqayyah was yearning for her father; therefore, they placed the head of her father in front of her. Ruqayyah died in Syria at the age of five from all the torture and grief that she had experienced.

Peter J. Chelkowski, Professor of Middle Eastern and Islamic Studies at New York University, wrote:

> Hussein accepted and set out from Mecca with his family and an entourage of about seventy followers. But on the plain of Karbala they were caught in an ambush set by the caliph, Yazid. Though

defeat was certain, Hussein refused to pay homage to him. Surrounded by a great enemy force, Hussein and his company existed without water for ten days in the burning desert of Karbala. Finally, Hussein, the adults and some male children of his family and his companions were cut to bits by the arrows and swords of Yazid's army; his women and remaining children were taken as captives to Yazid in Damascus. The renowned historian Abu Reyhan al-Biruni states: "Then fire was set to their camp and the bodies were trampled by the hoofs of the horses; nobody in the history of humankind has seen such atrocities."[287]

One dimension of this entire event that inspires me until this very day is the actions of Hussain's sister Zainab, who took on public relations duties for her family after the tragic massacre of Hussain and his family. She began to inform nations of what had happened to her brother. While held hostage, she delivered a powerful speech in Yazid's castle, humiliating him. She said: "It's shocking O' son of Hind* that you would dare bring us to Damascus as slaves. Therefore, strive and plot, but you shall never erase our remembrance from the minds of people."[288]

When Lady Zainab was asked about the massacre that resulted in the tragic murders of her brothers and nephews, she remembered the solidarity of Hussain and his companions who refused to pledge allegiance to the terrorist Caliph Yazid. She looked the enemy in the eyes and said, "I see nothing but beauty." Indeed, it is beautiful to remain strong when truthful, resilient when victimized, and never to shake the hand of an unscrupulous Islamic terrorist who has massacred innocent nations.

Today, tens of millions of people from around the globe walk towards the shrine and burial site of Hussain to commemorate his martyrdom in an annual pilgrimage called Arba'een. Hussain has become the symbol of freedom and reform, the symbol of love and victory. Hussain and his loyal companions proved to the world that it is possible for blood to become victorious over the sword. Hussain did in

---

* Hind was the mother of Yazid. She is famously known for participating in the Battle of Yarmouk against the Muslims on August 15, 636. After the battle, Hind mutilated the corpses of the dead Muslims. She cut off noses and ears and made them into necklaces and anklets. She then gouged out the liver of Hamza, the uncle of Prophet Mohammad, and bit into it; while other Islamic scholars claim that she cooked it before eating it.

fact lose the battle, but he won the war. In contrast, Yazid is hardly
ever remembered, and if he is mentioned he is always cursed.

The Holy Shrine of Imam Hussain, in Karbala, Iraq.

Great influential and leading figures have mentioned the tragic
massacre of Hussain in Karbala. This shows that Hussain doesn't only
belong to Muslims, but belongs to all those who want to see humans
live an honorable life without tyranny, humiliation and oppression.

Edward Gibbon, considered the greatest British historian of his
time, wrote: "In a distant age and climate the tragic scene of the death
of Husain will awaken the sympathy of the coldest reader."[289] While
Ignác Goldziher, a Jewish Hungarian orientalist and scholar of Islamic
studies, considered the founder of modern Islamic studies in Europe,
said: "Ever since the black day of Karbala, the history of this family has
been a continuous series of sufferings and persecutions."[290]

Anyone with a sound conscience and healthy mind will truly
comprehend the heartrending events at Karbala, and what tragedy
befell upon Hussain. He opposed violence in the name of Islam,
standing for reform, freedom, dignity, and for a better tomorrow. Such
a person deserves respect and honor, not a poisoned arrow in his eye.

Hussain inspires me until this day never to shake the hand of any radical extremist, and to strive towards global peace.

CHAPTER 7

A Religion of War

After all the internal conflicts and murders within Islam, the Islamic caliphs set out to expand their kingdoms. Since they did not have the skill to convince nations to convert to Islam by intellectual arguments, instead they resorted to violence. Amongst those terrorists was my own ancestor Adi Bin Hatim, son of the legendary Arabian poet Hatim al-Tai. They imposed Islam and Sharia Law upon defeated peoples, with death as the only punishment for those who opposed them. This time, a new situation had emerged, a new, untried political formation known as the global Islamic caliphate.

To me, the question is not why Arabs conquered most of the Middle East, Northern Africa, and Spain among other places. It is: How did Islam gain its reputation as a religion of war in the first place?

The Islamic Conquests

Prophet Mohammad had sought revenge on the tribes and chiefs of Mecca, his own city, for their plots to assassinate him during the first months of the emergence of Islam, which forced him into exile in Medina in September 622. As mentioned earlier, he returned to conquer Mecca on January 11, 630. I personally do not consider his return to Mecca a conquest, because he was simply returning to his home town with more followers and power than he had when he left. However, it is understandable why many would target Prophet Mohammad, and wonder why he would engage in battles. His monotheistic message was seen as a threat to the idol worship that was common at that time, and he belonged to a prominent Arabian family that adhered to the Abrahamic faith, which the chiefs of Arabia were terrified of.

Islamic historians and seminaries refer to the occupation of land by Islamic caliphates as "Holy Conquests," but in political science these "Holy Conquests" constitute invasions. As examined throughout this book, it would have been impossible for Prophet Mohammad to conquer other gigantic and established empires with 3000 lazy and disobedient soldiers. Not only were they disobedient and rebellious to their own prophet whom they claimed to love, but the soldiers who later became caliphs were in fact well-known cowards, and most of their "conquests" and "achievements" were a result of commands and expeditions, and not their personal participation in battles.

The Masters of Genocide

In July 628, Prophet Mohammad ordered his father-in-law, Abu Bakr, to lead a military campaign to scare off some tribes of Nejd,* after he had received information that they had suspicious intentions.[291] The plan was to scare them by walking through the region as a show of strength, similar to today's military parades. However, in those times they would conduct these shows in other cities so that potential political opponents were made aware of their military capabilities. As the acting commander of the army, Abu Bakr ordered the massacre of the Nejd people and tribes.[292] The army killed a large number of civilians and took many more as prisoners.[293] Minority denominations within Islam believe that Mohammad's intention was to show strength by parading only, and that Abu Bakr took matters into his own hands. Their justification for this claim is that the campaign was later named after Abu Bakr as "the Expedition of Abu Bakr," and he took credit for all the murders committed.

Four years later in 632, Abu Bakr was announced as the first caliph of Islam after the death of Mohammad. This succession caused many Muslims to rebel against Caliph Abu Bakr, not only because he was unsuitable for the caliphate and had a tarnished reputation, but also because many Muslims believed that they had submitted to Mohammad's prophecy alone, not to Abu Bakr. During this ongoing

* A geographically central region of Saudi Arabia that was home to many prominent Arabian tribes prior to the emergence of Islam.

dispute, a number of Arabians claimed to be prophets from God after Mohammad.** This matter angered Abu Bakr, as these false prophets gained thousands of followers. As a reaction, he declared the Wars of Apostasy,*** a series of military campaigns against rebel Arabian tribes that took place between the years 623 and 633 CE. The reason for these wars was that Abu Bakr believed the emerging self-proclaimed prophets were threatening the unity and stability of his Islamic caliphate. Abu Bakr defeated most of the tribes, with many of them being integrated into his caliphate. Abu Bakr's success came as a result of his strategy and planning. He studied the Muslim army and its strength, and divided it into several corps. The strongest corps was that of Khalid ibn al-Waleed, the terrorist described in Chapter 4 who attacked innocent civilians without prior warning, and beheaded Malik then cooked and ate his head before raping his widowed wife.

Once the wars against the apostates and ex-Muslims were over, Abu Bakr began to pave the way for the Islamic conquests that would lead to one of the largest empires in the history of human existence. In 633, Abu Bakr assigned Khalid once again as army general to invade the Sasanian Empire in Iraq.[294] After completing the conquest of Iraq in 634, Abu Bakr sent Khalid with four armies to invade the Roman province of Syria.[295]

Men, women, and children were massacred by the armies of the Islamic caliphates. Although the first Caliph Abu Bakr had led and sent out expeditions to massacre non-Muslims, they were minor events which cannot be compared to the crimes of Caliph Omar, as they were only paving the way for the Islamic "conquests" to officially begin during the reign of the second caliph, Omar ibn al-Khattab.

By now, the army of the Islamic caliphate* had become well established. *Military History Online* published an article describing the army:

> The Muslims not only knew the locations of vital desert oases, but also traveled with the camel, an animal evolved for the hot sands ... Recruited from their tribes and commanded by emirs the Muslim army fell into the two basic categories of infantry and

** Tulayha, Musaylima, and Sajjah all claimed prophethood after Mohammad's death.
*** Also known as the "Ridda Wars."
* Also referred to as the "Rashidun Caliphates."

cavalry. The Arab cavalryman, the faris, was armed with lance and sword, his main role being the attack of the enemy flanks and rear. Armor was relatively light, often consisting of a chainmail shirt and segmented helm. Unlike later Middle Eastern field armies the early Muslims relied heavily on their infantry. Muslim infantrymen were armed with spear, short sword, and composite bow. Defensively the Muslim infantry were equipped with chainmail shirts, segmented helms, and large wooden or wickerwork shields. On the attack Muslim infantry would weaken the enemy with arrow volleys, followed by a spear/sword charge, pining the enemy in place for a cavalry attack on the flanks and rear. Defensively the Muslim spearmen would close ranks, forming a protective wall for archers to continue their fire.[296]

Caliph Omar reigned as the second caliph of Islam during 634–644. His invasions incorporated present-day Iraq, Iran, Azerbaijan, Armenia, Georgia, Syria, Jordan, Palestine, Lebanon, Israel, Egypt, and part of Afghanistan, Turkmenistan, and south-western Pakistan into the empire of the Islamic caliphate. Islamic history reports that the Byzantines lost more than three fourths of their territory, and in Persia the Sasanian Empire was completely annihilated.[297]

An entire encyclopedia could be published regarding the massacres and invasions conducted by our second Caliph Omar, and how he utilized this army to invade, conquer, and even annihilate cities. Every region they dominated and conquered was instantly transformed into an Islamic State with a violent Sharia Law system. They forced nations into Islam by the sword, changed their religions by force, and sent the male forced converts to conduct jihad against their own people.

The Annihilation of Arab Soos

One of the massacres committed by Caliph Omar, which Muslim scholars worked effortlessly to erase from the books of Islamic history, was the massacre and complete destruction of the village of "Arab

Soos" (Arabic: عرب سوس). Arab Soos no longer exists and is infrequently mentioned in historic texts.

The massacre of this village occurred when Caliph Omar appointed Umayr bin Sa'd (Arabic: عمير بن سعد) as governor of Homs, a city in western Syria which was sought after by Muslim caliphs and dynasties, due to its strategic position in the area. For 2000 years, Homs had played a vital role in the economy of the entire geographic region, and was known for its provision of security services to surrounding areas and its ability to prevent any invasions. However, at first, Umayr knew the weight of this responsibility and tried to decline the offer as he preferred jihad, but Caliph Omar insisted that he became governor of Homs, while young Umayr was in his twenties.

During his time in office, Umayr sent a letter to Caliph Omar, informing him of a village within his territory situated between the Byzantine Empire and the Islamic caliphate called "Arab Soos," and that the people of this village were conspiring and plotting against his caliphate and government. Caliph Omar instantly ordered Governor Umayr to give the citizens of Arab Soos two options: receive financial payments for their assets and relocate to another country immediately, and their village will be destroyed, or take one year to relocate, and their village will be destroyed. The chiefs of the village refused the first option, and refuted the accusation that they plotted against the caliphate. Thus, Umayr allowed them one year to remain in their village, and when the year had ended, he massacred all of its citizens, and the entire village was annihilated.[298] Ironically, when Caliph Omar heard of this news he became extremely furious and beat Umayr viciously, and Umayr yelled, "I did so according to your written orders!", and he presented them to Omar; to which Caliph Omar responded saying, "Why didn't you remind me of this before I hit you?"[299]

I find it difficult to understand which is worse, Caliph Omar ordering the massacre of an entire village, or forgetting that he had issued orders for the destruction of a community living within his jurisdiction.

The Invasion of Roman Syria (634–638)

Throughout the 630s, Christians and Jews throughout Syria were dissatisfied with Byzantine rule and acted as a religious opposition against the values of the government. This meant that their loyalty no longer lay with the government, and they were not willing to defend it from any potential invasions; in fact, they welcomed the Muslim invaders and the army of the Islamic caliphate.[300] Along with the political and social tensions in the region, the Roman Emperor Heraclius had fallen ill, and was unable to personally engage in any military combat. As a result of this, he was unable to challenge the invasions of the Islamic caliphate, making the Muslims decisively victorious in their battles in 634,[301] paving the way for another invasion in Damascus during the same year.[302]

Two years later, in 636, the armies of the Islamic caliphate lured the Byzantines into a planned battle, which proved a death trap for the Romans[303] and left Heraclius saying, "Peace unto thee, O Syria, and what an excellent country this is for the enemy."[304] The following year, in 637, the Islamic army held the entire city of Jerusalem under siege. They raped and massacred its citizens until the Patriarch of Jerusalem, Sophronius, surrendered to the caliphate. English historian Steven Runciman describes the event:

> On a February day in the year AD 638, the Caliph Omar entered Jerusalem, riding upon a white camel. He was dressed in worn, filthy robes, and the army that followed him was rough and unkempt; but its discipline was perfect. At his side rode the Patriarch Sophronius, as chief magistrate of the surrendered city.[305]

They weren't content with all the land and wealth they had already gained, and their greed led them to Gaza, which they conquered along with its surroundings in 637.[306] As for northern Syria, most of its armies surrendered peacefully and agreed to pay *jizyah*.*

---

* Jizyah is the protection tax that non-Muslim citizens of an Islamic state are obliged to pay to the government to secure their safety and wellbeing.

Joannes Zonaras, an eleventh-century Byzantine chronicler and theologian, referred to his conquered hometown and massacred nation, saying: "[Even after the fall of Syria] They did not cease from invading and plundering the entire territory of the Romans."[307] Once they had terrorized the entire geographic region and announced dominance over the land they had conquered, they departed to Egypt in 640, with the intention to invade Armenia the following year. They conducted simultaneous campaigns in the entire northern African region.[308]

Invasions of Armenia (638)

In 638, Caliph Omar ordered the conquest of Armenia. The whole of Armenia was captured, followed by strategic raids targeting northern and central Anatolia. There wasn't much that Heraclius could do to prevent the rape and murder being carried out by the radical and terrorist armies of the Islamic caliphate, which led to him abandoning all the strongholds in this part of his empire. In order to prevent genocide, he withdrew and created a "No Man's Land" as a safe zone between the remaining land of his empire and the land conquered by the caliphate.

Caliph Omar hated the Romans because most of them would not accept Islam, even by the sword, and he didn't wish to engage in a counterproductive battle, when there were many other "productive" battles to be fought and other lands to invade. Therefore, it has been reported that he sealed his mission in Armenia with his famous saying: "I wish there was a wall of fire between us and Romans, so that they could not enter our territory, nor we could enter theirs."[309]

The Invasion of Egypt (640–643)

The invasion of Egypt was not one incident; it was rather a series of massacres and atrocities that took place in North Africa, and the north and south of Egypt. Although the rule of the Islamic state in Syria was still not firm, Caliph Omar was convinced that the Byzantine influence in Egypt was a continuous threat to Muslim rule in Palestine. At the time, Egypt was a wealthy country, if not the wealthiest, and was seen as a financial opportunity by the Islamic caliphate. An Islamic "parliament" deliberated on the matter in Medina, and the invasion of Egypt was announced in December 639 by Caliph Omar who then shed the Egyptian people's blood.[310]

Unlike the time of Prophet Mohammad, when the Muslim army didn't exceed 3000 fighters, in the year 640, the army of the Islamic caliphate had substantially increased in number. One general alone, Ibn al-Aas, had 3500–4000 troops under his command. Another, Al-Zubayr, had 12,000 skilled fighters. They joined forces, conquered Babylon and joined the armies of the Islamic caliphate in attacking Alexandria, Egypt. During these invasions, Gregory the Patrician* was murdered. The invasions and massacres in Egypt continued until 642, one day before the caliphate army decided to invade another nation; this time it was Persia.

The Invasions of Persia (633–642)

Continuing the conquests of Caliph Abu Bakr, Caliph Omar ordered a full invasion of the Sasanian Empire, leading to the complete conquest of the Persians around the year 651. These massacres and genocides in Persia (modern Iran) were "a series of well-coordinated, multi-pronged attacks which became Omar's greatest triumph."[311] However, the Persians decided to take back their invaded territories and defeated the Islamic caliphate in the Battle of the Bridge, led by the Persian warrior Bahman Jadhuyih in November 634.[312] This angered the Muslim armies and triggered an even greater massacre of the Persian people which commenced on the 13th of the following Holy Month of Ramadhan, coinciding with April 635.[313]

Caliph Omar sent delegates to all parts of Arabia, inviting the Arabs to participate in the war against the Persians. He announced the Battle of the Buwaib against the Persians beside the Boyab Stream. It was

* A relative of the ruling Heraclian Dynasty who declared himself emperor.

without a doubt the most violent conflict ever conducted by the Islamic armies as the Persians numbered over 120,000 fighters with 100,000 of them being skilled horsemen, while the Muslims consisted of 12,000 soldiers only. With all the Islamic motivation towards martyrdom and paradise and the myth of the 72 virgins, the Islamic army butchered over 100,000 Persian soldiers, causing the remaining soldiers to flee. It is also reported in Islamic history that every Muslim soldier killed 10 Persians on that day, resulting in the day being named "The Day of Ten." [314]

After this bloodbath, Caliph Omar's army took its war booty to Medina, which included the crown and golden garments of Khosrow II, the last great king of the Persian Empire who rejected the invitation to hear Prophet Mohammad's message about Islam. When Caliph Omar saw the crown of Khosrow, he began to pray, saying:

> Allah, You did not reward this wealth to your Prophet, and he was closer to You and loved by You more than I, neither did You reward this wealth to Caliph Abu Bakr and he was closer to You and loved by You more than I, and You gave it to me. [315]

This left the Persian King Yazdgerd III with no option but to seek an alliance with Emperor Heraclius of the Roman Empire in 635. The Persians and the Romans had a history of conducting war and revenge against each other, but they were prepared to unite against the common enemy: the Islamic Caliph Omar. Heraclius married his granddaughter to Yazdgerd III, to show alliance and possibly also to secure his loyalty. They both formed considerable armies to push back the Islamic caliphate and to end the conquests of their mutual opponent, Caliph Omar. The Persian army drew troops from every corner of its empire and was led by its chief generals. Their army included fearsome war elephants that were brought for the sole purpose of vanquishing the Islamist terrorist soldiers. Even then, the Islamic army was victorious, effectively ending Persian rule. After the battle, the Islamic army held the imperial capital of the Persian Empire under a three-month siege, forcing its collapse in March 637. This victory played a big role in the growth of the Islamic caliphate, inspiring the Islamic armies to utilize the war booty gained to invade Persia's neighbors, starting with Iraq.

The Invasion of Iraq (636–637)

During the caliphate of Abu Bakr, a region that is now known as Iraq was invaded by the Islamic armies in 633, killing thousands of innocent citizens in order to control their rich and fertile land. In 634, Caliph Abu Bakr sent his army general, Khalid, to Syria to massacre the Romans. Khalid took a large number of soldiers along with him which left the Islamic army dangerously exposed to a Persian counter-attack, resulting in them fleeing the scene and residing in the Arabian Desert.

Caliph Omar was very frustrated by this defeat. Therefore, without wasting much time, he sent a massive Islamic army to strengthen the position of the Islamic caliphate in Iraq. This began the bloody year of 636, wherein the Islamic armies massacred and annihilated the Romans in Syria and Persians in Iraq. Two years later, in 638, the Islamic caliphate returned to invade Ahvaz, a city in the south-west of modern Iran famous for its strategic position and economic wealth. This invasion forced the dominant Persian commander-in-chief, Hormuzan, to enter into peace treaties with the Islamic caliphate. After refusing to live under violent Sharia Law, he broke the treaty three times, and was forgiven each time he did. However, the situation escalated, and he was arrested and relocated to Medina for imprisonment. When they made him stand before Caliph Omar, he was asked to convert to Islam. Hormuzan refused to embrace Islam, and thus Caliph Omar called upon his executioner to behead him. He then converted to Islam out of fear for his life.[316] Hormuzan was then forced to act as an advisor for Caliph Omar, where he provided important guidance on economic and institutional developments. As mentioned earlier in this book, Hormuzan was falsely accused of plotting to murder Caliph Omar, and was killed by Omar's son, Abdullah, in the year 644.[317]

The Truth about Palestine

Since the mid-twentieth century, there has been an unending struggle between Jewish Israelis and Muslim Palestinians over the rule of the geographic region of Palestine. Muslims recognize Islamic Palestine as the only legitimate country, while the majority of Jewish people believe Israel is a legitimate state. Every year, especially during the Month of Ramadhan, Muslims protest against what they call "the Israeli Occupation of Palestine," or what has been referred to as the world's most intractable conflict.[318]

I am not a politician, and all the political and diplomatic arrangements that led to the creation of Israel are irrelevant to me, because I am a religious figure, who views such situations through the lens of geography and Islamic history. However, if we were to briefly review the ongoing Israeli–Palestinian conflict though a political lens, we would find that Palestine did have the chance of being an independent state of its own; in fact, this was an offer made to them by Israel, not once, but five times.[319] If Israel was a Christian or even a communist establishment, I highly doubt that the conflict would have turned out the way it has. Whether Palestine is Jewish land or whether Israel is a state are two completely different debates. A Muslim may reject Israel being a state, but cannot deny the fact that the entire region, including Palestine, is in fact Jewish land.

Messengers of both Judaism and Christianity had arrived in Jerusalem to preach their scriptures centuries before Prophet Mohammad. Therefore, it cannot be historically accurate to say that Mohammad brought Islam to Jerusalem before them. Up until the migration of Mohammad to Medina in 622 CE and the official establishment of Islam therein, Islam was a minority religion when compared to the two well-established religions of Christianity and Judaism. Besides, the citizens of Jerusalem who converted to Islam merely changed their own faith, not the entire history of Jerusalem.

Jerusalem was home for adherents of the Jewish and Christian religions, so how did Islam arrive in the region? Islamic scripture mentions that Prophet Mohammad arrived in Al-Aqsa Mosque (the

Farthest Mosque) during his time as a prophet. However, there is little evidence that this mosque is actually in Palestine, and there are a large number of Muslims who believe "the Farthest Mosque" is a reference to a mosque in the heavens, not on earth.

In reality, <u>Islam as a religion officially came to Palestine</u> in the year 636, <u>four years after Mohammad's death</u> and during the reign of the second caliph of Islam, Omar. The Islamic caliphate conducted an attack on Jerusalem, which was ruled by the Byzantine Romans. The city was placed under a four-month siege commencing in November of that year.[320] After four months of hardship and butchery, the Orthodox Patriarch of Jerusalem, Sophronius, surrendered Jerusalem to Caliph Omar in 637. When Caliph Omar realized that Islam was still a minority religion in the region, he adopted the *jizyah* system, forcing Christians and Jewish people to pay tax to the Islamic caliphate.[321]

Al-Aqsa Mosque

After conducting a massacre of the citizens of Jerusalem, our Caliph Omar came to Jerusalem to appoint his governors. He then built what is known today as "the Aqsa Mosque," which many Muslims mistakenly think was built by Prophet Mohammad.

Dome of the Rock

The mosque in Jerusalem with its golden dome is known to Muslims as "Qubbat al-Sakhrah"(Dome of the Rock), and it was completed in 691 CE by the Umayyad Dynasty, the following Islamic caliphate. It is arguably not permissible for Muslims to pray within the Al-Aqsa Mosque and the Qubbat al-Sakhrah, as they are built upon occupied and invaded land.* In fact, they should be boycotted because they spread hate, terrorism, and the ideology of **Salafi** Islam. It is also worth mentioning that these two premises are home to the past and present leaders of the global extremist Islamic party Hizb ut-Tahrir.

By the ninth century, the Fatimid Dynasty, a Shia Islamic caliphate, ruled a large area of North Africa. They were also terrorists who invaded Palestine and massacred Christians in Jerusalem for siding with the Romans of the Byzantine, who had attempted to regain their conquered land. The notorious caliph of the Fatimid Caliphate, Al-Hakim, caused much damage to the entire region, even killing John VII, the Patriarch of Jerusalem, a provocative act that laid the groundwork for the First Crusade.[322] Due to the defeat of the crusaders, Muslims became the majority, by the sword and not by the pen. By this time, the entire Mediterranean coast of Palestine had been

---

* According to Sharia Law, it is not permissible to pray on land without the permission of its owner.

captured, followed by a series of massacres of the Christian people and a genocide that spread all the way to Damascus and Beirut.[323] Islam became the established religion of Palestine by the ninth century, and became the majority religion of the region throughout the Mamluk Era, between 1250 and 1516.

Therefore, we Muslims did not enter Palestine as preachers and convert its nation into Muslims. We murdered their leaders and conducted serial massacres led by both Sunni and Shia terrorist Islamic caliphs. **The citizens of Palestine may convert to Islam, but in no way can Palestine be considered Muslim land.** Of course, many may dispute this position, but the fact is that the Jews were in this land long before even Christianity arose. Their ancient cultural links remain unbroken, as in the saying each Passover "next year in Jerusalem."

Our Arab-Muslim ancestors came out of their deserts as conquerors and not as learners, and as guiders who do not seek the guidance of others. The believed that they had sufficient knowledge and wisdom, and that they do not need to learn anything from others. This delusion of my co-religionists persists to this day, despite the fact that the world has changed.

Mohammad Defecates Towards Jerusalem

On the other hand, I do not understand the Muslim struggle for Jerusalem. Islamic laws strictly prohibit relieving oneself while facing Mecca, in fact, toilets in all Islamic countries and most Muslim homes do not face Mecca, out of respect to the holy city. Yet Bukhari reports that our Prophet Mohammad used to deliberately and repeatedly relieve himself while facing Jerusalem, even though he could have faced another direction instead.[324]

Is the most sacred Islamic book after the Quran spreading falsehoods about Prophet Mohammad, or is Jerusalem simply not a sacred Islamic city? Also, does it make sense that Palestinians are dying for Jerusalem when their own beloved Prophet used to prefer defecating towards it?

(14) Chapter: To defecate in houses

 Narrated `Abdullah bin `Umar:

I went up to the roof of Hafsa's house for some job and I saw Allah's Messenger (ﷺ) answering the call of nature facing Sham (Syria, Jordan, Palestine and Lebanon regarded as one country) with his back towards the Qibla. (See Hadith No. 147).

Reference   : Sahih al-Bukhari 148
In-book reference   : Book 4, Hadith 14
USC-MSA web (English) reference : Vol. 1, Book 4, Hadith 150
  (deprecated numbering scheme)

 Narrated `Abdullah bin `Umar:

Once I went up the roof of our house and saw Allah's Messenger (ﷺ) answering the call of nature while sitting over two bricks facing Baitul-Maqdis (Jerusalem). (See Hadith No. 147).

Reference   : Sahih al-Bukhari 149
In-book reference   : Book 4, Hadith 15
USC-MSA web (English) reference : Vol. 1, Book 4, Hadith 151
  (deprecated numbering scheme)

An online version of the reports in Sahih Bukhari. See endnotes for further references.

Courage and Jealousy

Upon examining the invasions and massacres conducted by Muslim caliphs, one wonders how "skilled and courageous" they really were.

Although the caliphs had powerful armies that committed massacres and genocides, the caliphs as individuals were nothing but cowards. Indeed, only a coward would kidnap, then rape and murder women and children, including members of his own family. This was the reality of our caliphs, and an honest Muslim would condemn this historical reality and seek reformation, and by doing so would find a community of like-minded Muslims waiting to embrace them.

Caliph Omar admitted to fleeing battlefields numerous times. On one occasion, he said: "During the Battle of Uhud, when we fled, I ran away and climbed the mountain, and I saw myself running and jumping like a mountain goat."[325] Aisha, the wife of Prophet Mohammad, testified that she went outside her house on the day of the Battle of the Trench and found Caliph Omar hiding in the garden. She said:

> I entered into a garden, and I saw a group of people who had been [hiding] there, among them was Omar ibn al-Khattab. Omar then said: "Woe to you, what brought you here?! By God you are a bold woman, what made you think that you are safe of being captured or getting into trouble!" She then said: "He kept blaming me so much." [326]

Caliph Omar often planned his escape from the battlefield in a manner that allowed him to blame others around him. In an authentic Islamic historical report, it has been recorded that, when Omar was sent out to war accompanied by a group of soldiers, he escaped the scene with his companions and came back to the Prophet. He then accused his companions of being cowards, but they insisted that he was the coward.[327]

Such cowardice was apparent from the early times of Caliph Omar. Skilled fighters who joined in the Islamic conquests and invasions to become prominent warriors in the eyes of the Muslim nation posed a threat to the throne and status of the caliph. To protect himself from an internal coup he wouldn't be able to challenge, Caliph Omar dismissed his own cousin, Khalid, from the leadership of the Islamic armies in the year 638. This decision by Caliph Omar was a result of Khalid's growing popularity, as he led most of the conquests from the era of the first Caliph Abu Bakr. Many Muslims were unhappy with the mistreatment of Khalid by Caliph Omar and began to protest against his decision in Medina. Caliph Omar then confessed his jealousy, saying: "I have not dismissed Khalid because of my anger or because of any dishonesty on his part, but because people glorified him and were misled. I feared that people would rely on him for victory." [328]

Internal Conflicts and the Rise of Ruthless Murderers

After the wars of the caliphs, many Muslims became fed up with the situation they were facing. They were fighting to make the caliphs more powerful and richer than ever, while in return they received nothing but injury, poverty, and endless social problems. As noted in Chapter 4, the Muslim nation revolted against the third Caliph Uthman in 656, sparking a civil war that ended with his murder and the overthrowing of the third caliph of the first Islamic caliphate. The Umayyad family came into power and established the Umayyad Dynasty. They were relatives of Prophet Mohammad as they were descended from a common ancestor,* and had also originated from the city of Mecca.

Although previous Islamic caliphs who had come after Mohammad were in fact kings, they did not announce a kingdom; rather they referred to themselves as caliphs. The Umayyad Dynasty, however, announced its empire, and played both roles: kings and caliphs. This culture continues until this very day, where Islamic leaders such as the House of Saud, or even descendants of Prophet Mohammad such as the Hashimite House of Jordan, refer to themselves as kings.

By the emergence of the Umayyad Dynasty, both foreign and civil wars had become the norm.** The Umayyads were no different in continuing the violence, except this time it was done strategically and under a different slogan. The wise Abdul Baha, son of Baha'u'llah the

---

* Muhammad was descended from Abd Manāf via his son Hashim, while the Umayyads were descended from Abd Manaf via a different son, Abd-Shams, whose son was Umayya.

** The Islamic civil wars were: First Fitna, Second Fitna, Third Fitna, Fourth Fitna, Abbasid Revolution, Berber Revolt, Fitnah of al-Andalus, and the Kharijite rebellions.

founder of the Bahá'í faith, said that "The Umayyad Dynasty rose against the religion of Prophet Mohammad." [329]

The Umayyad Dynasty (661–750)

The first action undertaken by the Umayyad Dynasty was genocide in the remaining Byzantine and northern Africa territories where they massacred the Christians.[330] They then invaded Spain, exterminating courageous men, women, and children while forcing the weaker ones into Islam. The Umayyads then formed an army of 40,000 who then decimated 30,000 people of the Byzantine Empire.[331]

Modern Tunisia was then used as a platform for further conquests and offensives. The *Cambridge History of Africa* described these campaigns, saying that the Umayyad Dynasty "plunged into the heart of the country, traversed the wilderness in which his successors erected the splendid capitals of Fes and Morocco, and at length penetrated to the verge of the Atlantic and the great desert,"[332] annihilating whatever and whomever they considered an obstacle in their path. The series of genocides conducted by this Islamic caliphate, which reached the borders of China and the Indian subcontinent, can be found in books specializing in this part of Islam's dark history. English historian Edward Gibbon covered a substantial amount in his book *The History of the Decline and Fall of the Roman Empire*.[333]

The Abbasid Dynasty (750–1517)

Alongside the Umayyad Dynasty there was the Abbasid family, the descendants of Abbas, the uncle of Prophet Mohammad. They believed themselves to be worthier of leadership than the Umayyads, simply because their bloodline was closer to Mohammad; a matter which has great meaning and significance amongst many Arabs. They also adapted a political strategy of character assassination of chief members of the Umayyad Dynasty. Tension rose between the two families, and majority of the Arab Muslims sided with the Abbasids against the

Umayyads, hoping that their rule would bring change to the condition of Islam.[334] The Abbasid family revolted and took control of the Islamic caliphate in the year 750, after leading a life of independent Islamic caliphs in Baghdad, in modern-day Iraq.[335]

Unlike the earlier caliphs who massacred Persians and invaded Persia, the Abbasids essentially elevated the Persians and established great ties with them.[336] This was merely a plan they had plotted to prepare a stronger army for their upcoming invasions. The Abbasids began by massacring the Umayyads after revolting against them. Yes indeed, the companions of Prophet Mohammad murdered his family and burnt his house, and now his relatives were butchering each other. Once the Abbasid Dynasty was established and they found themselves able to prevent a counter-attack from the Umayyads, they began to massacre the Christians. Once again, they waged war against the Byzantines, classifying them as polytheists and disbelievers. The Byzantine Empress Irene wanted peace, and she struggled with the Abbasid Dynasty.[337] They forced her to agree to pay up to 90,000 dinars to the Islamic caliphate for three years along with 10,000 silk garments, even though silk garments for men are prohibited under Sharia Law! They then invaded Cyprus, though they failed to capture it, and went on to commit genocides in other areas of Khorasan, a province in north-eastern Iran, all done in the name of jihad and expanding the Islamic caliphate.[338]

After the death of Rashid, the fifth Abbasid caliph, a civil war took place between two Abbasid brothers, Al-Amin and Al-Ma'mun, which resulted in Al-Amin being murdered in Baghdad while it was held under siege following a two-year brutal war.[339] After Al-Ma'mun came Al-Mu'tasim, who focused the war against the Christians once again in 833, reviving what the previous murderous caliphs had begun. When Abbasid Caliph Al-Mutawakil reigned, he invaded Anatolia, raiding the entire region, until he had annihilated its citizens in a massive genocide.[340] He was then assassinated by his son, Al-Muntassir, on December 11, 861.[341] Later, the story of his assassination would become tainted, with his son claiming that his father, the Islamic caliph, died choking on his wine.[342] This was despite the fact that this very caliph had prohibited drinking and executed people as punishment for intoxication!

The Abbasid Caliphate also interfered in other wars. On one occasion in the year 756, the caliph sent an armed force of approximately 5000 soldiers to support the Chinese Tang Dynasty against the An Lushan Rebellion. They entered China with the black flags of the Islamic state and butchered the Chinese opposition.

"The Golden Age of Islam"

Upon examining the history of Islam, we come across a time when the Islamic caliphate is believed to have flourished. This era took place from the eighth century until the fourteenth, under the rule of the Abbasid Dynasty. Historians have stated that during this era Muslims advanced and developed in culture, technology, education, law, mathematics, theology, philosophy, engineering, health care, science, commerce, travel, and even religious influence. However, upon pondering this development, one discovers that there are many imperfections to this history, resulting in many Muslims and non-Muslims alike believing that the Islamic golden age was nothing but a myth.

Paper, a simple requirement that made all of the developments and the advancements of the Islamic caliphate possible, had actually been imported from China,[343] while the most important texts used for education were actually translations of texts from the Persian, Greek, Indian, Chinese, Egyptian (Northern African), and Phoenician civilizations.[344] These texts were popularized in the Muslim world as a result of the Translation Movement introduced by "The House of Wisdom," a seminary founded by the murderous caliph of the Abbasids, Harun al-Rashid.

It is also my opinion that the Islamic caliphate of the time established this seminary as a political strategy to repair the image of Islam that had been tarnished and distorted throughout previous years. The amount of government funds invested in the Translation

Movement was incredible as it equaled twice the annual amount spent on research by the United Kingdom's Medical Research Council,[345] approximately £1,194,000,000 today.[346] Thus, I believe it was a government tactic, and not due to their interest in advancement or development, because they believed the Muslim *Ummah*, or nation, would never be honored in learning from the West. The Grand Mufti of Australia, Dr. Ibrahim Abu Mohammad, once "wrote in an essay published when he lived in Abu Dhabi in 1995": "The West does not bring to us any good, all they bring are their diseases, their designs and their shortcomings." He continued, saying that "modern society wanted women 'with legs and arms exposed, filling the shopping malls and the streets, competing for the glimpses of men.'" [347]

There are academics who propound the myth of an Islamic golden age of tolerance towards other nations and try to present the Islamic caliphs as wise individuals. Yet they admit that their goal is nothing other than

> to recover for postmodernity that lost medieval Judeo-Islamic trading, social and cultural world, its high point pre-1492 Moorish Spain, which permitted and relished a plurality, a *convivencia* [co-existence], of religions and cultures, Christian, Jewish and Muslim; which prized an historic internationality of space along with the valuing of particular cities; which was inclusive and cosmopolitan, cosmopolitan here meaning an ease with different cultures: still so rare and threatened a value in the new millennium as in centuries past.[348]

Professor Serge Trifkovic* stated:

> The problem with turning this list of intellectual achievements into a convincing "Islamic" golden age is that whatever flourished, did so not by reason of Islam but in spite of Islam. Moslems overran societies (Persian, Greek, Egyptian, Byzantine, Syrian, Jewish) that possessed intellectual sophistication in their own right and failed to

---

* Serbian American writer on international affairs, former director of the Center for International Affairs at the Rockford Institute, former spokesman for the Republika Srpska government, and a former adviser to Serbian president Vojislav Koštunica and Republika Srpska president Biljana Plavšić.

completely destroy their cultures. To give it the credit for what the remnants of these cultures achieved is like crediting the Red Army for the survival of Chopin in Warsaw in 1970! [349]

Therefore, the crimes of our caliphs must never be considered historical achievements. It is without doubt that the Islamic nation did advance and flourish between the eighth and the thirteenth centuries; however, their genuine scientific and educational development was in the field of Islamic studies and Islamic jurisprudence,[350] with the introduction of new Islamic concepts such as "juristic consensus" and "analogical reasoning," that is, the search for commonalities as opposed to highlighting differences.[351]

The questions that need to be addressed in this regard are: Was Islam's golden age during the caliphates a time of peaceful human development? Or was there violence during those centuries? The answer is that during these "golden" centuries of the Islamic caliphate, almost 300 major incidents of violence took place, ranging from murders to invasions of other nations.**

The Fatimid Islamic Caliphate (909–1171)

Shia Muslims were a minority amongst Muslims all around the world, separating themselves from invasions and conquests due to their opposition to the caliphs. As a result of this, they did not receive any rewards such as territory and influence. Therefore, their potential remained limited and their political power was close to nothing. In the year 909, almost three centuries after Prophet Mohammad's death, a minority denomination within the Shia Islamic school of thought established an Islamic caliphate in Northern Africa that expanded from the Red Sea to the Atlantic Ocean. This Islamic caliphate was governed by Ismaili Shia Muslims, and its economy and strength revolved around Egypt. By claiming that they were descendants from Fatima, Prophet Mohammad's daughter (hence the name "Fatimid Caliphate"), they managed to win the hearts and support of the Muslims of the entire

** For a list of these events see "Timeline of Islamic History," Wikipedia.

North African region.

However, their lineage is very difficult to authenticate, because the descendants of Fatima at the time were followers of what is known as the "infallible Imams," who are the grandsons of Prophet Mohammad, and who did not establish independent caliphates. Whether or not their lineage can be verified, Fatimids are in fact Shia Muslims. Although the Fatimids did show tolerance to other religions, they had an Islamist agenda of imposing their version of Sharia Law and belief systems onto the citizens of their Fatimid Caliphate.[352]

Being a Shia Muslim myself, I must condemn extremists from all Islamic denominations, including my own. The Fatimids were undeniably oppressed at the beginning, but they did develop into terrorists once in power. They conducted numerous invasions and were sectarian in their approach. In 909 they conquered the capital of Aghlabid,* an Islamic government that comprised what is known today as Tunisia, Tripolitania (western Libya) and the Constantinois (eastern Algeria), Malta, and Italy; and murdered many of their own Muslim co-religionists. By the year 969, they had conquered Egypt and turned Cairo into the headquarters of their Islamic caliphate, while they maintained another capital city in Tunisia.

The main terrorist figure in the Fatimid Dynasty was Abu Abdallah al-Shi'i, an Ismaili Shia Muslim who was a scholar and an army general at the same time. He conquered five surrounding cities and sent expeditions to conquer distant regions, while maintaining Ismaili Shi'ism as the faith of the Fatimid government. However, in the 1040s, the governors of the Fatimid Caliphate decided to declare their independence from the Islamic caliphate to join the caliph of the Sunni Abbasid Dynasty in Baghdad, Iraq. This matter, seen as treason of course, angered the chiefs of the Fatimid Dynasty, and they reacted by announcing an ethnic cleansing of the widespread Arabian tribes in North Africa.** Their conquests and invasions continued, which resulted in their caliphate expanding from Tunisia to Syria, as well as Sicily.

The Fatimid Caliphate came to an end after another Islamic terrorist, Saladin, invaded Egypt and massacred the Shia Muslims

* The Aghlabid was an Islamic Arabic dynasty that ruled the former Roman province of Africa Proconsu laris for over a century. The former Aghlabid lands are now parts of Algeria, Tunisia, Libya, Malta, and Italy.
** For example, the Banu Hilal tribe.

therein, establishing and founding the Ayyubid Islamic Dynasty, which invaded not only Egypt, but Syria and Northern Mesopotamia.[353]

The "Caliphate" of Ahmadiyyah Islam

Ahmadiyyah Islam is an offshoot of Sunni Islam that was established in India in the nineteenth century by Mirza Ghulam Ahmad, who claimed to be the divinely appointed and promised Messiah. Adherents of this school of thought number 10 to 20 million. The Caliphate of Ahmadiyyah Islam is not an actual caliphate in the form of a government; instead it is represented by its caliph and his international organizations.

While most Muslims don't consider Ahmadiyyah Muslims to be Muslims, I was the first imam to visit the Ahmadiyyah Muslim community in Australia. My visit was reported in the media, as it was a historic outreach to build stronger bridges and spread peace among Australia's diverse communities. However, although my intentions were pure, I soon came to regret my decision.

During my visit to the Ahmadiyyah Islamic centers, I was gifted with books and publications. Upon deeply studying their beliefs, mainly the writings and teachings of their founder, I began to question their famous slogan "Love for all, Hatred for None." A closer look into the teachings and ideology of the Ahmadiyyah faith could raise eyebrows, and keep you wondering whether their peacefulness actually matches the foundations of their belief system; whether this is an agenda of infiltration, or simply a calculated plan to expand their congregations. The love displayed by Ahmadiyyah Muslims towards other religions such as Christianity and the global Christian community is very attractive; however, the real question is: What does the Ahmadiyyah ideology teach about Christianity?

Mirza Ghulam Ahmad, founder of Ahmadiyyah Islam, believed that "Christianity is the perfect manifestation of Satan."[354] He alleged that Jesus was perhaps visited by Satan a second time and that he might have taught Jesus the doctrine of the Trinity.[355] He also believed that

"Jesus could not portray himself as a pious man because everyone knew that he was a gluttonous alcoholic ... His claim to Godliness was a result of his bad habit of drinking Wine." [356]

The founder of Ahmadiyyah Islam appears through his teachings to be a staunch enemy of the West. In *Victory of Islam*, he states:

O Muslims! listen, and listen attentively! All the intricate fabrications and the devious methods employed by the Christians to hinder the purifying influence of Islam, and the efforts made to spread them by the utmost exertion and by the spending of money like water, so much so that the most disreputable means, the details of which are best omitted to avoid tainting this book, have been fully used to this end — these are the crafty activities of the Christians and the believers in the trinity. And to combat their enchantment, until God the Most High shows His powerful hand which possesses the might of a miracle, and smashes this talisman of magic by means of this miracle, it is impossible to imagine that the simple hearts can ever be freed from the spell of this Western wizardry. Therefore, to destroy this magical influence, God the Most High has shown the true Muslims of this age the miracle of raising this servant of His to fight the opponents, having bestowed upon him His revelation, word and special blessings, and endowed him fully with the subtle knowledge of His way. And He gave him many heavenly gifts, signs from above, and the knowledge of spiritual truths and fine matters, so that with this Divine stone the waxen idol made by the Western enchantment may be smashed. [357]

Ahmadiyyah Islam appears to be founded on teachings that reject the West and preach hatred towards its inhabitants. In many instances, founder Mirza Ghulam Ahmad blamed Jesus Christ for the problems of the West: "The teachings of Jesus ruined the whole of Europe since it permitted unrestrained and unconditional liberty. So much so that it resulted in adultery and fornication like pigs and dogs." [358] He also claimed that the root cause of all the damage that alcohol consumption has had on Europeans was that Jesus used to drink alcohol, perhaps because of some disease or a previous habit.[359]

For someone who claims to be the promised Messiah in the likeness of Jesus, he seems to be somewhat delusional when referring to Jesus Christ, saying that "Jesus's three paternal and maternal grandmothers were fornicators and prostitutes, from whose blood Jesus came into existence."[360] The Ahmadiyyah Muslim community claims to have "love for all," but there remains a rather huge question mark about this due to their leader's belief that "Jesus had an inclination for prostitutes perhaps due to his ancestral relationship with them."[361]

In a lecture delivered by Mirza Ghulam Ahmad, known as the Lecture Ludhiana, he stated: "The Holy Qur'an and the Traditions of the Holy Prophets contain the prediction that Islam will spread and prevail over other religions and the doctrine of the Cross will be smashed." He continued: "I declare with all the emphasis at my command and with full conviction and understanding, that God has decided to demolish all other religions and let Islam triumph and be strong."[362]

With such a belief that promises the destruction of all other religions, a more suitable slogan for the Ahmadiyyah Islamic community would be "Love for None." As their founder clearly stated: "A believer can, therefore, have friendship, sympathy and goodwill for Christians, Jews, and Hindus and can exercise benevolence towards them, *but cannot love them*. This is a fine distinction, which should always be kept in mind."[363]

How such a hate-filled ideology has become successful in infiltrating western societies in the name of love and peace is totally beyond me. It appears to me that the founder of Ahmadiyyah Islam was a delusional individual. The following dream he shared with his followers, considering it a divine sign, shows his mental instability and perhaps love for animal cruelty:

I saw in a dream that a cat sought to attack our pigeon. It would not desist despite repeated efforts to turn it away. Then I cut off its nose and though it was bleeding it still persisted in its effort. Then I caught hold of it by its neck and started rubbing its face on the ground but it continued to raise its head, till in the end I said: Let us hang it.[364]

As the old adage goes, the Ahmadiyyah Muslim ideology proves once again that if something is too good to be true, it often is.

Twenty-First Century Islamic Governance

Tens of Islamic caliphates have been established since the emergence of Islam fourteen centuries ago. I have shed light on the invasions and genocides conducted by the most prominent of them in this chapter and, although there were other Islamic caliphates that were established by the sword such as the Almohad and Ottoman Caliphates, I wish to move on to shed light on Islamic governments affecting the world we live in today.

The Islamic Republic of Iran: Governed by Shia Islam, 1979–

The establishment of the current Islamic Republic of Iran has been a dark chapter in the history of Persia, but not as dark as the early Islamic caliphates. The former Pahlavi government wasn't infallible either and, like all other governments, they too had their errors and human rights violations. The corruption of the Pahlavi Dynasty was described by Stephanie Cronin of the Oriental Institute, Oxford, as "large-scale." [365] However, the difference is that they did not claim to rule or govern Iran on behalf of God, even though they were in fact Muslims.

In 1979, the forward progress of Iran ceased, and the Iranian nation began to be governed by a tyrannical government that showered them with waves of oppression. The human rights violations committed by the current Islamic government of Iran have been the norm for almost four decades. The culture of Islamism has spread, and Sharia Law has been imposed on all Iranians regardless of their beliefs. Public hangings and sexual assaults of women within prisons have been part of the doctrine of Imam Khomeini's revolution.

Khomeini and his notorious associate Khamenei "cleansed" the nation of any progressive scholars and intellectuals. Opposition members were seen as "God's enemies" and executed through the unjust trials of Chief Justice and Sharia ruler Sadegh Khalkhali, who earned his reputation as Iran's "hanging judge."[366] The government of Imam Khomeini sentenced hundreds of former government officials to death, even though many were Muslim, charging them with "spreading corruption on the Earth"– a punishable crime under Sharia Law. None of the executed members had access to lawyers nor a jury.[367] Some of those executed were simply taxi drivers or chefs employed in the former shah's castles.

Iran's political, cultural, and natural environments have been systematically destroyed by self-styled clerics and self-appointed leaders claiming to have divine authority and infallibility. Political corruption, bribery, substance abuse, prostitution, economic injustice, and human rights violations against youth are rampant; and suppression of women, irreverence towards military veterans and heroes, arbitrary imprisonment, humiliation, torture, and execution have been the norm.

The current leading terrorist, Ali Khamenei, orders millions of those infatuated with him to chant death slogans about western countries. He has destabilized the region by raising flags in Lebanon pushing for the establishment of Hizbullah, while constantly interfering in the political affairs of Palestine, and now Iraq, Syria, and Yemen.

I was studying in Iran when the popular Iranian uprising took place in 2009. It provided plenty of evidence that many Iranian citizens feel that the Islamic Republic of Iran is not an acceptable and legitimate form of government. Ali Khamenei and his mafia have managed to stay in power through brutal oppression and claims that he is God's chosen man.

The Islamic Republic of Iran sustains itself through terror, abuse, conflict, and war. The theocratic state was founded on Khomeini's principle that war is a divine gift bestowed upon the Islamic Republic by God. Today, many Iranians await the demise of Khamenei, hoping for a reformation in government to form a secular state, one that does not rape its women and threaten innocents with nuclear weapons. The 2017–18 Iranian uprising and protests, which the world witnessed, speak volumes about the solidarity within the Iranian nation, and the opposition to the tyrannical regime. I shall discuss Shia Islamic governance in the upcoming chapter.

The Kingdom of Saudi Arabia: Sunni Islam

The current government of Saudi Arabia was established after its founder, Ibn Saud, massacred his own people and conquered the Arabian regions of Riyadh, Najd, and Hejaz, announcing himself the ruler of central Arabia. The bloodshed and conquests began in 1902 and extended for three decades, concluding in the establishment of the Kingdom of Saudi Arabia in 1932. Since then, Saudi Arabia has had an Islamic government, imposing Sharia Law through a hereditary dictatorship.[368]

Just like the chief ruling clerics of the Iranian government, it makes no difference to the House of Saud that they are living in the twenty-first century. Today, Saudi Arabia's Ministry of Justice beheads women in the streets, while other corpses dangle from cranes after they have been hung.[369] When such bloody and shocking images invaded the internet, it revealed how disturbingly similar Saudi Arabia's punishments are to those of ISIS. In 2014, Saudi Arabia executed a record number of 158 people, 153 people were executed by the sword in 2016, and at least 146 in 2017 alone; 41% of those executed in 2017 were beheaded for simply attending political protests.[370]

The implementation of Sharia Law punishments has led to Saudi Arabia having one of the highest execution rates in the world.[371] Although the kingdom claims to have a fair legal system, people are executed for leaving Islam, arson attacks, practicing witchcraft, and even theft.[372]

The Founding and Funding of Wahhabism

Wahhabism is a worldwide Islamic movement inspiring the ideology of extremists. It was founded by Islamist extremist theologian Mohammad bin Abd al-Wahhab in 1703, after he made a pact with Ibn Saud, the founder of the current Royal Saudi Kingdom. Initially, this was a political strategy to unify and centralize the aggressive tribes of Arabia by bringing them under the control of the Saudi Kingdom. Wahhabism focused on ending any form of intercession of Prophet Mohammad, and denounced pilgrimages to saints' tombs, while issuing fatwas (verdicts) that their domes and shrines should be destroyed. Its founder wanted the whole world to return to the same lifestyle and traditions that were present during the era of Prophet Mohammad and opposed any form of innovation. It was a totalitarian and regressive ideology.

Wahhabism has become increasingly influential, partly because of Saudi money and partly because of Saudi Arabia's influence as protector of Mecca. In July 2013, Wahhabism was identified by the European Parliament in Strasbourg as the main source of global terrorism; with almost all Islamic terrorist organizations being subscribers to the Wahhabi ideology and faith.

Since the 1970s, Saudi charities have directed some of the wealth from petroleum exports to fund the expansion of the Wahhabi movement, including funding Wahhabi schools and mosques in other countries, causing "explosive growth."[373] The US State Department has estimated that over the past four decades Saudi Arabia – the world's richest Arab nation – has donated more than $10 billion to such charities in order to displace mainstream Sunni Islam and replace it with Wahhabism. Intelligence experts have suggested that 15 to 20 per cent of these funds have been diverted to Al-Qaeda and other extremist groups.[374]

The Funding of Universities

A report in 2005 revealed that a "Saudi prince had donated $20 million each to Harvard University and Georgetown University to advance Islamic studies and further understanding of the Muslim world."[375] The same Saudi prince "tried to donate $10 million to the Twin Towers Fund shortly after the Sept. 11 terrorist attacks, but it was denied by then-New York City Mayor Rudolph Giuliani," who said, "The check has not been deposited. The Twin Towers Fund has not accepted it."[376]

An article titled "National Security: Secret Saudi Funding of Australian Institutions" revealed that:

Many Australian universities, now driven entirely by financial priorities, have uncritically welcomed Saudi sources of funding, even though this creates a major national security problem ... Massive funding is presently being provided by Saudi Arabia to promote Wahhabism, the fundamentalist, exclusivist, punitive, and sectarian form of Islam that is both the Saudi state religion, and the chief theological component of Sunni versions of Islamism, the totalitarian ideology guiding jihadism and most of the active terrorist groups in the world.

Globally, this money is flowing to terrorist groups, political parties, religious and community groups, as well as to universities and schools. In Australia, there is concern that such funding could damage and even corrupt the Australian university system, especially given the existing ideological bias, political naivety, opportunism, managerialism, and the pseudo-entrepreneurial attitudes of many university academics and administrators.

The question of how foreign powers and agents are able to influence, direct or even control tertiary education in Australia and other Western countries is vitally important. This is because of the rise of Islamism [and] jihadism.[377]

The Worst Crime of Saudi Arabia

A name that shines within the never-ending list of Saudi Arabian human rights violations is Raif Badawi. He is a 34-year-old Saudi Arabian writer and freedom activist who has been sentenced to 1000 lashes and 10 years in prison under Sharia Law only because he set up a website that championed free speech. The autocratic kingdom of Saudi Arabia shut down the website once they arrested him in 2012.

He has already received his initial 50 lashes in public, with 950 lashes remaining. Even though many Muslims and non-Muslims alike have offered to take the lashes on Raif's behalf – which is permitted according to Sharia Law – Saudi Arabia's Ministry of Justice refuses to pay attention to the thousands of protesters and diplomatic missions demanding his release. I myself am honored to be an honorary member of the Raif Badawi Foundation, and also volunteered to take 200 lashes for him.[378]

Raif Badawi called for the liberation of women in Saudi Arabia and demanded that they be afforded basic rights, such as driving. The question now is why does the Saudi government insist on keeping Raif Badawi behind bars when women have now been given the right to drive?

Reform within Saudi Arabia remains an image more than a reality, and it would be safe to describe it as a revolution disguised as reform. In mid-2018, Saudi Arabia clearly hit the brakes on its so-called reforms when it expelled Canada's Ambassador after Canada expressed concerns over the unlawful arrest of award-winning gender rights activist Samar Badawi. Saudi Arabia then raced to play the "sovereignty card", saying that Canada had breached the principles of sovereignty. I call this diplomatic idiocy, simply because human rights are everyone's concern, and exactly what citizens expect from their democratic governments.

Today, hundreds of inhumane arrests and cold-blooded executions are still taking place within "reformed Saudi Arabia." If something sounds too good to be true, it most likely is.

The Islamic State of Iraq and Syria (ISIS)

After all you have read in this chapter, it is no longer surprising that a group of extremist Muslims would seek to invade land and establish an Islamic caliphate. This has indeed been the culture introduced to them by the early Islamic caliphs of Islam, and has continued until the twenty-first century. All of the crimes that we witness in the news being committed by ISIS are practices they inherited from the founding fathers of ISIS: Prophet Mohammad's fathers-in-law, the very first caliphs of Islam.

The recent success of the Islamic State in Iraq and Syria (ISIS) has been rapid and strategic. They began small in Iraq as the "Islamic State in Iraq" (ISI); with their parent group being Al-Qaeda of Iraq, established by Abu Mus'ab Az-Zarqawi, who pledged allegiance to Osama bin Laden. Abu Bakr Al-Baghdadi, the "caliph" of Muslims, is strangely enough Az-Zarqawi's student.

ISIS saw a unique opportunity in the conflict that has been raging in Syria. They invaded Syria at full strength and began calling themselves "ISIL," the Islamic State in Iraq and the Levant (Greater Syria). They began butchering and massacring all of those who disagreed with their ideology. The raping, trafficking, and murdering of women was and still is a daily practice within their Islamic caliphate.

It is indeed ironic that Prophet Mohammad and Imam Ali had already warned against the rise of extremism, saying:

> If you see the black flags, then hold your ground and do not move your hands or your feet. A people will come forth who are weak and have no capability, their hearts are like blocks of iron. They are the people of the State, they do not keep a promise or a treaty.
>
> They call to the truth but they are not its people. Their names are [nicknames like Abu Mohammed] and their last names [are the names of town and cities, like Al-Halabi and now Al-Baghdadi] and their hair is loose like women's hair. [Leave them] until they fight among themselves, then God will bring the truth from whoever He wills.[379]

Although Donald Trump has accused Hillary Clinton and Barack Obama of "creating ISIS,"[380] I don't adopt this accusation at all. What in fact did happen was that the adherents of the existing Islamist ideology were funded by the Democratic Party to give them more power and influence. The corrupt ideology of terrorism has existed since the early days of Islam; and it was simply revived in our time. ISIS and its crimes can be explained in one honest sentence: the culture of beheading opponents did not begin with ISIS; it began with our early Islamic caliphs. Yes, it is true that ISIS has been facing defeat, however, what is more important than tackling ISIS militarily is tackling the ideology that gave birth to ISIS.

CHAPTER 8

Difficulties of Shia Islam and Shia Islamic Governance

Islam consists of two denominations: the Sunni school of thought and the Shia school of thought. Shia Muslims are the minority denomination, making up only approximately 25 percent of the entire religion. Both Islamic denominations believe in the same fundamentals of the religion: one God, Mohammad being God's final prophet, the Quran as the word of God, along with the methods and directions of worship. Overall, they are very similar in practice, but differ in their theology with regards to the attributes of God, qualities of his prophets, and interpretations of the Quran.

As I mentioned several times throughout this book, I strongly oppose sectarianism, and I believe that one should always maintain a professional approach when discussing Islamic denominations. A reformer should not hold any regard for Islamic denominations, and rather should look at Islam as a whole while criticizing the wrong within all schools of thought.

Because I was born into a Shia Muslim family, and belong to a lineage of Shia Muslim scholars and jurists, I am able to speak with authority on Shia Islam and the difficulties within its theology. This chapter sheds light on the development of ideological, historical, and political difficulties within Shia Islam, as a result of ideas from outside Islam infiltrating the faith.

The First Difficulty: The Oneness of Existence

The "oneness" or "unity" of existence is a theological concept present in the doctrines of several religions, and it revolves around the belief that there is an inseparable bond between God and God's creations; to the extent that God is everything, and everything is God. Religions that maintain this belief may vary slightly in how they present this concept, but the foundations of this ideology remain the same: We are God, and God is us.

Belief in the oneness of existence means that whatever we see, whatever we experience, is only a manifestation of the eternal oneness of God. The divinity at the core of the human being is the same divinity that illumines the sun, the moon, and the stars. There is no place where divinity (or God), infinite in nature, does not exist.

Although this belief can be found in other religions such as Hinduism, specifically the Vedanta philosophy, the concept has always existed in some Islamic sects. The main Islamic sect that promotes the oneness of existence is the Sufi sect, through the major ideas of Sufi metaphysics. Because Sufism revolves around Islamic mysticism, this concept has become one of the main philosophies of Sufi Islam.

This concept was introduced into Shia Islam by the Shia Muslims who believed in mysticism after being influenced by the teachings of Ibn Arabi, a Sunni Sufi Mystic. After the Iranian Revolution and the establishment of the Islamic Republic in Iran in 1979, its founder, Imam Khomeini, began introducing the teachings of Ibn Arabi within Islamic seminaries and through his lectures. He wrote:

> There is nothing existing except God. Everything that exists is God's manifestation. The best example to use in this regard is that God is like the ocean and God's creations are the waves of that ocean. They are not independent from the ocean. There is no separate ocean or separate waves, but there are waves that belong to the ocean. When we look at the waves we think we are looking at the waves, but in reality, we are looking at the ocean. The same applies to this world, all of what we see is God.[381]

In another book, he wrote: "There are situations between us and God, where He is us, and we are Him, and He is himself and we are us."[382]

This might come across as sophisticated philosophy, but in reality, the concept simply means that God is everything, including all of God's creations.

The trap that Shia Muslims and the followers of Imam Khomeini have fallen into while believing in the oneness of existence is that it contradicts their core fundamental beliefs about God. In Shia Islam, God does not have and cannot have any material form, and there is nothing like God. Also, Muslims consider pigs, dogs, urine, feces, alcohol, and blood to be impure. Therefore, if God is everything that exists, and manifests in everything that our eyes see, then this also applies to what God considers "impure." This is a major contradiction within the theology of many Shia Muslim scholars, and perhaps is the reason why, before Khomeini died, he wrote: "I regret that my life that has gone like dispersed dust, after being spent in the path of ignorance and deviation."[383] It now becomes safe to say that believing that God is manifested in impurities is nowhere near the belief that God is a golden burqa-wearing child who is obese, as discussed in Chapter 2.

What makes the Shia belief in the teachings of Ibn Arabi shocking is the fact that Ibn Arabi himself believed Shia Muslims to be "pigs" and "dogs." In his books, Ibn Arabi highlighted the fact that, through metaphysics and his spiritual practices, he used to reveal the realities of Shia Muslims and they appeared to him as pigs, and he would yell at them saying "Repent to God! You Shia!"[384] On another occasion, Ibn Arabi said, "I have a sign from God where I am able to see Shia Muslims in the form of dogs"[385] and "Satan has deceived them."[386]

Therefore, how can we take our doctrinal beliefs from the teachings of an individual who believes that, in reality, we are pigs and dogs that have been deceived by Satan?

The Second Difficulty: "The Science of Men"

Holy Islamic scripture consists of the Quran and hadiths, being Prophet Mohammad's sayings, teachings, and doings. The Science of Men analyses and examines the authenticity and truthfulness of the chain of narrators who reported the teachings of Prophet Mohammad. Some narrations are classified as weak, meaning hard to prove, because the chain of narrators includes liars, thieves, and untrustworthy people; while other narrations are considered authentic. <u>The problem with this science is that it's not really science</u>. It's a political tactic used by clerics to weaken and strengthen the authenticity of historical reports to benefit themselves and to further their political motives. This has resulted in an ideological catastrophe within the Shia faith, because what is considered a true and authentic prophetic teaching to one person is considered to be weak and unacceptable by others. The Science of Men has destabilized the entire faith of Shia Islam, and revolves around gossip about people whom we have never met.

Historical Hypocrisy Towards "the Companions"

Shia Muslims have always maintained a negative attitude towards the companions of Prophet Mohammad, considering a number of them to be oppressive tyrants and terrorists. In return, they curse them in their events, prayers, and sermons. Shia Muslims also celebrate the death anniversaries of Mohammad's companions. This is well known amongst all Islamic schools of thought. Personally, I proudly and unapologetically reject the authority and example of the majority of Mohammad's companions and fathers-in-law because of their unethical behavior and terrorism when conducting their invasions.

However, it is not fair to criticize the companions of Prophet Mohammad and not the companions of Ali, the cousin of Mohammad, and the main Shia faith icon. If we are going to criticize the wrong, then we must criticize the wrong in all schools of thought, including the wrong within our own faith and history. Anything else would be plain sectarianism. The following are two of many Shia Muslim figures that deserve criticism, but are sometimes praised instead.

The First Companion: Kumayl Bin Ziyad

Kumayl was one of the most loyal companions of Ali, and is held up as one of the most venerated Islamic figures by Shia Muslims. He converted to Islam during the time of Prophet Mohammad and became known for his loyalty to him. During the caliphate of Ali, Kumayl was appointed Governor of Hit, a city in Iraq.[387] Kumayl was also a chief tribal leader with over 100,000 soldiers under his command. When Hussain was held under siege in Karbala, Kumayl did not make any effort to travel for two hours to protect Hussain, the grandson of his own Prophet, and neither did he order members of his tribe to go and rescue Hussain from the massacres of the terrorist Caliph Yazid.

Ali, the main figure in Shia Islam, states regarding Kumayl:

> It is wrong of a person to disregard and neglect the duty entrusted to him and try to take up the work entrusted to someone else – and at a time when he is not required to do it. Such an attribution indicates a weak and harmful mentality. Your desire to invade Kirkisiya and to leave your province undefended and unattended shows the confusion in your mind.[388]

Despite being criticized by Ali, Kumayl still enjoys a prominent position among Shia Muslims, displaying a great contradiction in faith.

The Second Companion: Hujr bin Adi

Hujr was one of the most prominent companions of Prophet Mohammad. After Mohammad's death, he became a loyal companion of Ali. He opposed the Umayyad Dynasty when they began cursing Ali, and launched a counter-campaign to curse them from pulpits instead. After his assassination in 660 CE, Shia Muslims built Hujr a massive shrine where he is visited and revered.

The major trap that Shia Muslims have fallen into is the fact that Hujr approached Caliph Ali's son, Hassan, who led the Muslim nation as the infallible caliph after Ali. After disagreeing with Hassan's treaty with the Umayyad Dynasty to prevent the shedding of more blood during civil conflicts, Hujr spat on the face of his own divine leader, and said, "You have humiliated the believers." How can such a person be glorified?

Shia Muslims built shrines and exalted whoever was killed by their enemies, regardless of whether they were good or bad individuals.

Islamic Unity Deception

Since the Islamic Revolution of Iran in 1979, many Shia Muslims have been staunch advocates of unity amongst all Muslims. They primarily call for unity against the enemy Israel and the United States, as Iran's leaders have chanted "Death to America, Death to Israel" after every congregational prayer and event since the rise of the revolution. Personally, I am in favor of Muslims uniting and ending the civil conflict that has been going on for decades. In an article I wrote for *Huffington Post* in 2016, titled "Islamic Unity: Realistic Aspects of Success," I presented political, economic, and social methods for Muslims to achieve unity.[389]

However, the advocacy for Islamic unity that has been heard in Iran for the past four decades is a deception introduced by the chiefs of the Iranian Revolution to politicize religion, and to brainwash citizens of Muslim nations into the belief that we must all unite against the West, because the West plans to massacre us all. The conferences on Islamic unity in Tehran have become politicized to the extent that religion no longer plays a role within their agendas. Shia Muslim clerics have tried to achieve political and social benefits under the banner of "Islamic unity," whereas in reality there will never be an ideological unity amongst all Muslim sects.

Al-Barrak, an Islamic scholar and former faculty member at the Imam Muhammad ibn Saud Islamic University, issued a vicious fatwa regarding Shia–Sunni unity, saying that"the Sunni and Shia beliefs are completely contradictory and cannot be reconciled; the talk of Sunni–Shia rapprochement is utterly false."[390]

Yusuf al-Qaradawi

Yusuf al-Qaradawi, an Islamic theologian and chairman of the International Union of Muslim Scholars, was a regular participant in the Conferences of Islamic Unity held by the Shia leadership in Iran. He later appeared on his Al-Jazeera TV program *Sharia and Life* declaring that he had wasted his life on Sunni–Shia unity. In an interview with the Turkish Anadolu news agency, he stated:

> At the beginning, I advocated [interfaith dialogue] with the Shiites, but later, we had disagreements on many issues. *I realized that they were trying to invade the Sunni belief.* We sent forty preachers to African countries, and they detected in all the Islamic countries there were millions of dollars and thousands of Shiites invading Sunni [territories].[391]

Qaradawi went on to praise hardline radical, Wahhabi, fundamentalist, and extremist Islamist clerics for being "more mature and far-sighted" than him with regards to Shia Muslims.[392] Qaradawi then became an opponent of Shia–Sunni unity and warned of the "Shiitisation" of the Middle East, claiming that Shia Muslims were "invading" Sunni Muslim countries through political means and unity conferences.[393] He warned that "If there is preaching of the [Shia] doctrine, others will stand up against them. Then there will be civil strife and endless massacres."[394]

The Iranian government has managed to maintain its deceptive mask of seeking unity amongst all Muslims, going to the extent of banning the publication of Shia doctrinal books that are somewhat displeasing to other Islamic sects. However, the true colors of the Shia advocates of "Islamic unity" showed when they responded to Al-Qaradawi by accusing him of being a spokesperson and "a front for International Freemasonry and Jewish Rabbis."[395]

Ayatollah Mohammad Taskhiri

During my 2016 trip to Iraq, I bumped into Ayatollah Mohammad Taskhiri, Iranian Shia Muslim scholar, diplomat, and the chief organizer of the Islamic Unity Conference in Iran. I greeted him and gradually began to criticize him and his agenda that places the lives of many Muslims in danger. Quickly, his bodyguards removed him from the scene, as they feared members of the public might begin to video record the confrontation.

What makes this media show of unity amongst Muslims in the face of the infidels a ridiculous performance based on a deceptive and insincere political agenda is the fact that the patriarch and founder of the Shia Islamic government invested large amounts of money and time into defaming the sacred icons and role models of Sunni Muslims. In his book *Islamic Purifications*, we learn that Imam Khomeini believed that the divine leaders of the Sunni Islamic denomination, including **Mohammad's wife Aisha,** "were all **filthier** than dogs and pigs."[396]

Muslims Kill Muslims

While Muslims generally appear peaceful towards each other, there are various attitudes towards Shia Muslims that can be found among the worldwide majority Sunni community, and vice versa.

Leading scholars from the majority Islamic denomination do not consider the minority Shias to be actual Muslims. In fact, they are seen as more "heretical" than Jews, Christians, and polytheists; and often compared to the Crusaders and Mongols.[397] Prominent Sunni scholars consider Shia Muslims "the source of all deviant groups in Islam history,"[398] while others have gone as far as issuing fatwas ruling that Shias are *Kuffar* (non-believers),[399] and that they are to be considered atheists and apostates, resulting in the prohibition of marriage to Shia Muslims.[400]

Throughout Islamic history, prominent Sunni Muslims have compared Shia Muslims to Jews. Amir al-Sha'bi (عامر الشعبي), a companion of Islam's second Caliph Omar, stated:

> The Shia are the Jews of this nation. They hate Islam as the Jews hate Christianity. They embraced Islam, not because they longed for it or because they feared Allah, but because they detested the Muslims and intended to overpower them.[401]

In modern times, Ehsan Elahi Zaheer, Islamic theologian and leader of a Pakistani Islamist movement, insisted that all Shia Muslims, approximately 300,000,000 people, were infidels and Zionist agents.[402]

As for the radical jihadists that stem from the Sunni sects of Salafism and Wahhabism, they see Shia Muslims as walking-dead individuals, whose murder grants entry into paradise, hence the constant butchering of Shia Muslims by ISIS and Al-Qaeda. This results from the teachings of Muhammad ibn Abd al-Wahab,[403] founder of Wahhabism, and Al-Tartusi.[404]

Sunni Muslims have also been oppressed by Shia Muslims. Iran is considered the Shia bastion, and has been persecuting Sunni Muslims since the Safavid era, even before the current Islamic government.[405] There are 47,291 Shiite mosques and 10,344 Sunni mosques in Iran; however, Sunnis are limited in their preaching and activities, while being infested with spies and strict monitoring. It is common for Shia government officials to demolish Sunni Muslim mosques and turn much of their spaces into rubble.[406] For decades now, Shia governments have been supporting the suppression of Sunni Muslims in Syria, Iraq, and Lebanon. This is done both directly and indirectly, through militias funded by Iranian Shia authorities.[407] Leaders from both Islamic denominations take advantage of political tensions to butcher the adherents of the other faith.

Black Turbans and Black Hearts

A black turban indicates a Shia Muslim scholar who is also a descendant of Prophet Mohammad. They are also referred to as "sayeds," meaning princes. Descendants of Prophet Mohammad are expected to be of high morals and excellent character; however, while there are many respectful sayeds, this is not always the case. Imam Khomeini, Ali Khamenei, and Hassan Nasrullah are seen as the face of Shia Islam, and lead the current development and growth of the entire denomination, both religiously and politically. In order to assess the current situation of Shia Islam, it is vital to take a closer look at the two main characters who have assumed leadership of the Islamic hierarchy, Imam Khomeini and Ali Khamenei.

"Imam" Khomeini

The followers of Imam Khomeini consider him to be a descendant of Mohammad. The legitimacy of this claim is unknown as there is no authentic family tree that traces his ancestry back to the Prophet Mohammad. The claim has been strongly refuted by his top student, Ayatollah Ahmad Ali Mesbah, who travelled to India with the sole intention of investigating Khomeini's family. During a video recorded interview, Ayatollah Mesbah confirmed that Khomeini's grandfather was a Sikh who wore a black turban. When his father converted to Islam, people mistook them for offspring of Mohammad, when in fact they were Indian migrants in the Iranian city of Khomein. Years later, documents emerged which proved Khomeini's Hindu ancestry.[408] By claiming to be a descendant of Mohammad, Khomeini made his decisions appear to be divinely approved by God, making his opposition "enemies of God" who deserved execution.

Initially, Khomeini was not known as a scholar – a status required to rule an Islamic government. The presence of high-ranking Islamic authorities and jurists with millions of followers made it intensely difficult for him to rule in the name of God. His strategy was to associate himself with the greatest and most noble Islamic scholar at the time, Shariatmadari, and to receive legitimacy from being amongst his followers. His activism against the Shah of Iran earned him a death sentence in 1963, but he managed to escape it after Shariatmadari raced to issue Khomeini a certificate which gave him recognition as a Grand Ayatollah ("High-Ranking Sign of God"), since the Iranian constitution at the time stated that a Grand Ayatollah could not be executed.[409] The shah decided to exile him instead, and after Khomeini's return to Iran on February 4, 1979 to establish the Islamic State of Iran, Shariatmadari welcomed him,[410] which then led to the nation's uprising against the Shah of Iran and the Islamic Revolution.

From the beginning of Khomeini's religious mission to establish an Islamic state, he said: "I will appoint a government. *I will slap this nation on the mouth*,"[411] referring to his own Iranian nation.

Khomeini then gathered thousands of Muslim youth on the eve of the Iranian New Year, and ingrained in them his ideology and love of jihad. Addressing the youth, he said:

> We *should try hard to export our revolution to the world*, and should set aside the thought that we do not export our revolution, because Islam does not regard various Islamic countries differently and is the supporter of all the oppressed people of the world. On the other hand, all the superpowers and all the powers have risen to destroy us. If we remain in an enclosed environment we shall definitely face defeat. We should clearly settle our accounts with the powers and superpowers and should demonstrate to them that, despite all the grave difficulties that we have, *we shall confront the world with our ideology*.[412]

Khomeini preached the mercy of God but showed little mercy to those he executed, who were, he said, opponents "who got what they deserved." He executed at least seven prostitutes, fifteen men accused of homosexuality, and a Jewish businessman alleged to be spying for Israel.[413] In November 1979, his intelligence services raided the US Embassy in Tehran and held fifty-two American diplomats hostage for 444 days, making it the longest hostage crisis ever recorded.[414]

Shariatmadari, the grand jurist who gave Khomeini legitimacy and recognition as a scholar, was put under pressure by the nation and held responsible for the crimes of Khomeini. He condemned the hostage crisis, and demanded the release of the US diplomats in 1981.[415] At this time, Khomeini realized that, even though he was the leader of the country, Shariatmadari still had a powerful influence on the nation's citizens and Islamic scholars. Therefore, he spent the remaining months of 1981 paving the way for the arrest and assassination of Shariatmadari. In 1982, Shariatmadari was accused of plotting to assassinate Khomeini and to overthrow the Islamic state. Therefore, he was placed under house arrest in his late 70s, and assassinated in 1986. Current living grand jurists who were present at the time – and whose names cannot be mentioned for their own personal safety – informed me in 2010 that Shariatmadari was buried inside the toilet space of his own house as a form of humiliation to him, disregarding his black turban which truly symbolized a lineage back to Prophet Mohammad.

Upon consolidating his power, Khomeini launched a bloody campaign of wiping out his political opposition. In one year, Khomeini murdered more people than the shah had executed during his entire quarter-century reign! All this was alongside the imprisonment, torture, and execution of progressive figures.[416]

In 1988, just two years after assassinating Shariatmadari, Khomeini ordered a massacre, executing more than 30,000 political prisoners without trial: "Secret documents smuggled out of Iran reveal that, because of the large numbers of necks to be broken, prisoners were loaded onto forklift trucks in groups of six and hanged from cranes in half-hourly intervals" and that "children as young as 13 were hanged from cranes, six at a time, in a barbaric two-month purge of Iran's prisons on the direct orders of Ayatollah Khomeini, according to a new book by his former deputy."[417] Due to these violent crane hangings, five major crane manufacturing companies ended their business in Iran and cut ties with the Iranian regime.[418]

Khomeini, dubbed the "Sign of Allah," managed to fool and later persecute many dedicated, humane followers. He may have gradually changed his public stance for a variety of reasons to lead the Islamic Republic in such a demonic direction. The religious fervor of these crimes makes them even more shocking. For instance, a woman's rape was frequently the last act that preceded her execution in Iran, as under the violent "Sharia" Law guidelines of Khomeini, the execution of a virgin female is not permitted. According to him, and as he stated very clearly, Islamic justice is based on simplicity and ease. It settles all criminal and civil complaints in the most convenient, elementary, and expeditious way possible. As Khomeini expressed it: "All that is required is for an Islamic judge, with pen and inkwell and two or three enforcers, to go into a town, come to his verdict on any kind of case, and have it immediately carried out."[419]

When Grand Ayatollah Hossein Ali Montazeri's son, Ahmad, a moderate cleric, posted a confidential audio of his father on his website wherein he confessed to the crimes committed by the regime,[420] he was ordered by Iran's intelligence service to remove it.[421] Montazeri,who was second in line to rule after Khomeini but was later placed under house arrest for objecting to mass executions, stated before his death:

> You [Iranian officials] will be in the future etched in the annals of history as criminals. The greatest crime committed under the Islamic Republic, from the beginning of the Revolution until now, which will be condemned by history, is this crime [mass executions] committed by you.[422]

While walking towards the Holy Shrine of Qum, I was accidentally involved in the protests between Montazeri's supporters and the Iranian revolutionary guards during his funeral in December 2009, and had to flee beneath the nearby bridge over the drying Qum River after being attacked by the officials of the Islamic State of Iran.[423] I knew Montazeri on a personal level. The internal clashes between the founders of the Islamic government led to investigative journalism and detailed research into the fight for power, resulting in the publication of many books, including one about Montazeri himself, titled *The Dissident Mullah: Ayatollah Montazeri and the Struggle for Reform in Revolutionary Iran*. As for Montazeri's son, Ahmad, he received a 21-year sentence for disclosing the audio file containing confessions of the mass execution of Iranian political prisoners conducted by the government in 1988.[424]

To justify all of these tyrannical oppressions and mass murders, Imam Khomeini has been declared a prophet who is better than all 123,999 prophets who preceded Mohammad whom Muslims believe in.[425] Being considered a prophet, his decisions are treated as divine rulings that nobody can dare object to. This is how the religious administration has managed to rule, and continue to groom new terrorists such as Khamenei and Nasrullah, who later founded Hizbullah.

The "Supreme" Leader Ali Khamenei

Since the very beginning of the Islamic Revolution in Iran, the loyal followers of its leader Khomeini have tried to boost the religious and political authority of Khamenei by linking him to Islamic holy figures such as Ali and the Mahdi, whom Muslims believe will be the redeemer of Islam and the savior of humanity at the end of time. They also claim that he is an associate of the awaited savior who will appear to bring peace and justice on earth.

Khamenei's status as a scholar has always been controversial. Even though the Society of Seminary Teachers declared him a grand jurist, countless prominent and senior grand jurists of Islam have declined to recognize him as such. Khamenei didn't forget this position of theirs, and immediately sought revenge by launching attacks on their offices and placing them under house arrest once his power was established.[426] Nevertheless, his followers remain a handful compared to other grand jurists, as he remains a political figure, not a religious one. Al-Fayyad, one of the most senior living grand Islamic jurists, considers Khamenei a political cleric, and said in one of his lectures: "There is no value in a political cleric."[427]

Ali Khamanei in his modified vehicle

During Khamenei's trips around Iran, fabricated copies of his family lineage are distributed to show that he is a descendent of the Prophet Mohammad. To create a holy and divine appearance, his car is fitted with strategic lighting aiming to give him an artificial halo. *Foreign Policy Magazine* has stated that "he has allowed, if not encouraged, sycophants to proclaim him the prophet's representative on earth." [428]

A brief examination of Khamenei's Islamic education will show that he is an imposter:

1. He was born in 1939, making him 79 years of age.

2. He travelled to the Iranian city of Qum in 1958, and remained there until 1963 to engage in Islamic studies (approximately five years).

3. He was occupied with administering the affairs of Khomeini, while

his leader was in exile in France, imprisonment and preparations for a revolution in 1965–1979.

4. He did not engage in any studies from the beginning of the revolution, nor during the life and rule of Khomeini 1979–1989, as he was fully occupied with the fledgling Islamic government and the Iran–Iraq War, which lasted eight years.

5. He became the supreme leader of Iran in 1989, at the age of 49.

6. He did not engage in any studies after 1989, as he assumed the highest political and religious position in the Islamic government, and who would dare teach the supreme and divinely appointed leader?

The tricks of Islamist politics once blinded me so that I truly believed that Khamenei was an infallible being, incapable of sinning or committing error.[429] Growing up, I was infatuated by him. I wore the white scarf around my shoulders which symbolized the victory of the Islamic Revolution and its martyred jihadists. My entire belief system revolved around his jurisprudential and political views. Looking back at my early years, which I now refer to as my "years of ignorance," I begin to understand why I was enamored and enraptured by the character of Ali Khamenei. His office and entourage play a central role in creating a divine and heavenly appearance for him, which is also a physiological strategy to mesmerize his followers and to attract more innocent and vulnerable people, who in return will give their money and even lives for him.

Holy Wombs and Islamic Governments

Shia Muslims have always been a minority, hence the number of Islamic governments established by Shias cannot be compared to the hundreds established by the adherents of Sunni Islam. It is understandable for Sunni Muslims, and they are the majority, to demand an Islamic government or caliphate to deal with their affairs as a nation, but that cannot be the case for Shia Muslims. This is because

Shia Muslims believe that a ruler of an Islamic government must be infallible – a characteristic which doesn't exist in any human today.

Ruhullah Khomeini

In modern times, a group of Shia Muslim scholars have altered the teachings of their own faith by establishing an Islamic government, known as the Islamic Government of Iran; also referred to as *Wilayatul Faqih*, i.e. "Government of the Islamic Jurist." Now, to give this government religious legitimacy, and a coating of divinity to gain support from Shia Muslims around the globe, its leaders have attributed divine characteristics and qualities to themselves, such as infallibility. They claim that they are infallible and do not commit any mistakes, errors, or sins. In other words, they have amended their own faith to suit their current political policies and to further their own agendas, making it seem possible for regular human beings to reach the status of God's prophets, and even higher.

To begin with, they groomed jurists and promoted clerics who were loyal to their regime. Then those clerics began to claim that the leader of the 1979 revolution and founder of the Islamic Government of Iran, Imam Khomeini, was "better than God's prophets," **despite**

him being a terrorist with pedophilic teachings, as I will explain in Chapter 11.

Ali Khamanei

When Iran's current supreme leader Ali Khamenei succeeded Khomeini, the paid political clerics knew that establishing his credibility amongst the Muslim world would be a difficult mission, because he lacks knowledge in the most basic fields of Islamic studies. Therefore, they painted a divine image for him by claiming that when he was born Khamenei was <u>no ordinary baby</u>.

They have elevated Khamenei to a level as close to a prophet as possible. They have groomed "scholars for dollars" and placed them in leading positions to make claims such as, "Khamenei pronounced the names of Islam's saints as he exited his mother's womb!" That would be exactly like telling the Catholic world that Pope Francis was born pronouncing the name of Jesus, a claim which is extremely hard to sell.

The Friday prayer leader of the Iranian Holy City of Qum, Ayatollah Mohammad Saeedi, said that Khamenei, the supreme leader, said, "O Ali" at birth. The midwife responded saying, "May Ali protect you."[430] Ali refers to the cousin of the Prophet Mohammad, who was the first Shia imam and saint. In Muslim philosophy, Ali is a divinely appointed leader who is respected and revered for his courage, knowledge, belief, honesty, unbending devotion to Islam, and deep loyalty to Prophet Mohammad.

Linking Khamenei to Ali makes obedience to him an obligation, and opposition is to be punished by death! But what kind of a government requires such brainwashing to be able to govern? The answer is simple: a theocratic government, because every government that claims authority on behalf of God needs to paint a divine image for itself.

Ali Khamanei behind a pulpit that claims his authority to be the same authority of Prophet Mohammad.

The second claim fabricated in favor of Khamenei was that the Islamic state, or caliphate, that he leads is the Islamic government that existed during the era of Prophet Mohammad. On his pulpit, a large text faces the audience saying, "The Authority of the Jurist is the same Authority of the Messenger of God [Mohammad]." The entire arena is also decorated with verses from the Quran that refer to divine leadership and authority, such as the verse: "O you who have believed, obey Allah and obey the Messenger *and those in authority among you*."[431] This verse refers to the divinely appointed successors of Mohammad who are appointed by God, but is quoted on banners to imply that Khamenei is one of "those in authority." This façade of divinity is applied to a man who has absolutely no qualifications to lead a minor congregation, let alone an entire Islamic nation. As clerics and missionaries, we were aware of this reality, but we chose to continue to promote this idea for personal benefit throughout those years.

The Islamic government of Iran operates upon the philosophy that, in order for law to ensure reform and the happiness of the people, there must be an executive power and an executor: a government based on Sharia Law.[432] It also holds that, in addition to revelation (the Quran), God's messengers undertook the implementation of Sharia Law and the establishment of the ordinances of Islam, thereby bringing into being the Islamic state.[433]

Even though, as I demonstrated in Chapter 3 of this book, Mohammad never had an Islamic government, the chiefs of the Islamic revolution of Iran insist that "The nature and character of Islamic law and the divine ordinances of Sharia furnish additional proof of the necessity for establishing government, for they indicate that the laws were laid down for the purpose of creating a state."[434]

In other words, according to the Islamic government of Iran, *belief in and application of Sharia Law is not a personal matter, but must be imposed upon all human beings through the authority of an Islamic state.* And, because <u>Muslims have been brainwashed to believe that without the presence of Islamic governments the West will take over Islamic lands and annihilate them</u>, they have become tolerant of oppressive Islamist regimes, and have sacrificed their lives for them during wars and conflicts. For the past four decades, they have propagated the idea that Muslims are in need of a Sharia Law–based government to overthrow oppressive and tyrannical governments, i.e. whoever doesn't agree with the Islamic government.

Despite the fact that this Islamic government claims that it "does not correspond to any of the existing forms of government"[435] and that "it is not a tyranny,"[436] its past and current leaders have been extremely sensitive to any opposition, and the slightest form of criticism attracts imprisonment, torture, and even death. Journalists and bloggers have been put on trial by the Iranian intelligence agency for the charge of insulting Khamenei. Several journalists have been sentenced without the right to obtain legal aid or a lawyer, because criticism of the leader of an Islamic government is considered blasphemy. They received lashes and jail time, with some dying during the process.[437]

Four decades have passed and hundreds of thousands of lives have been lost due to a government founded in the name of Shia Islam that has no religious roots within the Islamic religion. In fact, the greatest Islamic authorities of Shia Islam admit that the authority of a jurist "is limited to the *guardianship of widows and orphans* and that it *could not be extended* by human beings to the political sphere." [438]

I support the United States in its desire to bring an end to the theocratic regime in Iran. Islamic governments have always been a scam, because religion exists to guide, not to kill and govern.

Family Empires and Secret Societies

As in all religions, there is a governing body directing the affairs of Islam and its adherents in every region, and sometimes continent. Islam revolves around the mosque. Muslims head towards local mosques for all of their affairs in life: paying religious finances, prayers, marriages, weekly sermons, celebrations, Qur'anic lessons, dispute resolution, inheritance matters, and so on. Islam also depends on clerics and mosques for expansion and survival, as it is the scholars and clergymen who invite people to Islam, also known as *Dawah*. Such a situation has resulted in Islamic scholars being highly revered and idolized amongst Muslims, especially if the clergymen are also descendants of Prophet Mohammad – or at least claim to be.

It is undeniable that we have erudite scholars who have spent decades studying and preaching Islam; however, their children do not inherit this merit. The son of a religious leader should not automatically become a glorified figure amongst the Muslim community, without any study or effort. Sadly, this is the case. In recent decades, prominent Islamic authorities have passed away leaving behind a fortune gained from Islamic taxes. These finances are usually taken by the children of the scholar as an inheritance for themselves. However, if they are pious, they hand the money over to the next living scholar they believe is the most knowledgeable. Although this sounds like a generous thing to do, there is always a catch. Unfortunately, it is often witnessed that when the sons of the deceased scholar visit a living scholar to pass on the remainder of the religious finances (since they have greater authority in religion), they place a condition on the scholar and say that they will give over the Islamic finances their father left behind on the condition that the other half is gifted back to them.

This legalized scam has been occurring for many decades and has become even easier now that transactions are private through the availability of online banking. This has allowed both parties to avoid being questioned, since before this online system members of the public could overhear or witness the transaction taking place. Nowadays, the children of the greatest scholars are corrupted to the extent that they make financial agreements with the children of a dying scholar before he dies, without their father knowing! It is similar to an auction, in that whoever is willing to gift them more receives the money their father leaves behind.

In May 2009, I was still engaged in my first years of Islamic studies in the Iranian Holy City of Qum, and witnessed the city raise black flags throughout all the streets as the great and prominent scholar Ayatollah Bahjat had passed away at the age of 92. Bahjat left behind a fortune, as his followers who paid him annual religious finances were spread all around the globe. There was not one country with Muslims without followers of Bahjat. A former employee within Bahjat's office informed me that the amount left behind was over $500,000,000 USD.

The Islamic government of Iran, claiming that it is the divine rule of God, intervened and seized all the money Bahjat had left behind. They were also motivated by the fact that Bahjat's son was an opponent of the Iranian government and by inheriting such great wealth he could become a threat to the government. However, in a very cunning and calculated manner, they distributed all the money to the students of the

Islamic seminaries and missionaries within Iran. By doing this, the money returned to the economy of the country through trade, and was received by the government as "trade money" as opposed to "religious finances," which would have had incurred a responsibility to spend the money only on expanding the religion. Shifty!

Other leading families occupy mosques and other similar venues to host events. However, they don't leave these venues after the events. Instead, they transform them into offices for themselves. The owners of these properties are fearful of issuing a complaint against a prominent scholar with ties to the government. Thus, they allow their property to be used by the "pious scholar" for religious purposes, hoping they will enter paradise even though the "pious scholar" has just robbed them!

It is worth mentioning an incident that took place in the year 1817 within one of the holiest cities of Shia Islam in Iraq, which led to the brutal murder of a prominent and eminent grand Islamic leader by other prominent and eminent grand Islamic leaders. That year, a group of scholars identified themselves as ideological jihadists who fought for the "pure teachings of Islam," and made sure that its teachings remained in accordance with its foundations. They began targeting a prominent leader by the name of Mirza Mohammad al-Akhbari, simply because of their jealousy of his great following amongst Muslims that extended from Iraq to Turkey and Arabia. They issued an Islamic fatwa regarding Mirza, stating:

> It is an Islamic obligation for every lover and loyal person to this religion, to strive in killing him, and rob his wealth. Otherwise, their prayers and fasting is no longer accepted by God, and they shall occupy a specific place in hell-fire.

All the ideological jihadist scholars signed the fatwa and began announcing it from the pulpits of the mosques, which resulted in Muslims flooding to Mirza's house that night to murder him. He was beheaded along with his student, which led to his family escaping to southern Iraq, to live in exile amongst the Mesopotamian Marshes.[439]

Sayid Kazim Rashti.

If you thought the murder of Mirza was appalling, an even more tragic incident occurred just 27 years later, on December 31, 1843 in the Holy City of Karbala, Iraq, which many Muslims, specifically Shia Muslims, found to be a safe place to hide from enemies. It involved the brutal killing of one of Islam's greatest scholars, Kazim Rashti, by another prominent Shia family of scholars. Kazim was descended from a lineage of erudite Islamic scholars, and his family were renowned merchants. His students ranked the highest in Islamic education and knowledge. Kazim became controversial after informing his students that the savior would appear at the end of time along with the return of Christ. Mainly due to jealousy and the fact that his congregation was large due to his knowledge and charisma, other Islamic authorities saw him as a threat, and raced to hold private meetings where they'd agreed to publicly declare him a deviant deceiver who must be boycotted. Soon enough, he was considered an apostate. He was beheaded in his home and buried in Karbala in the Holy Shrine of Hussain, the grandson of Prophet Mohammad. A few years later, his son Ahmad was beheaded, and they began hunting for his youngest son Qasim, a young boy who hid in his father's home. When Qasim grew, they plotted to assassinate him as well, and he fled to Baghdad, then Turkey and sought asylum within the Ottoman Empire.

Ayatollah Mohammad Reza Shirazi before and after his murder.

Assassination plots amongst Muslim hierarchies within various Islamic denominations are common, and continue to this day. In the year 2008, our teacher Mohammed Reza Shirazi, a prominent and influential ayatollah who is also a direct descendant of Prophet Mohammad, was found murdered in his home in Iran. Just like all other prominent scholars from his family and lineage, he too was against the role of religion in politics, which led to his suspicious killing, which is yet to be solved. His father, who ranked as one of Islam's greatest scholars, was murdered in hospital by the Iranian regime in 2001. His body was then stolen from his funeral and buried in the women's section of a holy shrine. The main reason why the opposing prominent scholars urged the intelligence services to bury him in the women's section was to utilize the complete segregation of men and women to prevent any men from visiting his grave, as prominent scholars gathering around his tomb would revive the story of his murder for the public.

In the West, these secret meetings amongst prominent and leading families take place. However, due to the force of law, they cannot do much harm other than plot the character assassination of a public and influential figure. A well-known victim of these dirty tactics is Professor Sayed Ammar Nakshawani who, due to his independence, knowledge, and charismatic preaching, has been subject to much oppression by the corrupt sons of other Islamic scholars. These character assassinations led to him being banned from certain television channels, cancellation of programs, and ongoing rumors. What I find ludicrous about these strategies of character assassination due to jealousy is the fact that most of the conspirators are the direct offspring of Prophet Mohammad, and have forgotten the teachings of their own faith leader and saint, Imam Ali, as he said: "Envy is a great trap of Satan." [440]

Such underground plotting and crimes wouldn't have such an effect if it wasn't for the obedience of Muslims to their scholars, and the fact that they are idolized as God-like figures, something that contradicts the very reason behind the prophecy of Mohammad, who came to end idol worship.

The Grooming of Clerics

Offices of Islamic authorities preserve their empires through not only the children and relatives of other living scholars, but also through their students. Senior students who allow themselves to be used as decoration beside the grand scholar and act as their entourage usually receive great incentives; annual trips to Mecca, qualification certificates, and high wages are part of the deal. These students remain beside the grand scholar at all times, even more than their own sons, and in a few years' time they are given honorific titles such as "Eminent" and "His Excellency." When their beards have turned white, and they are considered elders, they are funded and made independent. Each of them establishes an organization and/or office where they preach the virtues of their teacher and grand scholar.

When the grand scholar wishes to issue a death fatwa against a singer or journalist, they all approve the fatwa and begin to propagate it. These groomed scholars also know that it is highly likely that one of them will occupy the position of leadership once the grand scholar dies, and therefore they compete in displaying their loyalty to the office and jurisdiction. This also entails more work at the office, and less time at home. This is how grand scholars establish their empires and support their base at the expense of other people's families. It's also considered shameful for a wife of one of these groomed scholars to complain about her husband's long working hours, because she should never object to her husband serving the representative of God on earth!

A marriage office in Iran.

Such figures are offered great incentives, such as holidays to Georgia and Azerbaijan, where they are given financial gifts and surrounded with sex workers. Although adultery is not allowed in Islam, these clerics engage in what is known as the Islamic concept of temporary marriage or *mutah*, which allows them to become intimate with strange women. According to Islamic jurisprudence, a Muslim man is allowed to marry four permanent wives, and an unlimited number of temporary women, all at the same time. Since clerics are funded by their Islamic authorities, the money of innocent and devout Muslims is also used for sex and vacations. During my time in Al Mustafa Islamic University in Qum, Iran, my teachers would inform me of the permissibility of these actions. In fact, there are offices set up in Iran's holiest cities known as "Daftar-e-Izdivaj" (marriage offices, pictured), which provide matchmaking services for permanent marriage, temporary marriage, and polygamy. The sexual abuse of young boys also occurs but is practiced outside the holy cities to maintain the image and reputation of the Islamic Revolution of Khomeini.

Scholars for Dollars

Islamic leaders who pledge allegiance to the Islamic government live a life of luxury and endless benefits. Throughout my time within the holy cities of Shia Islam, I worked for a number of grand ayatollahs and high-ranking jurists, either managing their office affairs or translating and supervising their publications.

Makarem Shirazi

Grand Ayatollah Makarem Shirazi

As I recounted in Chapter 1, I worked for grand Ayatollah Makarem Shirazi for one year and a half, as the head of his English publications department. Shirazi, who has been described as the "Verse of God," actually lives a double life. Without going into all the details of his personal life and his three wives, Makarem is also known as the "Sultan of Sugar" or "Mafia of Sugar." As *Voice of America* TV has exposed, he has a deal with the government to receive all royalties and taxes from the sugar being imported and exported from Iran, just as Khamenei receives from petrol and the late Rafsanjani from top-quality pistachios.[441] Despite him being strictly a religious figure, he receives a monthly payment of over $50,000 from the local government, alongside the religious payments he receives on an hourly basis through his offices across the Middle East. His castles, disguised as "research centers," are located in just about every major city in Iran, with his offices in every Islamic city including those outside of Iran.

A theatre within the "Cultural Complex of the Theological School of Imam Kadhim". Picture: RASA.

The latest castle built by Makarem is located in the Holy City of Qum, Iran, and was given the name the "Cultural Complex of the Theological School of Imam Kadhim." The smallest theatre within these castles costs millions of dollars, all established from religious income and illegal royalties, without the slightest sympathy towards the fact that between 44.5 percent and 55 percent of Iran's urban population lives below the poverty line.[442]

In return, Makarem's entire jurisdiction is placed under the service and command of the government. To support the tyrannical regime, he issued a fatwa banning women from attending football matches in stadiums on April 25, 2006,[443] followed by another fatwa on June 20, 2015 banning women from attending volleyball matches, resulting in the complete ban of women from sports arenas.[444]

In 2010, there was a rise in the pet trade within the Islamic government, with advertisements related to buying and selling pets filling the main streets of Tehran. Since dogs are considered filthy and prohibited animals under Sharia Law, the government requested Makarem to intervene once again. He issued a fatwa on June 19, 2010, this time banning pet dogs, saying "Friendship with dogs is a blind imitation of the West."[445] He continued, saying, "There are lots of people in the West who love their dogs more than their wives and children." He also claimed that owning dogs would result in "evil outcomes."[446] Despite the fact that his ancestors were Jews who had sought refuge in Iran,[447] he stated that "The Holocaust is nothing but superstition," only to please the Islamic government.[448]

In 2012, I assisted in the development of his $12,000 website (www.makarem.ir). I recall his office director, Mr. Masoud Pirani, informing the website developers to ensure the website functioned at high speed. The speed needed to compete with the high-speed internet available to followers in the West. In September 2014, I was shocked to hear that Makarem had issued a fatwa denouncing high-speed internet, saying that "3G mobile services are against Sharia Law" and violate "human and moral norms."[449] Such hypocrisy left me confused, and reminded me of the phrase, "Do as I say, not as I do."

During his career as an Islamic leader, Ayatollah Makarem has attempted several stunts to elevate himself amongst the Muslim world. In 1986, he turned against Shariatmadari, the most senior Shia cleric in Iran,[450] leading to his house arrest along with his family members by Khomeini, and the brutal torture of his daughters-in-law.[451] In 2015, he issued a death fatwa against Mohammad Ali Taheri, an Iranian researcher on alternative medicine, who remains in prison while suffering torture to this day.[452]

Although this loyalty to the Islamic regime made him a prominent and wealthy religious leader, he tried to paint a legendary image for himself, similar to that of Mirza Hassan Shirazi, leader of the Persian Tobacco Protest. Makarem released a fatwa banning smoking, expecting national outrage against the importation of American and other western cigarettes.[453] However, this stunt failed miserably as the leaders of the government are addicted to cigarettes and pipes themselves.[454]

Misbah Yazdi a.k.a. "Professor Crocodile"

Another grand jurist who has sacrificed his integrity for money and power is Misbah Yazdi, who now sits in the Assembly of Experts within the Islamic regime of Iran. He has been nicknamed "Professor Crocodile" due to his harsh and violent Islamist conservatism,[455] and because his first name Misbah rhymes with *timsah*, the Arabic word for crocodile.

Ayatollah Misbah Yazdi

Vali Nasr, an Iranian-American academic specializing in the Middle East and the Islamic world, has described Misbah as the most conservative and the most powerful clerical oligarch in Iran's leading center of religious learning.[456] Despite Misbah being described as "a theoretician of the radicals" by scholars within the Islamic seminary and "the theoretician of violence" by Iran's former President Khatami,[457] he has managed to elevate himself into the high ranks of government scholars who are loyal to the supreme leader Khamenei by issuing extremely controversial and inflammatory statements that benefit the Islamic state. An example is this statement from 2009: "When the president is endorsed by the leader, obeying him is similar to obedience to God."[458] Akbar Ganji, an Iranian pro-democracy journalist, said that Misbah "encouraged or issued fatwas, or religious orders" for the 1998 chain murders and assassinations of five Iranian dissidents.[459]

Throughout the election campaign of Ahmadinejad, Iran's sixth president, Misbah received large financial incentives including promises of future benefits should he support Ahmadinejad. Misbah, being someone who's ready to sell his soul in exchange for money, did so.[460] Not only did he claim that Ahmadinejad was his student and should be elected, he also guaranteed him victory after issuing a religious verdict in 2005 urging the nation to vote for him.[461] He then declared his election a miracle[462] and a gift from the Mahdi.* The matter did not end there. Misbah went on to issue a death fatwa on electoral candidate Mir Hossein Mousavi, whose popularity threatened Ahmadinejad's.[463]

When Ahmadinejad finally won the election and his colors of tyranny and oppression began to show, Misbah was widely criticized. To maintain his reputation and status, he turned against Ahmadinejad, saying that he needed to be "saved"[464] because he had been "bewitched."[465]

During the years 2009–2013, I attended lessons and sermons by Misbah Yazdi, studied his books and participated in his weekly lectures on Wednesday evenings. During his lectures and lessons, Misbah openly and publicly advocates stripping all citizens of their basic human rights, including the right to vote in elections. He claims that a genuine Islamic government must not hold elections, and that the only option citizens have is to express allegiance to the supreme leader, Khamenei.[466] When asked about the right of citizens to vote, he stated: "It doesn't matter what the people think. The people are ignorant sheep."[467]

He teaches that in a situation of war between Muslims and non-Muslims, Muslims must take as many non-Muslims as possible as slaves and convert them to Islam by force.[468] Among his teachings are that western culture, especially American culture, must be completely

* In Islam, the Mahdi is the awaited savior and divine Islamic authority, who is expected to appear at the end of time.

opposed,[469] that Jews are all Zionists, and that Zionists are the fundamental source of evil on planet Earth.[470]

It would be safe to say that Misbah is one of the main reasons why there has not been an Islamic reformation, as he is a vicious opponent of any reformist movements in the Middle East. His well-regarded students and large following from among the clergymen and Islamic seminaries has given him sufficient power and diplomatic influence to end any reformist voice within any Islamic government. Misbah is also a violent man, who compares the ideas of reformers to "injecting the Aids virus" into society,[471] and urges: "If someone tells you he has a new interpretation of Islam, sock him in the mouth."[472]

Professor Crocodile is opposed to academic education, and claims that western universities teach Muslims "psychological warfare" against Islamic governments.[473] Ironically, his son Ali, whom I associated with at the time, had studied at McGill University in Montreal, Canada.

In an Islamic government like that of Iran, a career of dirty politics and death fatwas against innocent people has earned Misbah a high standing. Today, there are rumors that he will be the one to succeed the supreme leader, Khamenei.[474]

CHAPTER 9

The Governing Muslim Body in Iran

Human beings are not infallible and therefore our decisions will not be infallible, but those who assume positions of Islamic leadership and represent "infallible" Islamic teachings have a responsibility they must live up to. During my ten-year journey throughout the holy Islamic sites and seminaries of Iran and Iraq, I witnessed many behind-the-scenes meetings and decisions made in secret that directly influenced social developments. I enjoyed a healthy relationship with offices of numerous grand ayatollahs, including the Khomeini family and ambassadors of the Iranian Revolution. I have plenty of evidence to back this claim, as images of my meetings and interactions with these grand Islamic authorities have already been circulated on social media, and receipts of their payments to me are reproduced in the first chapter of this book.

The following incidents present an idea of how the Islamic hierarchy in Iran functions, and how corruption is legitimized in the name of religion.

Islamic Finances: From Where and to Where?

On Friday June 3, 2011, I was still a full-time Islamic studies student in the Iranian Holy City of Qum. Early in the morning, I ran into a friend who had travelled to Iran from London, UK, and we decided to walk to a nearby café to have breakfast together since we had not seen each other for over three years. My friend, whom I shall refer to as Ahmad, is the son of a multi-billionaire who once owned a massive real estate agency in London. He had travelled to Iran to deliver his father's religious payments to the Islamic authorities, but had no idea where the office of his father's particular ayatollah was. Ahmad said that he had brought a large amount of money with him, and he was hoping to deliver it that very same day as he feared anything could happen to him as a foreigner in Iran. I could not help but inquire about the amount, so I said "How much money did you bring along?" and Ahmad replied, "700,000 pounds." He informed me that his father transferred the money to him when he landed and settled in the city of Qum. Immediately, I decided to try to persuade him against taking the money to his grand ayatollah, as I knew of his corruption, and to convince him to pay another grand ayatollah who would give him a receipt for the money and inform him where exactly the money would be spent.

He was convinced, but after making a phone call to his father, he found that his father wanted the money to go to his particular grand ayatollah, even though it is permissible in Islam to deliver it to another. It was also a public holiday to mark the birth of Prophet Mohammad's grandson, but I knew that with such a large amount in the rapidly declining economy of Iran, Ahmad and I could even meet with the president of Iran if we wanted to. The year 2011 marked the beginning of the current economic sanctions on Iran, and the value of the Iranian rial had begun to drop substantially.

I drove Ahmad to the office of his grand ayatollah, telling him that his decision was a grave mistake. I clearly remember saying, "Your money will be spent on cigars, sex, travel, and luxury living for them and their sons." But Ahmad truly believed that I had biased views which were not necessarily true. We reached the office of the grand ayatollah and I tried once more to prevent him, but he insisted on delivering the money. So, I knocked on the door of the office. The receptionist answered and said that the grand ayatollah was not available. I informed him that we had come to deliver religious finances to his eminence. He allowed us to enter the office as he made a phone call to the home of the eminent grand ayatollah. After the phone call had ended, we were told to come back the next day, as it was a holiday that day.

I turned to Ahmad and said to him, "They think we've come with only $10,000. Watch what will happen now." I said to the receptionist, "Tell the son-in-law of the eminent grand ayatollah that it is an amount we cannot return with." The receptionist instantly asked, "A large amount?" I said, "Yes, very large." Once the second phone call was made to inform the grand ayatollah that it was a large amount, we were told to wait as they would be sending a vehicle to pick us up and take us to the grand ayatollah's home. I left my car parked outside the office and travelled with the grand ayatollah's chauffeur as I truly believed it would not take longer than an hour, since this was not the first time I had delivered religious payments. To our surprise, the grand ayatollah and his sons-in-law were not in town; they were in their other property located about two hours' drive away from the city. Immediately, it clicked in my mind. I knew where we were going as I had heard of this place, and my previous doubts about its existence began to vanish as we got closer to our destination.

We finally arrived at the location and were escorted into the residence of the grand ayatollah which included an enormous orchard, a natural stream, a massive garden, and a pathway of marble leading to the castle-like home of his humble eminence. I noticed that Ahmad's face began to change color once he had seen the lavish lifestyle his grand ayatollah was living, all financed by his followers, as ayatollahs don't work a day of labor during their entire lives. But it was too late now; he should have trusted me and taken my advice seriously. We entered the massive mansion to find it furnished with what appeared to be luxurious Turkish and Italian furniture, and waited in the living room that contained a three-meter fish tank and what appeared to be a custom-made top-quality Persian rug.

It became clear that we were not his only guests, as there were sounds coming from his meeting room. Now it was time to enter the meeting room of the grand ayatollah and, on doing so, I was surprised to find one of America's black-turbaned Islamic clerics sitting beside him, eating strawberries. After I greeted the grand ayatollah, the American cleric quickly gathered himself to greet me and excuse himself from the meeting room. He appeared to be startled as he was not expecting my arrival. It then became crystal clear where the Islamic finances of the American Shia Muslim community go, and how they are spent.

The grand ayatollah then sat to welcome us, and thanked us for travelling such a distance. He ordered cups of tea for Ahmad and myself. The tea came instantly, and he wanted us to drink it as we spoke about Australia and the current situation of the Muslim community. After taking the first sip of tea, I realized that it was made with saffron leaves, the very year the value of Iranian saffron had exceeded the value of gold. Grand ayatollahs have offered me unique beverages, such as pure pomegranate juice from the trees of Naisapour, but this saffron tea was on a whole new level. Out of respect, we had to complete drinking the tea before the topic of the finances could be addressed.

After Ahmad had witnessed the lifestyle the grand ayatollah was living, he was certain that his father would refuse to pay him a penny. Therefore, he tried to bargain with the grand ayatollah by keeping half of the money to be spent on orphans. This excuse wasn't going to work as the ayatollah fired back, saying, "We have an orphanage ourselves where it will be spent." His employees were called, and Ahmad handed over the large bag of money. A moment later we began to hear the money-counting machines in the other room as they counted the money. The employees returned with a note and handed it to the grand ayatollah that contained the amount we brought to him, £700,000. He raised his hands to the ceiling and began to pray for our success and blessings. On behalf of Ahmad, I requested a receipt for his father. But the grand ayatollah said that the book of receipts was in the office, and that we should come the next day.

The next evening, I drove Ahmad to the office of the grand ayatollah to receive the receipt, which was indeed prepared for him in an envelope. However, the problem was that the receipt was for only £700 and not £700,000. When we returned to the office of Islamic finances to ask them to correct the receipt, they said that they had deliberately written £700 in order that nobody would know that the grand ayatollah had received £700,000 from only one of his followers. When we exited the office, I said to Ahmad:

If you had given it to the other grand ayatollah, he would have given you a receipt for the full amount. Now, there is no record for your father's finances, and you cannot hold the ayatollah's office accountable for anything more than £700. Next time you bring finances, don't give it to someone who is dishonest.

Ahmad asked: "What about all the money?" I replied, "Now that they have your money, say goodbye to your £700,000. You won't hear about the money again." This is how ayatollahs affiliated with the Iranian regime operate, and have been operating since 1979.

Alcoholic Hypocrisy

One of the main problems with the Islamic authorities and government is hypocrisy, in the sense that what applies to the regular Muslim does not necessarily apply to the Islamic clerics, nor to their close associates. Violent Sharia Law only applies to poor and helpless Muslims.

One of the greatest sins in Islam is the consumption of alcohol. It's a red line no practicing Muslim ever crosses. The punishment for drinking alcohol is severe, and the social backlash ruins reputations and lives. In some cases, Muslims who consume alcohol are murdered by their community members or their own conservative families. This violent culture that holds no regard for religious advice and/or counselling is taught and promoted by Islamic clerics. However, some of these same clerics drink alcohol and smuggle it into the holy cities of Islam; and some sons of the greatest jurists consume alcohol with the knowledge of their holy fathers.

In the conservative Islamic seminaries, alcohol is secretly referred to as "fesenjoon," which is an Iranian and Iraqi stew flavored with pomegranate syrup and ground walnuts. Hypocritical clerics use it as a secret code-word between themselves: So Adam, how was the *fesenjoon* last night?

A Story from My Teacher

My teacher, who descends from the lineage of Prophet Mohammad and who is currently serving a prison sentence in the dungeons of Iran's Evin Prison, would spend hours each week speaking to me about his experiences as a faith leader in Iran. He is an erudite scholar, powerful orator, and great author who comes from a prominent family. He is also the brother of the son-in-law of one of the greatest living authorities on Islam in Iraq. I am unable to mention his name at this time for his own personal protection. He lived with the secrets of the Islamic institutes and knows how leaderships are formed. He witnessed the corruption, filth, and hypocrisy of what appears to be a holy and sacred body of prophet-like clergymen, and at one point was part of it.

The stories my teacher told me were shocking, and some of the stories brought tears to his eyes as he articulately narrated each incident to me. Despite being a descendent of Prophet Mohammad, he lived much of the last two decades of his life before his imprisonment as an outsider, and a stranger amongst his own people. He is now being held by the Iranian authorities with the aim of stopping him from exposing the corruption of their groomed grand Islamic clerics.

In 1962, during the rule of the shah, my teacher was visiting Iran. One night in Tehran he was walking in a beautiful park in Darband, formerly a village inside Tehran's metropolitan limits. He came across one of the spoilt sons of a grand Islamic leader in Iraq who was publicly drinking alcohol, seemingly without a care in the world, to the extent that he was dribbling saliva onto his shirt. He was dressed in casual clothing and defiantly was not wearing his turban and clerical robes. My teacher was infuriated and began to yell at him, saying, "What are you doing here?" As the son of the Islamic leader noticed him, he responded, "Please don't inform my father." My teacher walked away, shocked and angry from what he had just witnessed. Upon his return to Iraq, he came across the son's father and asked him, "Dear Grand Ayatollah, where's your son?"

The grand ayatollah responded, saying that his pious cleric of a son was in Iran undergoing medical treatment. My teacher then informed the grand jurist that he had seen his son drunk and in a completely unacceptable condition in public! The grand jurist turned the accusation against my teacher, saying, "And how do you know what alcohol does to the human or what it smells like? Have you consumed alcohol before yourself!?" My teacher responded saying no, and went on to explain that during his travels throughout Iraq the taxi drivers would often consume alcohol while driving and this is how he became familiar with people's attitudes, odors, and personalities when under the influence of alcohol.

After being confronted with the hypocrisy of the actions of his own household, the grand jurist responded: "Do you have proof that my son consumed alcohol? Maybe he only gargled with it!" My teacher, being an erudite scholar and son of a lineage of grand jurists, responded: "And was there nothing else for him to gargle with, only alcohol that could lead to his punishment by death, if his father was a just and honest ayatollah?" and walked away.

The Global Scam of Halal Certification

While I am not against kosher or halal food, I have always considered "halal certification" to be the greatest scam ever established in the name of Islam. Islam is over 14 centuries old, and the idea of the need for halal certification was introduced to Muslims less than one hundred years ago. The question isn't really "Why do we Muslims need halal certification on products?" It's rather: "How were our Muslim ancestors dealing with food 13 centuries ago? Why is it that we need halal certification *now*, and not back then?" The answer is clear. It's a money-making business opportunity. Islamic institutions need money to survive and, even though donations from devout Muslims towards religious projects and events exceed billions each year, the clerical system also invests these finances in business projects.

Muslim communities in the West have been made paranoid about the food in major retail stores. Growing up in Australia, our local mosque cleric Shaikh Imran once said: "Do not drink tap water. This land and its water is not pure," while Shaikh Hassan promoted the idea that Pepsi was short for "Pay Every Penny Serving Israel." We were also told that "Coca Cola" read "No Mohammad, No Mecca" when written backwards in Arabic.

A claim that Coca Cola reads "No Mohammad, No Mecca" in Arabic.

After creating these rumors about many western products, Islamic clergymen promoted the need to designate all products as halal or haram (prohibited and permissible to consume). They conducted an investigation into the ingredients of Pepsi and Coca Cola, and demanded that both highly-sought-after products undergo the process of "halal certification" before being sold to Muslim nations.[475] Obviously, neither of the products contain animal fat nor pork extracts, but to obtain the halal certificate to certify that they don't costs money.

The matter doesn't end with what can be consumed, but also extends to other ridiculous matters, such as halal-certified toilet paper.[476] *The Daily Telegraph* reports that the halal certification mark sits on almost every item in an Australian shopping basket, and that the "Islamic Federation of Islamic Councils, in the last financial year, had an income of almost $6 million, which added nicely to its $63 million worth of assets."[477] An investigation discovered that "Worldwide, the halal market is valued at $2.1 trillion. In Australia, it is worth about $8.5 billion, $1.5 billion of which is in the meat sector."[478]

Muslims can find out if a product is halal or not by reading its ingredients to make sure that it doesn't contain pork or animal fat. Alternatively, the major Islamic communities in every country could set up a mobile app or website that lists all halal and non-halal products. However, this would mean that major companies no longer need to pay a hefty annual fee to Islamic councils for the halal logo on their products. This is why I consider it to be a business using the name of God.

What almost all non-Muslims don't know about the sneakiness behind the halal industry is that it affects Muslim retailers as well. Islamic jurisprudence allows a Muslim to buy meat and other products from a Muslim individual or a Muslim market without asking whether or not it is halal. Due to the mutual trust among Muslims, a Muslim customer will automatically assume that a Muslim retailer only sells halal food. But the clerical institutions want as much money as they can; therefore, even Muslims are required to obtain halal certificates for their retail shops. Muslims who don't abide by the rules set by the community clerics often become the subject of rumors which may then result in the end of their careers and bankruptcy. One of the rumors they spread is that they sell pork, and in order to prove that they do not sell pork they need to obtain a halal certificate.

One common concern about halal certification is whether it funds Islamic terrorism. While I have not come across any solid evidence to support this concern in Australia, there is a matter I find worth mentioning. In 2015, I was invited to Indonesia to host an Islamic event for the Shia Muslim community. During my visit, I was welcomed to Jakarta by its former governor, Basuki Ahok, to whom I presented a proposal about my projects in Jakarta. Shia Muslims within Jakarta were concerned about the authenticity of halal certification, and asked me to visit the local halal certification authority to view the procedure and whether or not it was in line with the jurisprudential teachings of all Islamic sects, including Shia Muslims. Upon visiting the halal certification authority of Indonesia, I noticed that they were affiliated with members of Jemaah Islamiyah, a militant extremist Islamist rebel group responsible for the 2002 Bali Bombings. The halal certification authority displayed images at their offices that included the Jemaah Islamiyah logo. The question worth asking ourselves in the West is: Indonesia's halal certification authority influences many of the halal certification authorities in the West, so are we indirectly funding terrorism?

The Clash of the Turbans

A famous phrase by Prophet Mohammad is "the disease of scholars is envy"; and indeed, it's near impossible to find a more eloquent description of the disease that clerical societies suffer from. Even though, to the majority of Shia Muslims, clerics appear to have a good relationship with each other, the truth is exactly the opposite. The hate and envy amongst Shia Muslim scholars is difficult to fathom. Shia Muslim scholars compete for speaking venues and go as far as investigating who is invited to prominent places to speak, and who is paid more money. The plotting then begins to cancel each other's events.

In the USA for instance, some prominent Shia families dress their fledgling young men in black turbans and consider themselves the voices of Islam. In reality, they are nothing but corrupt individuals who have taken advantage of the ignorance of Shia Muslims, abusing their women and misusing their Islamic finances. Some clerics also compete about who has the most beautiful wife, or the latest vehicle. It is a morally and ethically corrupt community.

In 2015, I was directly involved in a case which concerned an Islamic scholar in Orange County, after both him and his married son, who also claims to be a scholar, had made sexual advances to a married lady from their Islamic congregation on several occasions. After investigating the case with her, she informed me that the senior scholar (the father) had given her financial support to open a window to her friendship. In an earlier case, the son had travelled to Seattle to deliver sermons for the Muslim community. During his stay at the hotel, he engaged in sexual activity with a minor girl (aged 16) from the very Islamic community he had travelled to serve. No charges were laid as the victims' fear the consequences of exposing such a prominent Islamic scholar. In their belief, maintaining the image and reputation of their Islamic center is more important than the safety of their bodies. This belief has been taught to them by the very scholars that sexually abuse them.

Those who rank the highest in corruption within my Shia Islamic denomination are the representatives of Iran's Supreme Leader Ali Khamenei. They are violent, arrogant, manipulative, and promote a revolutionary Islamist agenda in the West. When I was studying in Iran's Al-Mustafa International University, clerics from the office of Ali Khamenei or other government departments would take my friends out for a "journey." This "journey" usually resulted in the young student performing an obligatory washing ritual, one usually performed only after intimacy. Some clerics had links to sexual escorts and would work as pimps, providing western students with women in exchange for dollars, a more valuable currency than the Iranian rial. What would be the benefit of this, one may ask? The benefit is rather simple. Should a student then decide to turn against the teacher, they have something to use against him. This is exactly what happened to a cleric currently residing in Sydney, who was taken to Tehran to engage in sexual activities with an Iranian lady. Once he decided to leave the clerical system, he found himself in deep trouble, with marriage to this woman being his only option to avoid charges.

These clerics' sexual activities are not limited to women. Iran's supreme leader, Ali Khamenei, has sexually abused young boys according to a letter written by his brother-in-law, Shaikh Ali Tehrani, to Khomeini.[479]

Prominent Shia clerics such as Khamenei who thrive on dominance, and exploiting both boys and girls, begin to suffer from a delusion – that somehow the world revolves around them. Their titles begin to grow in length, from a simple "cleric" to "Authority of God"; and, knowing that there are pious and respectful scholars more loved by the majority of Shia Muslims, their envy begins to show. Their dark past and actions begin to haunt them, and the only solution in their minds is to take down the pious and clean scholars, to remain the only ones in charge. Shia Islam, which consists of over 350 million adherents, is governed entirely by two individuals: Ali Khamenei of Iran and Ali Sistani of Iraq, with Sistani's entire office and entourage being controlled by the Iranian intelligence services.

Amongst senior Islamic scholars and ayatollahs, Ali Khamenei is referred to as "the Pharaoh." This title was given to Khamenei because the pharaoh of Moses' time is a condemned figure in the Quran. All Muslims believe that he, the pharaoh, assumed and claimed divine positions that he was never worthy of, oppressed those who didn't believe in his message, and spread corruption on the earth. Khamenei is extremely sensitive to criticism, and it leads to imprisonment.

One of the leading voices against the Iranian regime is Ayatollah Hussain Shirazi, son of the Grand Ayatollah Sadiq Shirazi, who comes from a lineage that exceeds 150 years of Islamic leadership. After the killing and arrest of hundreds of innocent protesters in early 2018, Ayatollah Hussain Shirazi delivered a powerful speech criticizing the Iranian regime and its theocracy, labelling its leader as a "Pharaoh." As a result, the Iranian intelligence services committed the public crime of kidnapping Ayatollah Hussain Shirazi in the Holy City of Qum, Iran. He was accompanying his father to his home after delivering his morning lesson, when three vehicles belonging to the intelligence authorities forced their vehicle to stop in an unsafe manner. They then forcefully assaulted Hussain Shirazi by dragging him out of his vehicle in an inhumane manner, causing him to collapse on the floor. Finally, they turned to Grand Ayatollah Sadiq Shirazi and began threatening him, saying: "Your day shall come soon!" Hussain Shirazi was then taken to an unknown place and released after twelve days in need of serious medical attention.[480]

The strive for dominance is clear in Shia governments and theocracies. Grand ayatollahs use their political and financial powers to bring each other down, with some maintaining links with foreign intelligence services for increased power and protection. Shia Muslims may very well be the victims of ISIS and other hardline Sunni Muslim groups such as Al-Qaeda, but they are also the victims of themselves and their own ideology. Shia Islam must be cleansed from the contradictions introduced to it by unqualified scholars, which have resulted in grave theological and doctrinal contradictions within the Shia school of thought. They must maintain a separation of mosque and state, and especially a separation from terrorist leaders, in order to be accepted as a legitimate faith and not the ideological and political cult that Hizbullah wants it to be.

CHAPTER 10

Twenty-First-Century Islamic Terrorism

The world's greatest think tanks have gathered countless times to discuss the evolution of Islamic terrorism within both political and academic platforms, all presenting their thoughts on how the religion of Islam does or does not directly influence terrorism. While terrorism is not solely an Islamic phenomenon, many terrorist acts, and the contemporary terrorist attacks that have caused a great number of deaths, have been perpetrated in the name of Islam. This has led to ongoing debate in the West and within the Muslim world regarding the link between terrorism and the teachings of Islam.

Modern international Islamist terrorism is a product of both major Islamic denominations, Sunni and Shia. Sunni Islamic terrorism, which introduced ISIS and its like, is a natural offshoot of seventh-century Islamic fundamentalism. It was revived in the eighteenth century through the Wahhabi movement. Shia Islamic terrorism became officially recognized after the Iranian Islamic Revolution in 1979, although its roots stem from the tenth-century invasions of the Fatimid Dynasty.

Researchers studying Sunni Islamic terrorism believe that:

The underlying element in the radical Islamist worldview is historic and dichotomist: Perfection lies in the ways of the Prophet and the events of his time; therefore, religious innovations, philosophical relativism, and intellectual or political pluralism are anathema. In such a worldview, there can exist only two camps – Dar al-Islam ("The House of Islam"– i.e., the Muslim countries) and Dar al-Harb ("The House of War"– i.e., countries ruled by any regime but Islam) – which are pitted against each other until the final victory of Islam.[481]

When Imam Khomeini was asked whether his policies in Shia Islamic governance had taken the Islamic religion back many years, he said, yes, it was his aim to take Islam back to the seventh century.

The ideology of jihad breeds a mentality of "I fight, therefore I exist." The one main issue that has been overlooked and is essential to mention in this regard is the fact that what you and I believe is terrorism is defined by Islamic fundamentalists as a religious and moral duty that is rewarded with entry into paradise. Therefore, the roots of our definition of terrorism differ from the roots of what Islamic fundamentalists see as jihad. The fundamentalist attitude is "my way or the highway," and this is exactly what it has evolved into: it is either my way or you do not deserve to live.

The definition of jihad or Islamic terrorism according to the US Department of Defense is the "unlawful use of – or threatened use of – force or violence against individuals or property to coerce or intimidate governments or societies, often to achieve political, religious, or ideological objectives."[482] However, the definition of jihad, according to Islamic teachings, is a beautiful journey to paradise through martyrdom after fighting for the establishment of the rights of God on earth and bringing victory to the glorious message of Islam by all means possible.

Governments and security agencies will never succeed in tackling radical religious educational programming through applying their traditional measures of security, because an ideology can be tackled but can never be eliminated. Moderate Islamic leaders such as myself who oppose suicide and the killing of innocent people will always struggle, as we remain the minority. In contrast, terrorist groups like Al-Qaeda and ISIS assert the legitimacy of their motives through reference to the holiest Islamic books of hadith, making their form of Islam, known as "Islamism," a justified and holy war. Therefore, I believe that the only realistic way to tackle Islamic terrorism is to understand the structure and formation of its ideology.

Sacred Books of Terrorism

While I received my initial Islamic education in a conservative and private Muslim school in Western Australia, my Islamic studies teachers taught me that it was useless and unwise to question the history of Islam. My teacher and Islamic scholar Sheikh Mahmoud summarized this matter in one phrase: "What happened has happened, and only Allah can judge." I couldn't help but question many occurrences within the history of Islam, because they paved the way for problems the entire globe is suffering from today.

On my teacher's desk sat a book titled in beautiful Arabic calligraphy, *Sahih al-Bukhari*, a compilation of prophetic traditions, or hadith, by the grand Muslim scholar Muhammad al-Bukhari. As mentioned earlier in this book, Muslims view this as the most trusted collection of prophetic teachings and the most authentic book after the Holy Quran. The Arabic word "Sahih" translates as authentic, and Bukhari refers to the author, so the title means "The Authentic [Teachings of] Bukhari."

This sacred book was written during the ninth century, more than two hundred years after the death of Prophet Mohammad. The author, Mohammad al-Bukhari, was a Persian Islamic scholar who not did not meet Mohammad nor live during his era. Unfortunately, he was also blind.

When I decided to study *Sahih al-Bukhari*, I went to the local Muslim bookstore in Western Australia and purchased it. I found it available in only one volume translated into English, titled*Sahih Al-Bukhari: The Early Years of Islam*.[483] I became somewhat suspicious about why the four Arabic volumes were not all translated into English. It appeared to me that the one English volume was prepared to impress non-Muslim readers, and it only included translations of the sections that maintain a favorable image of the history of Islam. However, I insisted on obtaining the original four Arabic volumes of the *Bukhari*, which I eventually bought from an Islamic superstore in Melbourne, Australia.

Shortly after commencing my study of the *Bukhari*, I was both shocked and disgusted by its contents, and by the fact that such corrupt teachings had been passed on for centuries and considered divine and sacred. Our "most sacred book after the Holy Quran" teaches violence in all aspects of life, and in fact revived the ideology of violent jihad after it had been almost extinct for two centuries, presenting it in the form of scripture that is now considered holy and sacred by almost two billion Muslims. It is true that jihad did exist in practice, but it could have vanished through the evolution of society, and by strengthening of diplomatic relations among countries and nations. However, Bukhari presented jihad as a doctrine coated with prophetic reports nobody had heard of before him. This is one of the reasons why many believe that revered Islamic scholars within the early centuries of Islam were actually politicians in religious garb, introducing policies of war as Islamic doctrine that is obligatory to follow.

No chapter in the *Bukhari* is free from violence, including the chapter on medicine, a subject that sounds far from terrorism. Ironically, even methods of supposed "medicine" were as barbaric and as terrorizing as one could ever imagine.

As mentioned earlier in this book, Bukhari reported:

Some people of the Arabian tribe of Ukl came to Medina and its climate did not suit them. So the Prophet ordered them to go to the herd of [milk] camels and to drink their milk and urine as a medicine. So they went as directed and after they became healthy, they killed the shepherd and drove away all the camels. The news reached the Prophet early in the morning and he then sent men in their pursuit and they were captured and brought at noon. He then ordered to cut their hands and feet, and it was done, and their eyes were branded with heated pieces of iron, they were put in a hot cabin and when they asked for water, no water was given to them.[484]

Among the many corrupt cultures Bukhari promoted in his "authentic" book is the culture of jihad and unconditional love Muslims should have for death. He reported:

> Prophet Mohammad was asked about "the best deed" in life, and he replied saying, "To offer the prayers at their early stated fixed times." I asked, "What is next in goodness?" He replied, "To be good and dutiful to your parents." I further asked, "what is next in goodness?" He replied, "To participate in Jihad in Allah's Cause." And "Paradise is under the shades of swords."[485]

Hatred for this world is planted in the hearts of young Muslims by teachings such as:

> A single endeavor of fighting in Allah's Cause in the forenoon or in the afternoon is better than the entire world and whatever is in it.[486]
>
> I would certainly never remain behind any Sariya' [army unit] setting out in Allah's Cause. By God! I would love to be martyred in Allah's Cause and then get resurrected and then get martyred, and then get resurrected again and then get martyred and then get resurrected again and then get martyred.[487]

The fear of hellfire is engraved in the hearts of Muslims from a very young age, and they are forced to grow up looking for what guarantees them entry into paradise. Twelve centuries ago, Bukhari used his social and politically backed status to attract vulnerable youth to himself by guaranteeing them access to paradise should they engage in jihad. In this book, he said: "Allah's Apostle said, 'Anyone whose both feet get covered with the dust of Jihad will not be touched by hell fire.'"[488] Such comforting statements from revered grand Islamic jurists act as a guarantee of entry to paradise. Once Bukhari had established a love for death, it became the duty of Islamic clerics to instill the attraction of the afterlife in the minds of the mosque congregation; a topic that inevitably leads to a discussion of jihad as it is the quickest path to paradise.

My Islamic studies teachers used to give validity to the myth of the beautiful virgins awaiting jihadis in paradise by linking it to the Prophet Mohammad. They taught us:

> The Prophet said, "A single endeavor of fighting in Allah's Cause in the afternoon or in the forenoon is better than the entire world and whatever is in it. A place in Paradise as small as the bow or lash of one of you is better than the entire world and whatever is in it. And if a *houri**from Paradise appeared to the people of the earth, she would fill the space between Heaven and the Earth with light and pleasant scent and her head cover is better than the entire world and whatever is in it."[489]

This aspect of Bukhari's writing, which Islamic scholars commonly preach, is a myth prepared to impress and brainwash sexually deprived individuals for political gain. <u>This was also a tactic I once used to create the much-needed vibe and appropriate atmosphere for the spread of Islamism.</u>

The myth of the 72 virgins in paradise is an example of the heavenly promises made to Muslim youth that drive them to blow themselves up in suicide attacks as a shortcut to paradise. Bukhari not only promoted this idea, while knowing very well that it would pave the way for uneducated radicals to believe in an imaginary shortcut to paradise, but also fabricated reports about his own Prophet. There is no evidence linking those claims directly to Prophet Mohammad, yet they were taught to us and we taught them to our congregations. The theory of God rewarding good deeds with women is both morally and logically unacceptable. God cannot reward good deeds with women, because women are not objects.

Our early Islamist scholars, including Imam Bukhari, were simply politicians wearing the dress code of science and religion, who were glorified by the Islamic rulers of that time for their abundant services to

---

* An individual member of the virgins in paradise is referred to as a "houri" or "houriya."

them. They did not hold any regard for any prophet nor religion, and strived to introduce violence in the name of religion. They promised Muslims divine rewards in the hereafter so that the kings could utilize Muslim youth to oppress and massacre people under the umbrella of Sharia Law, a concept originally containing only the laws about praying and fasting.

Just like Bukhari, many of Islam's greatest scholars only became great because their words were deemed sacred, leaving no room for objections and being completely protected by Islamic governments. The religion of Islam only being 200 years old at the time, it was easy for revered scholars to introduce concepts they saw as "fit and beneficial for the Muslim nation." Today, this deception continues, as our Islamic seminaries teach us that it is permissible to lie for the benefit of the religion.

Jihad as a Doctrine

Whether it was defined as war or self-defense, militant jihad existed in the early years of Islam. However, it was a chapter in Islam's history that could have evolved or ended with the advancement of society and passing of time, as there was no actual "doctrine of jihad." The practice of jihad depended on the orders of Islamic army leaders, not religious scripture, and the passages about war in the Quran can be interpreted in many ways. One of the prominent interpretations is that the passages about war and self-defense are limited to a time and place and are not absolute verses that are to be applied at all times and in every place. Therefore, they reflect the historical development of Islam, and do not order war against non-Muslims until the end of time. The words "fight the disbelievers" can been interpreted as referring to the Meccans who plotted to kill Prophet Mohammad, not to all those who don't believe in Islam.

Sahih al-Bukhari was the first book to include an entire chapter on jihad, introducing it as a doctrine that must be considered an essential part of one's faith. Once Bukhari had compiled the history of terrorism and Islamic invasions during the early caliphates of Islam, he then introduced the concept of jihad against non-Muslims in the form of actual scripture. He needed to do this because the jihad mentioned in the Quran can be interpreted based on the reason for the revelation of the verses, which only refer to a specific time and place. In contrast, *Sahih al-Bukhari* is a set of absolute and sacred teachings that do not fall within the boundaries of time and place; and can in fact be applied at any time or place on planet Earth. This expanded and strengthened the power and control of Islamic governments over both Muslims and non-Muslims. It also means that many Muslims who form armies to defend Imam Bukhari and Islamic governments are now victims of the violent Sharia Law that he introduced. Violent aspects of Sharia Law such as beheadings can also be applied to Muslims who disobey a ruler.

Stoning, a Monkey Practice

Bukhari, along with every other Islamic cleric at that time, knew very well that stoning was a practice of the ignorant ages of Arabia, and that it was not mentioned in the Quran. But the governing Islamic bodies fabricated the law of stoning and attributed it to Amr bin Maimun, one of the companions of Prophet Mohammad, claiming that he said: "He saw a she-monkey surrounded by a number of monkeys. They were all stoning it, because it had committed illegal sexual intercourse. I too, stoned it along with them."[490] By this fabricated teaching about monkeys, stoning became an Islamic concept for Islamic governments to implement, and this continues in the twenty-first century. Even today, Bukhari's loyal followers and faithful believers in his book become extremely offended when the authenticity of the "authentic" Bukhari is questioned. Perhaps it has now become clear why these disturbing beliefs were not translated into English and made available for the non-Muslim world to read. All you need to do today is visit an official website of *Sahih Bukhari* (such as www.Sahih-Bukhari.com) and search for the word: Monkey.

Tackling the Jihadi Ideology ("Jihadi-ology")

There is no doubt that the violent confrontation between Islamic radicalism and the rest of the world has been one of the defining features of the first decade of the twenty-first century. The wars in the Middle East and a series of modern-day terrorist attacks have shown how the resurgence of Islamic fundamentalism has fostered the belief that a religious war against the infidels is an obligation. Jihad means "to strive" or "to struggle" in Arabic. However, the term has a dual religious connotation, involving an outwardly directed struggle against oppression and tyranny, and an inwardly directed personal struggle for holiness. When discussing religious jihad in the West, we are certainly not discussing the "inner struggle" of a human being, as there is nothing that calls for such a struggle in the West. The jihad being discussed on a political and social level has always been the struggle against non-Muslims. Furthermore, all Islamic scriptures that discuss jihad do so in a violent way. The books that discuss the inner struggle of one's self are books about ethics, which have been published by regular scholars since the twentieth century.

There are two main forces that have worked to spread Islamic fundamentalism around the globe. One is grassroots, a non-governmental effort, and the other is sponsored by Islamic governments, mainly the governments of Saudi Arabia and Iran.

The Islamic obligation of jihad, if taken seriously, is no less of a religious imperative than the other five pillars of obligatory worship in Islam. In the case of an "infidel occupation," it becomes a de facto sixth pillar: a Muslim who does not perform it will go to hell. What needs to be understood is that such a philosophy ascribing significance to the duty of jihad is not an innovation of twenty-first century radical Islam. Seventh-century Islamic sects took this position and implemented it, even though moderate Muslims rejected this doctrine as a heresy. It is true that the overwhelming majority of Muslims reject terrorism and the jihadists' call for a war on the West, and that they view jihadist or radical Islamist beliefs as a perversion of Islam. But in reality, they are not a perversion of Islam, and they actually come from the very heart of the seventh century when the first Islamic caliphates were established by the fathers-in-law of Prophet Mohammad.

Islamic states prosper through jihad as it boosts their leadership status and, in some cases, expands their territories. The western attacks on Islamic governments have given birth to jihadists who rose to emulate their seventh-century heroes and sacred icons. These consequences show that attacks on terrorist elements throughout the Middle East have not been entirely successful, as the facts show that the present terrorist crisis is connected to radical Islamic movements within the region. As the crimes of ISIS become more extreme, more governments of Muslim countries and more citizens in the Islamic world are beginning to oppose them. However, they are not always working together to counter the threat. During a live interview in 2017 with *Sunrise* on Channel 7, I stated that our governments are mistaken to think that a healthy relationship with Muslim communities can prevent a lone wolf attack. Befriending communities is one thing, while having control over the spread of a radical ideology is another.

At present, organizations such as the Muslim Brotherhood and Hizb ut Tahrir exist in more than 70 nations in the world, including western nations such as the UK, USA, and Australia, despite the fact that they have been banned in Muslim countries such as Iran and Saudi Arabia. These Islamist organizations aim to establish a global caliphate, or a global government of Islamic jurists. The only way this could be achieved is if the Muslim masses were gradually brought back to fundamentalist Islam, which was indeed mainstream Islam during the eighth century. These extremist organizations disguise themselves as peaceful organizations by caring for orphans, helping war-torn countries, preaching generosity, family, and social values, while preventing women from receiving an education and restricting them to their traditional role as cooks and cleaners in their homes.

Islamic governments operate based on Sharia Law, believing that it is the rule of God, and every Islamic government has a designated budget to spread Sharia Law. Proven oil reserves in Iran make it the fourth largest oil-producing nation in the world. Iran, along with Saudi Arabia, which is home to one-fourth of the world's known oil reserves, produces great wealth. Saudi Arabia spent nearly three centuries funding a hardline Sunni Islamic ideology (Wahhabism), while Iran has been central to creating, arming, and financing numerous radical Islamist groups and militias such as Hizbullah.

Western and other non-Islamic nations need to understand that they must change their approach to tackling modern Islamic terrorism. Powerful Islamic state-backed organizations and individuals operating within their societies as social and charitable groups cannot be tolerated. These organizations preach a radical, fundamentalist, and extremist ideology, and have, without a doubt, gained influence over members of parliaments and universities – either through ideology or funding – so that they can enjoy the benefits of being able to operate both on land and through satellite channels. They cannot be tackled through public relations alone, with governments hoping to "befriend" the radical or hoping their citizens will try to understand where extremists are coming from. What citizens expect from the politicians they elect is an absolute crackdown on jihadi mosques and a complete ban on extremist preachers entering the country, and these demands are yet to be fulfilled.

Both state and federal governments in the West should closely monitor mosques within their jurisdictions, and carefully examine all new proposals for the establishment of new Islamic centers. Moderate and peaceful Muslims should be championed and given a platform along with protection, so that they can confront the extreme Islamist ideologies and prevent radicals from operating.

It must also be kept in mind that "Islamic extremism" is an actual belief system. It cannot be treated as an opinion or a theory. Extremist Muslims do not consider themselves to be extremists, rather devout Muslims who expect all Muslims to be exactly like them. De-radicalizing an extremist Muslim is a form of conversion into another belief system. There is a big difference between "the duty to kill the non-believer" and "the duty to respect human life regardless of their beliefs." Progress begins when an extremist is initially convinced that he or she is an extremist, and then shown a different path.

The One Islamic Nation

Islam teaches that Muslims are all brothers and sisters in faith, and that which affects a group of Muslims should affect the entire Islamic population. There are numerous Islamic teachings that describe this concept. One of them is verse 23:52 of the Holy Quran, which states, "And surely this nation of yours is one nation, and I am your Lord." Prophet Mohammad also taught that: "All Muslims are like one body, if one limb is affected, everyone is affected."[491] Such divine and prophetic teachings have introduced the concept and belief in the "one Islamic nation."

These teachings were initially intended to strengthen the Muslim nation, to create a spiritual bond between all Muslims and a religious obligation to protect the lives and interests of one another. However, due to the mixing of political and regional interests with Islamic governance, Muslims have been victims of each other. Muslim nations have been attacking each other since the early Islamic caliphates, each of them claiming to be the true Islamic nation, while labelling their opponents the enemies of God. This divide in the Muslim nation has resulted in many sects within the religion. While the majority of Muslims do believe in the one Islamic nation, many of them do not engage in activities to promote or strengthen it.

A clear example of this in modern times is the Israeli–Palestinian conflict, whereby the Palestinian authorities and "freedom fighters" expect the rest of the Muslims around the world to join them in the war against Israel; while their call has been pretty much ignored. Some Islamic leaders refuse to refer to the conflict as the "Palestinian–Israeli" or "Arab–Israeli" conflict, and refer to it as the "Muslim–Israeli" conflict instead. However, Muslim governments around the world treat the conflict as Palestinian–Israeli only, and sometimes even side with Israel against the Muslims of Palestine. Therefore, the concept of the one Islamic nation no longer has the weight and value it once had during the times of the Islamic conquests.

Within nations where Muslims are a minority, and particularly amongst the fundamentalist and Wahhabi groups, the belief in the one

Islamic nation plays a key and essential role in their daily lives. They depend on the concept of the one Islamic nation in order to recruit members into their circles, which brings us to the issue of Islamic terrorism in non-Islamic countries.

Fundamentalist Muslims living in the West have two citizenships, the citizenship of the country they live in, which is a physical legal document, along with a religious "citizenship" making them a member of the one Islamic nation, which is an obligation engraved within their very beings. Therefore, if an Islamic authority sitting in Mecca issues a fatwa of war against non-believers, a young Muslim man living in London will ram a truck into the "non-believing" public, or if Muslims in Syria are attacked by non-Muslim forces, a Muslim living in the USA will conduct a terrorist attack as a form of retaliation; both believing that they are serving the cause of God in protecting the one Islamic nation. Thus, in reality, Islamic terrorist attacks are not a wave of a special kind of mental illness; it is simply their allegiance.

Islamic Extremists are Equal to Dangerous Gangs

It is important that laws apply equally to all radical groups. Many of the laws which apply to motorcycle gangs should apply to radical Islamic groups and organizations. The foundations of their respective views mean that such an alliance in some ways is a natural one. Both groups share the same view that legal authorities are tyrants that need to be brought down. Both outlaw gang members and radical Islamists believe that their version of justice and governance should be established upon the land. The initial contact between these groups, it seems, is forged in prisons.

Both radical Islamists and motorcycle gang members largely come from a common economically and socially depressed environment. In both cases, radical Muslims and motorcycle gangs use their numbers to inflict terror upon their opponents. They also use their numbers to send an intimidating message to any would-be opponents and the media. Each group has their own recognizable uniform: for the gangs it is their colors, and for radical Muslims traditional Middle Eastern clothing and long, messy beards.

Motorcycle gangs provide radicals with an ally from the mainstream western community, and radical Islamists are a potential source of money and weapons from the radicals' home countries. As only a small percentage of containers entering ports can be carefully searched, it is difficult to cut off the supply of brand-new weapons. Weapons that have been fired may be detected by trained sniffer dogs, whereas new weapons are simply pieces of metal. This is alongside the fact that large sums of cash are regularly detected in the process of being sent to foreign destinations. The gangs and radicals present a potentially unholy two-way trade. Some countries under sanctions would then be in receipt of western currency. In return, if there is one thing not in short supply within these countries it is weapons.

One assumes that imprisoning radical Islamists would safely isolate them from the mainstream community. While imprisoning them is certainly a necessary legal sanction, there is a terrible flaw in this idea. In fact, imprisoning them within regular jails opens a new set of problems. During my 2016 meeting with the Australian intelligence services, I informed them that non-radicals are being exposed to radicalization by this particular subset of prisoners. One of the tactics outside radicals use to bring the extremist ideology into prison is using misleading book covers. The books they bring into prison may appear to be harmless books, but the content is all about jihad. There are prisoners who enter the prison system as thieves, thugs, and fraudsters, and emerge as Islamic radicals looking for an opportunity to vent their frustrations upon society at large, while believing that they are doing God's work and will be rewarded for it in paradise. These radical groups provide a sense of belonging and meaning to persons living marginalized lives.

In this regard, an important question worth asking is: who are the Islamic clerics visiting our prisons? One would hope that the majority of these clerics are moderate and integrated individuals. However, how can we be certain that there are not a number of radical clerics using their privilege of access to prisoners to promote their extreme views?

Investigative journalism reports show that violent and dangerous inmates are trying to force other prisoners in some of Australia's worst prisons to convert to Islam against their will, in a practice now known as "jailhouse jihad."[492] These groups need to be treated as the special category of criminals that they are. The solution must include association laws to prevent them gathering in groups, and they must be completely separated from all other categories of prisoners when they are inside the correctional system. Only imams with a proven social record of moderation and indeed patriotism should be allowed to engage with them as spiritual advisors.

Radicalizing the Vulnerable

Radical Muslims are now looking at yet another highly marginalized and vulnerable part of some western communities, the indigenous people. The increasing number of indigenous people identifying on the census as Muslim, is a clear indication that there are inroads being made into this community. I believe in freedom of religion; however, we as Muslim imams need to make sure, that if Islam grows, it grows in a direction compatible with humanity, democracy, and good values. At present, there are no credible sources to state whether those proselytizing are radicals or moderates, but this is a matter that I believe needs closer examination. In recent times, it has been reported that Australian Indigenous celebrity and boxing champion Anthony Mundine appeared on social media supporting the Sharia Law concept of beating wives.[493] This is highly troubling considering the unfortunate levels of domestic violence within the Indigenous community.

Misguided Moderate Muslims

The mind set of misguided "moderate" Muslims is made up of two major factors: Islamic traditions and ethnic cultures. Islamic traditions teach principles and discipline, while ethnic cultures teach what is accepted within the society that Muslims were raised in. This does not necessarily mean that Islamic traditions and ethnic cultures do not clash. In fact, they clash very often, which can be demonstrated by the fact that there are twenty-two Arab nations in the same broad geographic area today; however, in the early years of Islam, these countries were all united under one caliphate, forming a large Islamic empire. The main reason that this tradition did not continue was the traditionally clashing regional cultures within the caliphate, and it is indeed true that these differences may still be seen today. In some states, such as Saudi Arabia, beheading and chopping off hands is taught by the violent version of Sharia Law, whereas in Kuwait this would be considered horrific behaviour.

In the light of this history, it may be understandable why some moderates feel that they must not criticize other Muslims, irrespective of which Middle Eastern cultural tradition they come from. This belief has hindered moderate Muslims in their opposition to radical Muslims, and limited their ability to reclaim their Abrahamic religion from the extremists. We see a lack of condemnation of radicals by Islamic scholars and community leaders, which raises many questions about why Muslims are not speaking out against the corruption encircling their religion.

I must add that, from amongst the Muslims living in the West whose mentality has been somewhat influenced by their traditions which promote that westerners are infidels, it becomes very difficult for them to rise against fellow Muslims, since they fear that it could strengthen the cause of the infidel. The terrible trap that these people have fallen into as a result of this attitude has meant that the small minority of violent extremists can operate with minimal criticism, knowing that there are misguided politicians fighting for their radical agenda to have a platform under the principle of freedom of speech in a democratic society. This thinking by some politicians is fatally flawed because radicals don't believe in democracy.

On the other hand, the mind set of radical Muslims focuses on what they believe is God's expectation from them. Radical Muslims believe their main land is Islamic land, and that their presence in the non-

Islamic land of disbelief is merely a test from God, and confers a greater responsibility upon their shoulders to spread their faith and ideology. This agenda justifies their long-standing presence within the land of the "infidels." This understanding is of course only a result of wrong teachings, such as the belief that children who are born in non-Islamic lands are not blessed, or that they will grow up to be deviants. A true follower of God would know that all land belongs to God and geographic borders do not make the citizens of one nation worse or better than another. The total rejection of western democracy and people of the West is taught to Muslim radicals from a very young age. They are taught that "we are not like them." As a man of religion, I do not support their position.

In the current time, it is safe to say that the great majority of Muslims in the world have no desire to join a jihad or to politicize their religion. However, in many Islamic countries where migrants to the West come from, the radical ideology does not represent a marginal and extremist perversion of Islam but rather an increasingly mainstream interpretation. Friday prayer sermons which are broadcast weekly from Mecca and Tehran cannot be easily distinguished from those of ISIS or Al-Qaeda.

Consequently, even when pressure is put on Muslim communities after a terrorist attack, there exists a political asymmetry in favor of the radicals. Many moderate Muslim imams who engage in interfaith events in the West and cooperate with the police become somewhat reluctant to condemn radical imams as they risk being accused of apostasy and "siding with the infidel." Thus, they lose ground to radicals in their societies.

CHAPTER 11

The Fatwa Disaster

Another ongoing tragedy within Islam is the continuing series of bizarre fatwas and religious rulings issued by senior Islamic authorities. You might have heard of a number of strange or ridiculous verdicts in the past, such as men being allowed to eat their wives in case of severe hunger or having sex with them immediately after their death.[494] Here however, I wish to present to you several fatwas which I were taught by my teachers, as well as those that were circulated within the mosques I previously attended.

Eating a Rock Melon

My Islamic ethics teacher informed me that the early scholars of Islam were great and honorable people who had many notable merits and virtues. Our books report that Ahmad Bin Hanbal, the founder of one of Islam's greatest schools of thought, was revered due to him following the very footsteps of Prophet Mohammad, to the point that he did not eat rock melons because he did not know how Prophet Mohammad used to eat them. He conducted an investigation into the books of Islamic history in pursuit of the true and accurate way Prophet Mohammad consumed rock melons, but failed to find any historical reports on the issue. Therefore, he refrained from eating rock melons.[495]

Foolish matters like this are what is used to create the basis for a fundamentalist ideology that revolves around strictly following the footsteps of the Prophet and his companions. I personally found this hypocritical as all Islamic clerics have tasted modern dishes such as pizza, pasta and maybe a hot dog, none of which were consumed by Prophet Mohammad. Also, it also appeared to me that, according to such an extremist view of the world, every fruit and vegetable needs to be accompanied by a manual on how to eat it, because it seemed to me that eating a rock melon is a highly sophisticated task in need of philosophical reasoning and historical analysis.

Mickey Mouse Must Die!

In 2008, Sheikh Muhammad Munajid, a renowned Saudi Arabian scholar and founder of the world's most popular Islamic website (IslamQA.info) issued an Islamic fatwa on LIVE TV saying, "mice are one of Satan's soldiers." He then went on to say, "For children they've become something great and beloved. Like this Mickey Mouse, who is seen as a great figure, even though under Islamic law Mickey Mouse should be killed."[496] He later clarified that his fatwa was against all mice and not specifically against Mickey Mouse.

Gifting Roses is Illegal

In 2012, Imam Kheld Abdul Alim issued a fatwa ruling that it was not permissible for Muslims to gift flowers or roses to each other during happy events or illness, because it is an act widely performed by the non-believers; and doing so makes Muslims similar to non-believers.[497]

Beware of the Fly!

On matters concerning purity before engaging in acts of worship, we were taught to perform a washing ritual known as *Wudhu*, or ablution. Certain acts make this state of purity void, such as purposely touching a strange woman. I burst out laughing when my teacher taught that, "If a fly (or any other insect) was to fly and enter into the anus and comes out with no injury, your purity will not be void."[498]

Sharia Law and the Laws of Sex

Masturbate Using a Cucumber

My Islamic studies teacher, Imam Omran, taught us in the private Australian Islamic College, that one of the main books of Islamic jurisprudence explains: "In a situation where a woman is far away from her husband, she is able to masturbate by using a cucumber or anything similar."[499] On the other hand, there are rulings banning women from going anywhere near bananas or cucumbers to "avoid sexual thoughts," and pronouncing that they must chop them into pieces before consuming them.[500]

The Banana, Cucumber and Carrot

In our jurisprudential studies, we were taught that it is the ruling of our highly revered and prominent scholars that women are not allowed to touch or handle bananas, cucumbers, carrots, or any other penis-shaped fruit or vegetable because their phallic shape may make them think of sex.

One fundamentalist Islamist cleric said: "If women wish to eat these food items, a third party, preferably a male related to them such as a father or husband, should cut the items into small pieces and serve."[501] Another fundamentalist cleric living in Europe added eggplants to the list, because "they resembled male genitalia."[502]

Mannequins to Wear Burqas

When ISIS took over parts of Iraq and Syria, they enforced Sharia Law completely, including the law which "forbids statues or artwork depicting the human form." Middle East news agencies reported that "Mosul shop keepers say they've been instructed to drape the heads of not only their female mannequins but also their male mannequins in black cloth."[503]

Sex with Sheep

A book of Islamic law issued by a senior committee member at Al-Azhar, Islam's most prestigious university, teaches:

> If a man penetrated a sheep and impregnated it, causing the sheep to give birth to a human being. In a case where the baby was to grow older and learn his Islamic duties, and then was to lead the prayers for the Muslims, and then be slaughtered as a feast sacrifice, it is allowed for the Muslims to do so. Simply because the son is like his mother in decree, and because it is correct to sacrifice his sheep mother, it is correct to sacrifice the son.[504]

Young, Intentionally, and Forcefully

One of Islam's most revered scholars, Al-Nawawi, reports:

> If the penile head has penetrated a woman's anus, or a man's anus, or an animal's vagina or its anus, then it is necessary to wash [yourself]; whether the one being penetrated is alive or dead, young or old, whether it was done intentionally or absentmindedly, and whether it was done willfully or forcefully.[505]

As long as you wash afterwards …

Suppose You Cut Your Penis in Half …

During 2006, my teacher in Islamic jurisprudence taught us a book which contained the rulings and ethics of sex in Islam. The book is authored by prominent Islamic jurist Al-Shafi'i and it states:

> If a man cuts his penis in half and enters half of it into one of his wives and the other half into another one of his wives, a *Ghusl* [religious bathing ritual after sex] will become obligatory on him,

but not on his two wives. However, if he enters half of it into the wife's vagina and half of it into her anus, the bath will become obligatory for both of them.[506]

The Criteria of a Good Cleric

When studying the books of one of Islam's prominent scholars of jurisprudence, Al-Hanafi, I stumbled upon a fatwa he issued regarding the laws and characteristics of clerics leading congregational prayers. He said if we were to choose between two clerics to lead congregational prayers, we must choose the one with the best voice for recitation,

> the one whose wife is more beautiful, then the one who has more money, then the one who has more possessions, then the one whose clothes are cleaner, then the one whose head is larger and his penis is smaller.[507]

Violent Sharia Law Allows Incest

One of the most important Sharia Law books that was taught to us was Al-Muhalla, and it preached that:

> There is no limit for the one who marries his mother that gave birth to him, and his daughter, and his sister, and his grandmother, and his father's sister [aunt on the father's side], and his mother's sister [aunt on the mother's side], and the daughter of his brother, and the daughter of his sister, when knowing their relativity with him, and knowing their prohibition from him, and [the prohibition] of having sexual intercourse with them.[508]

Sex with Minors

We received extensive lessons on the laws of marriage, which also included laws on child brides. I present to you a sample of the texts we were taught:

- Islamic scholar al-Shirbīniy ruled: "It is permissible to have sexual intercourse with the girl even if she is a baby that is incapable of sexual intercourse."[509]

- Ibn Abidin, a prominent Islamic scholar and jurist wrote a special and central reference for Islamic law that was delivered to Muslim scholars alone, not the general Muslim public, and in it he ruled: "It [sex with babies] does not depend on age, because the thick and fat baby can bear intercourse, even if she is at a minor age."[510] The following is a scanned image from the original book, indicating that it is a "Special Print".

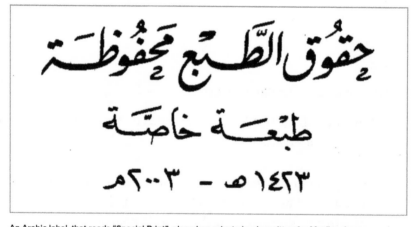

An Arabic label, that reads "Special Print", placed on private books written for Muslim clergymen alone.

- Prominent Islamic scholar Al-Nawawi ruled: "As for sleeping with a minor-aged wife and having intercourse with her, if the husband and the guardian of the wife [father or brother] agree that it is not harmful for her, then it is legitimate."[511]

- In one of the commentaries on *Sahih al-Bukhari*, we were taught:

"Marriage of a minor age from an adult is allowed, there is consensus of scholars on this, even if she was in her cradle. However, the husband should not sleep with her until she can bear it."[512]

- Another book of Islamic law taught to us was *Badā'I al-Fawā'id (Amazing Points of Benefit)*, written by Ibn Qayyim, a revered Islamic jurist and theologian, that said: "If a man has a 'slave girl,' whether be it a girl or a little child, he can masturbate using her hands; and if she was a non-believer, he can have intercourse with her in other than her vagina."[513]

My Shia Islamist teachers were no better either. During my studies in Iran, we were taught the books of Imam Khomeini in Al-Mustafa International University – one of the many reasons that caused me to withdraw from the university, alongside its attempts to groom us into militant Islamists. In our main book of *Fiqh* (Islamic jurisprudence), we were taught:

It is not permissible to sexually penetrate the wife before the age of nine, whether it be permanent or temporary marriage. As for all other pleasures, such as touching and hugging with lust or "thighing" [having sex with the thighs] – there is no problem with that, even if the girl was an infant.[514]

In more recent times however, these mullahs have advanced in their foolishness. The following are an example of what some Islamic jurists spend their long hours discussing before issuing a religious verdict for all Muslims to follow.

Sexual Jihad

The Arabic term jihad al-nikah describes an evident phenomenon of extremist Muslim women traveling to the Middle East in order to provide comfort as well as sexual favors for jihadists. These hardline women consider such practice a legitimate complement to holy war, and that God will reward them greatly in the hereafter.

During a national security address to members of the National Constituent Assembly, Tunisian magistrate and Interior Minister Lofti Ben Jeddou said that these women "have sexual relations with 20, 30, 100" militants, and that "After the sexual liaisons they have there in the name of 'Sexual Jihad' they come home pregnant."[515]

Women Can't Sit on Chairs

Islamic extremists have banned women from sitting on chairs or sleeping beside walls, simply because the Arabic words "chair" and "wall" are masculine, and should be treated like strange men.[516] The "reason" behind this is that "it is believed that evil male spirits penetrate the woman" without her knowing.[517]

On the same note, female Islamic scholar Um Anas (الداعية أم أنس) released a fatwa stating that there was no difference between sitting on a chair and committing the great sin of adultery.[518] In recent times, reports from the Middle East have shown prominent signs saying, "It is absolutely forbidden for women to sit on the chairs, according to the instructions of the authorities."[519]

Bestiality

Islamic scholar al-Marghinani, author of *The Guidance*, one of the most influential compendia of Islamic jurisprudence, ruled that: "Whoever performs sexual intercourse with an animal, there is no punishment for him."[520]

And the list of outrageous fatwas goes on ... from other sexual fatwas which cannot be included in this book, to fatwas that prohibit men from wearing jeans, advertising for beauty salons as well as cutting off the hand of a taxi driver to cutting off his head if he charges more than the Islamic government allows.[521]

Indeed, we have reached a stage in Islam where backward thinking is considered a virtue.

CHAPTER 12

Our Reform Delusion

Throughout the centuries, Islamic fundamentalist scholars have exhorted maximum effort to maintain the "true Islamic teachings." These teachings include the violent Sharia Law which orders Muslims to kill non-Muslims and classifies them as hypocrites, pagans, disbelievers, and even infidels. Islamic fundamentalist scholars have always relied upon religious and devout Muslims to defend the religion and, in the majority of cases, these devout Muslims are educated in the fundamentalist teachings of Islam and Sharia, and hence radicalized.

Islamic reformation is one of the greatest threats to Muslim fundamentalists. With the world discovering the violent teachings of scriptures considered sacred by the majority of Muslims, they have become aware of the threat that comes with Islamic fundamentalism.

Although the thought that many around the world consider me one of the leading faces of Islamic reform is indeed humbling, the truth is that Islam, as a whole, shall not undergo reformation in the foreseeable future. However, I sincerely believe that Muslim individuals may be reformed, or that we may see a reformation within the Muslim communities throughout the West.

The Road to Real Reform

The notion of Islamic reform provides hope for future generations. It promises much safer societies, particularly in non-Muslim countries, which is why we must treat Islamic reform as a concept, not a theory. Realistically speaking, a complete reformation of Islam will not happen – at least within the twenty-first century – which means there must be other steps towards reform that can be taken to pave the way for a reformation in the coming centuries. And in my opinion, the most realistic approach would be to target the ideology of Islamic communities living in the West, in order to produce a reformed Muslim community in as many countries as possible. This would be a fruitful method, as the key element required for a reformation is freedom of speech, which is mainly found in the West.

Reformed Muslim communities within cities that influence the world, such as Washington, DC, New York, Sydney, and London create a new field for both discussion and belief, by challenging the current paradigm which politicians have gotten used to and benefited from. Having said that, I believe in reforming Muslim individuals and groups, as opposed to trying to reform the corrupt clerical system that governs a school of thought inherited from rotten allies in Iran or Pakistan.

A closer look at every counter-terrorism organization or democracy forum led by Muslims willing to reform Islam proves that Islamic reform is nowhere near being achieved in our current century. It is not only an uphill battle, but it is a battle that requires strategy, timing, and accuracy – because Islamic extremists may be foolish enough to blow themselves up for 72 mythical virgins, but they are very intelligent in their calculations and recruitments that lead them to such an abominable crime.

What's Stopping an Islamic Reformation?

The Calculated Plan

In order to prevent true Islamic reformation, Islamic fundamentalists have introduced a new group of people to act as reformers. However, they are not true reformers and neither have they reformed anything in the past. They are a front to spread Islamic fundamentalism through a very calculated and strategic plan. To begin with, these "reformers" don't dress in the same style as Islamic radicals. They dress in suits and ties; however, their ideology is that of the extremist supporter of ISIS. They do not face any threat from radical Islamists and lead a very normal life. A true reformer, on the other hand, lives under constant threat and needs protection. I have had the experience several times now of reaching out to "reformers" to later discover that they have been trying covertly to neutralize my message. Publicly they are silent or offer only muted criticism of my work, while privately they desperately lobby politicians and media not to engage with me. My suspicions of their true motives and allegiances are growing.

A leaked video from 1989 showed American Muslim activist Sharifa Al-Khateeb stating:

> Education is one of the most important areas that Muslims have to address, and while our final objective is not just to become part of the system that we experience now and that we see, our final objective is to create our own Islamic systems and not only create Islamic systems for Muslims, but to look at all the other people who are sharing this country with us as potential Muslims. And if we look at them as potential Muslims, and feel that we have the obligation which Allah has told us to try and bring them into the same style of thinking, way of behaving and objectives that we have, then we have to have some way that we can communicate with them and some way that we can work with them. And in that long-range process, of making America Muslim, all of America Muslims, then we have to have some actual short-range goals. We have to have some way of dealing with them, and know how we are going to deal with them, and in which ways, and be very calculated about it, or else we will not accomplish our goals.[522]

Years after Sharifa Al-Khateeb delivered this speech, in September 2004, she received the Community Service Award from the Islamic Society of North America, making her the first woman ever to receive the honor. During her life, she worked as a diversity consultant with Fairfax County Public Schools, was managing editor of the *American Journal of Islamic Social Sciences*, and co-wrote *Arab World Studies Notebook*, which is used throughout the American public-school system in the United

States. She was also the president of the Muslim Education Council and founded the North American Council for Muslim Women (NACMW). Al-Khateeb was also elected to participate in the Fourth World Conference on Women convened by the United Nations in Beijing, China. In conjunction with the Department of Justice, she established the Peaceful Families Project and became the Muslim Team Leader for the Community Resilience Project, funded by the Federal Emergency Management Agency.

It is indeed safe to say that, since 1989, the Muslim community of America and Sharifa Al-Khateeb have progressed in their goal of making the whole of America Muslim. They have infiltrated government departments and received funding for their Islamist missions. It is also without doubt that this seed is still growing, and radical Islamists are joining the United States Armed Forces, while posing as reformers to attract more people towards fundamentalist Islam. These agendas can be seen in books which call for the revival and restoration of "the soul of Islam," which without a doubt includes all forms of Sharia Law, instead of calling for a complete ban on what was appropriate 1400 years ago. Any "reformer" who does not call for a total rejection of extremist Islamic teachings is either ignorant of this problem and is therefore irrelevant, or they are the knowing covert supporters, or unwitting dupes, of radicals.

Fake Islamic Reformers

A fake reformer refuses to condemn terrorist figures and oppressive tyrant caliphs who transformed prophetic succession into kingship, simply because they were the companions and associates of Prophet Mohammad. They hold on very dearly to the old traditions attributed to the Prophet Mohammad, and do not condemn historical Islamic figures who spread Islam by the sword and who are revered until this very day by the majority of Muslims. An undercover radical Islamist appearing to be a reformer is always offended by these statements of true reformers when they announce their rejection of certain sacred Islamic books and/or teachings. For political reasons, when reviewing history, they side with the sacred caliph against those he beheaded and massacred. This matter can be clearly seen in their rejection of any symbolism that represents those beheaded by the caliphs or, as I call them, the fathers of ISIS.

An undercover radical is always the first to attack a true reformer by accusing him/her of being divisive and sectarian, sometimes even of being an extremist. In fact, it is these accusations that are extreme and intolerant. For a true reformer, Islamic sects and denominations are irrelevant and have virtually no meaning, because a true reformer would only be concerned with the core and essence of the religion and not how many groups it consists of. A true reformer condemns the violence and extremism in all sects of Islam and does not fall into the Shia–Sunni sectarian trap. I would invite readers to take note of Muslims who have been attacking my message. Are these people merely naive, or are they in fact a front for a more sinister agenda?

"Reformers" who attack other reformers and accuse them of having affiliations with an Islamic state are in many cases themselves affiliated with a foreign Islamic agenda. Alternatively, they might see the presence of other reformers as a financial threat to their empire-building aspirations. It is also safe to say that some fake reformers receive orders from a higher Islamic authority to bring down true reformers when they come to their attention or begin to influence the masses.

A fake reformer is always prepared to point out and condemn extremism within Islamic sects other than his/her own. It is not enough for a Muslim reformer to condemn ISIS alone. A true reformer condemns the fathers of ISIS: the terrorist companions of Prophet Mohammad, who transformed prophetic succession into kingship and dynasties, and spread Islam by the sword. These are facts no educated Muslim should deny.

Reformation is "Human Made"

All Islamic denominations and schools of thought teach that the foundations of Islam are divine revelations from God, in the sense that both Prophet Mohammad and the Quran came from God as the two main pillars of God's message: God is perfect, and what comes from God is also perfect. Therefore, Islam presents itself as a perfect belief system. Reformation however, if achieved, would be a human-made concept, and human-made concepts are not divine, nor can they be considered sacred or holy. As a result of this, a complete Islamic reformation shall probably never be achieved, because Muslims will only follow what they believe are interpretations of God's law, and not what other humans present and assume could be God's law.

On the other hand, Islamic reform will be achieved through the efforts of actual Islamic scholars, and not politicians. Politicians come and go; ideologies however remain forever. A genuine reformist scholar who manages to influence a handful of Muslims could in fact be paving the way for many lives to be changed, and many others to be saved from terrorism.

Why I will Not Join the "Muslim Reform Movement"

I am one of those who believe that a genuine and professional reformist movement within Islam is long overdue. With great happiness, I came to hear about the new "Muslim Reform Movement" (MRM) in May 2017, when its key founder Mohammad Zuhdi Jasser wrote an article for *Asia Times*, saying: "If Imam Tawhidi wishes to prove his reformist bona fides, we urge him to indicate his clear support for the Muslim Reform Movement declaration."[523] This was the first time I had heard of Zuhdi Jasser and his fledgling reform movement, which was established in December 2015. Therefore, I welcomed this invitation. In February 2018, I flew from Australia to the United States and Canada, to meet with six key founders of "The Muslim Reform Movement." They are six people whom I am glad to have met throughout my journey. They showed me great hospitality and respect, and I am looking forward to working with them as individuals in the future.

While they are pure hearted and sincere reformists, there is an elephant in the room, and it's a big one. With all the funding being poured into the MRM, they are yet to present any real results. Since 2015, there has been no printed review of the Quran, and nor have they been successful in de-radicalizing a single extremist Muslim. With all of the intellectual abilities, opportunities, and public relations skills of this movement, it has failed to influence mosques and local Islamic centers, not to mention the inability to reform a single jihadi fatwa or even successfully counter it.

The Muslim Reform Movement, as an organization, still has less than 20 members, and attracts only a handful of elderly non-Muslims to their best events; with barely any involvement of the actual Muslim community. If we want to be realistic, the founders of the MRM are not getting any younger either, and most of them are at least 50 years old. This isn't a matter of age, but it definitely prompts a legitimate question: Will we see a global reformation of Islam in the next 20 years? The best answer is that it is highly unlikely.

In an interview with *The Federalist*, Zuhdi Jasser said, "We reached out through snail mail, e-mail, and telephone to over 3,000 mosques and over 500 known public American Muslims. We received only 40-plus rather dismissive responses from our outreach, and sadly less than ten of them were positive."[524] So, are all of the 3000 mosques and 500 public Muslims who ignored Jasser fundamentalist extremists? Perhaps the problem is with Jasser himself.

The Islamist Reformist

Despite serving in the US Navy, Jasser has numerous troubling facts surrounding him. The following are three of many:

1. The Council on American–Islamic Relations (CAIR) was listed as a terrorist organization by the UAE due to its ties to the Muslim Brotherhood, yet the Militant Islam Monitor has uncovered that "Zuhdi Jasser's Islamic Center of the Northeast Valley (ICNEV) has a documented history of radical associations besides CAIR (a Saudi-funded front group for Hamas) yet Jasser remained a congregant

there for over a decade and headed their Dawah (proselytization) efforts in 2003 at least until 2011."[525]

2. Zuhdi Jasser's employee and Community Outreach Coordinator, Courtney Lonergan, was a member of the Islamic Community Center of Phoenix, the mosque attended by jihadists Ibrahim (Elton) Simpson and Nadir Soofi, who were killed in 2015 by private security officers after plotting to carry out a terrorist attack using automatic rifles at the American Freedom Defense Initiative Conference in Garland, Texas. Lonergan came to know Simpson at the same extremist mosque 10 years before he tried to carry out the terrorist attack. She told the media that "Simpson would never waver from the teachings he picked up in the mosque" and that "Ibrahim would die for an ideology and to protect a faith."[526] Throughout those ten years, the FBI had paid Dabla Deng $132,000 to spy on Simpson by pretending to be his friend, and had obtained a recording of Simpson talking about travelling to the Middle East to engage in jihad.[527] Old and public activities on social media link Simpson to Islamic terrorists halfway around the world. Lonergan is still Zuhdi Jasser's assistant today.

3. In his book, *A Battle for the Soul of Islam*, Zuhdi Jasser speaks about the people who have influenced his thinking. He says, "My own Islamic ideas were influenced by a host of others in my life," moving on to say "I was able to find [imams] who nurtured my faith. In my own readings, I was influenced by such leading reform-minded Islamic thinkers," then he listed Alija Izetbegović as an influence.[528]

If you haven't heard of Izetbegovic, he was the President of the Presidency of the Republic of Bosnia and Herzegovina, and also the author of the Islamic Declaration (1990),[529] a piece of work that drips blood and promotes militant Islamism. He was immediately accused of wanting to turn Bosnia into an Islamic state[530] because he referred to the Islamic Republic of Pakistan as a "model country".[531]

Also in the declaration, this man whom Zuhdi Jasser named as an influence says, "There can be neither peace nor co-existence between the Islamic religion and non-Islamic social and political institutions" and"the Islamic movement should and can start to take over power as soon as it is morally and numerically strong enough to be able to overturn not only the existing non-Islamic government, but also to build up a new Islamic one." These quotations align with the mission of Al-Qaeda and ISIS, and if this ideology isn't the very core of militant Islamism, then what is?

Hypocrites like Zuhdi Jasser will warn you about Islamists, but will work in their interests behind your back. Through his own words, Jasser has proven that his isn't a reformist project; it is in fact an Islamist project. In a few words, he is a radical of a different flavor.

This could very well be the reason why President Donald Trump has ignored the Muslim Reform Movement's request to meet with him, and did not invite them to the Ramadhan White House Dinner, despite a State Department memo advising Trump to push for an "Islamic Reformation."[532]

Funding of the Muslim Reform Movement

Among all Muslims, one of the most damaging factors is to be funded by right-wing or Zionist donors. You can't possibly bring about reform within a Muslim community when they know that you are funded by Zionists or right-wingers. This is the exact dilemma of the founder of the Muslim Reform Movement.

I believe that a movement to reform Islam should be totally independent – or funded by moderate Muslims themselves – and not funded by political donors or promoted by Fox News, CNN, and other agenda-based organizations. This could jeopardize the cause, and deter Muslims who could be de-radicalized from the entire movement.

Political donors enjoy throwing money around to add to their list of contributions, and they really cannot be blamed for this. Mr. Jasser has managed to convince a few donors that he is the awaited savior of Islam who has sided with the US constitution, and they are none the wiser.

Despite confessing in his book that he has been influenced by

Islamist ideologies, basic research shows thousands upon thousands of dollars being pumped into Jasser's organization.[533] A *Washington Post* report revealed that a major GOP donor, Foster Friess, gave Jasser $100,000,[534] making him a "total sell-out" in the eyes of most Muslims.[535] These realities are exactly what prevents the MRM from achieving actual results amongst Muslims, and in many cases could isolate them from other reformist scholars.

Distraction or Delusion?

I would be honored to support an actual reformist movement that had clear goals and strategies to achieve them. Telling the world that "We will reform Islam" does absolutely nothing. For Islam to co-exist with the rest of humanity, we need to make sure that we drive out the extremists and Islamists from our communities, and not promote their barbaric and intolerant ideology, as the founder of the Muslim Reform Movement does.

This is only a distraction from dealing with the actual problem and eliminating it. Al-Qaeda and ISIS consider themselves reformists who are fighting for the soul of Islam, and so does Zuhdi Jasser, as he titled his book *A Battle for the Soul of Islam*. In his case, however, it is a delusion that the early stages of Islam were peaceful.

This only strengthens my argument that Islam as a religion will never be reformed. The Muslim Reform Movement in the US have reached an unprecedented low, with no actual headquarters, "reformist mosque," or congregation, and it exists only on paper. Furthermore, its founder provides the West with empty hope and, with no relevant credibility nor training, is simply selling to his donors a form of Islam which does not even exist.

***

Speaking of Islamic Reform, I am very grateful to know great and honorable Muslims whom I have met throughout my journey. Democratic governments should support and protect them, as they are leading the current movement against the militant Islamist ideology. They are: Tarek Fatah, Tahir Gora, Maajid Nawaz, Asra Nomani, Raheel and Sohail Raza, Qanta Ahmed, Salim Mansur and Hasan Mahmud. They should be acknowledged and praised for their outstanding counterterrorism efforts.

The Touch of Jesus

All that you have read up until this page is only a drop in the ocean of problems facing my religion and its adherents. I have attempted to combine what I felt was worth mentioning into one volume. The one question – or thought – which remains is: Will the majority of Muslims ever co-exist, assimilate, and integrate with the rest of humanity, or will this struggle amongst us exist forever? This of course requires realistic solutions as well as revising educational curriculums within Muslim schools and societies.

As I stated earlier, I do not believe that Islam as a religion will undergo a reformation – and while presenting my reasons for believing so, I have also expressed my belief that Muslim individuals and communities may be reformed. Though we may find many generous non-Muslims willing to support reformist movements within Islam, I believe the answer and solution to this dilemma lies with Muslims themselves. Islamic extremism is our problem to own and solve, and we cannot continue to burden other societies with our own problems.

Perhaps the answer to our problem is: Jesus the Son of Mary. I am not asking Muslims to convert to Christianity but, since we claim to love Jesus, why are we not learning from Him? The heart and center of the Quran includes an entire chapter dedicated to Jesus and his mother Mary, yet our mosques and educational institutions fail to inform us about them out of fear that Muslims might convert to Christianity. Gone are the days where beneficial information is ignored in order to preserve a particular religious agenda, yet we still deprive ourselves of the example of a man such as Jesus, while spending our valuable hours listening to the repetitive and incompetent speeches of paid scholars.

The Quran teaches that Muslims must love all men sent by God and not to differentiate between any of them.[536] Thus, I ask my co-religionists: How much do you know about Jesus, the one you claim to love? The values taught by Christianity are part of the building block of western society and, in order for us to peacefully and successfully live together, it is essential that all migrants understand the values and foundations of western civilization.

Armah, the Christian King of the Kingdom of Axum (now Ethiopia) was the first to welcome Muslim refugees in the year 615, after Mohammad ordered his family and followers to flee the persecution of Meccans and to seek refuge in his kingdom. When King Armah asked the first Muslims why their Prophet sent them to his kingdom, they responded, saying, "Our Prophet told us to seek refuge in your kingdom, because it is ruled by a king who oppresses nobody."[537]

Mohammad could have sent the first Muslims to China, or any other country to seek refuge therein, but he knew that a true Christian kingdom is based upon values that put humanity before politics and religious differences; an essential factor to achieving peace. This is not to say that western values are not the values of our constitutions, rather, the fundamental values of today's western societies come from both Judaism and Christianity, and they have become the universal principles that formed the basis of modern civilization.

It is important for us Muslims to accept this reality, and find a common ground with the greater Christian community. This will not end all conflicts, but will surely and gradually eliminate the tribal mentality of wanting to conquer every Christian country we set foot in. If Christians and Muslims were to achieve peace, then Jesus is the best and only possible uniting figure who is common to both religions; especially since most Muslims believe in the second coming of Jesus and consider him a savior. As for all other religious groups and atheists, the road ahead is a long one, but there remains hope in future generations.

In order to achieve peace with the Jewish people, Muslims must start by stopping the distortion of historical Jewish claims to Jerusalem, while inflaming Jewish passions. Such a politically driven attitude only creates a vicious cycle that exacerbates problematic local and international stances. We must be honest with ourselves and admit that our terrorist caliphs were the ones who invaded Palestine and built mosques above sacred Jewish sites. It is also vital for us to realize that the conflict is between Palestinians and Israelis alone, and not Israel and the entire Muslim world.

Final Statement

In this book, I have presented the theological, doctrinal, historical, and social difficulties of Islam and my co-religionists. I have presented this humble volume containing valuable information that, for a long time, had been hidden from both Muslims and non-Muslims alike, and I have opened topics the Islamic hierarchy want closed. I have tried to maintain an objective position in my constructive criticism, especially when exposing the corruptions and difficulties presented earlier.

As explained in the preface, the aim of this work is to educate and raise awareness about what is taught within the Islamic seminaries in the Middle East, as well as the evident contradictions in such religious education. My intention was to educate my readers on what the Islamist sources contain, because these are realities that many people still do not realize. I am firmly convinced that truth must be presented without recourse to insults, curses, or profanity, which is why I have completed this book with a sincere commitment to maintain a very far distance from sectarianism, bigotry, and blind allegiance to traditions; because these are matters that do nothing but dissipate the spirit of peace and harmony.

After shedding light on sensitive aspects of Islam's history and historical figures, and highlighting its problems and difficulties, I shall now move on to the second stage, and that is writing a detailed manifesto of how future Muslim generations can save themselves and the rest of humanity.

***

This book was completed in 4028 hours over the span of 575 days.
I travelled twice to the Middle East to obtain physical copies of numerous sources that are now included in this book.
Thank you for joining me in this journey.

References

To view the original sources of these references, visit:
www.ImamTawhidi.com / References.

1. Ibn Qudamah, *Sharh Lum'atul-I'tiqaad*, with commentary by Ibn Al-Uthaymeen, 1995, p. 151.

2. Ibn Qudamah, *Sharh Lum'atul-I'tiqaad*, with commentary by Ibn Fawzan, 2003, p. 252; see also pp. 247–264.

3. Al-Dhahabi, *Siyar a`lam al-nubala' (The Lives of Noble Figures)*, 1982, Vol. 10, p. 92.

4. The Holy Quran, 42:11.

5. Ibn Taymiyah, *Bayan Talbees AlJahima Fi Ta'sees Bida'uhum AlKalamiyah (Criticism of Incorporation)*, 2006, Vol. 7, pp. 197–198, 289–290.

6. Al Haythami, *Majma' al Zawa'id, Kitab-ul Ta'beer*, 2001, Vol. 7, p. 265.

7. Al-Nishapuri, *Al Mustdrak Ala al-Sahihain, Book of Tafsir*, Vol. 2, pp. 430–431.

8. *Sahih al-Bukhari*, Beirut, Lebanon: Dar Al-Kotob Al-Ilmiyah, 2014, Book 10, Hadith 201; *Sahih Muslim*, Book 1, Hadith 358.

9. *Sahih al-Bukhari*, Book 80, Hadith 18;*Sahih Muslim*, Book 6, Hadith 201.

10. Ibn Taymiyah,*Minhaj Al-Sunnah Al-Nabawiyyah(The Way of the Prophet's Sunnah)*, 1986, Vol. 2, p. 631.

11. Al-Tabrani,*Al Mu'jam al-Kabir*, Cairo, Egypt, Vol. 19, p. 13, no. 18; Al-Tabari,*Tafsir al-Tabari*, 2001, Vol. 20, pp. 467–468; Al-Haythami, *Majma al Zawa'id*, 2001, Vol. 8, p. 126, no. 13182; Al-Bayhaqi, *Al-Asma' wa al-Sifat (The Divine Names and Attributes)*, 1991, Vol. 2, pp. 198–199, Hadith 761.

12. Ibn Asakir,*Tabyin Kadhibi-l-Muftari fee ma Nusiba ilal Imam Abu-l-Hasan al Ash'ari (The Exposure of the Culmniator's Lying Concerning What Has Been Imputed to the Imam Abul Hasan Al-Ash'ari)*, 1928, Vol. 1, p. 311; Ibn Asakir, *Tarikh Dimashiq (History of Damascus)*, 1994, Vol. 62, p. 161 [Original Emphasis].

13. Imam Saleh al-Fawzan, "The Law of Killing Non-Believers, Polytheists and Shedding their Blood", lecture. A link to the audio file can be found at www.ImamTawhidi.com/references

14. Ahmad ibn Ajiba, *Iqaadh Al-Himam Sharh Al-Hikam*, p. 34. This concept has also been refuted in Ibn Taymiyah, *Bayan Talbees AlJahima Fi Ta'sees Bida'uhum AlKalamiyah (Criticism of Incorporation)*,2006, Vol. 4, p. 375.

15. Imam Mohammad Bahjar al-Bitaar, *Al-Nafahat Al-Aqdasiyya*, Beirut, Lebanon, p. 338.

16. Quran, 9:30.

17. Quran, 5:51.

18. Quran, 5:60 (Muhsin Khan).

19. Quran, 7:176. The usage of the word "elevated" in this verse refers to the fact that dogs originally had a low status in Islamic thought.

20.   "US Pastor Supervises Quran Burning, Sparks Outrage in Pak," Times of India (Washington/Islamabad), March 22, 2011; "JuD Announces Rs 10 Crore for Killing US Pastor Over Quran Burning,"PTI, March 22, 2011.

21.   Camille Mann, "Pastor Terry Jones Receiving Death Threats After Quran Burning," CBS News, April 4, 2011.

22.   Brian Prince, "'Here You Have' Worm Floods E-Mail Inboxes," eWeek, September 9, 2010; "Iran Clerics Vow Death for Koran-Defilers," UPI, September 13, 2010.

23.   "US Accountable for Quran Desecration," Presstv.ir, September 14, 2010.

24.   Quran, 56:77–79.

25.   Ibn Abidin, Radd al-Muhtar ala al-Dur al-Mukhtar , 2003, Vol. 1, p. 365.

26.   Yusuf Khan al-Farghani, Fataawa Qadhi Khan , Beirut, Lebanon: Dar-al-Fikr, Vol. 3, p. 305.

27.   "Iraqi Leader's Koran 'Written in Blood'", BBC News, September 25, 2000.

28.   Imam Ashraf Ali Thanwi, Malfoozat Hakim-ul-Ummat , p. 182.

29.   Ibn Nujaym al-Miṣrī Yaqut al-Hamawi, Al-Ashbah wa al-Nadha'ir, Ghamz Uyoon al-Basa'ir, Beirut, 1985, Vol. 4, p. 286.

30.   Quran, 24:30, emphasis added.

31.   Imam Abul Hassan Al-Karkhi, Ta'sis al Nadhar – Usool Al-Karkhi , Beirut, p. 169.

32.   Ibn Maajah, Sunan Ibn Majah , Vol. 3, Book 9, Hadith 1944.

33.   Quran, 81:19–25.

34.   Sahih al-Bukhari, Book 76, Hadith 79; Vol. 4, Book 54, No. 490; Vol. 7, Book 71, No. 658.

35.   Ibid.

36.   Al-Zamakhshari, Tafsir Al-Kashaf, 1998, Vol. 4, pp. 204–206; Ibn Ishaq,The Life of Muhammad: A Translation of Ibn Ishaq's Sirat Rasul Allah ,trans. A. Guillaume, Oxford: Oxford University Press, 1955, pp. 165–167.

37.   Sahih al-Bukhari, Vol. 1, Book 30, Hadith 39.

38.   Quran, 49:1–4 [original emphasis]

39.   Sahih Bukhari, Prophetic Commentary on the Qur'an (Tafseer of the Prophet (pbuh)), Vol. 6, Book 60, Hadith 368; see also: Hassan A. Nahim, The Division after Prophet Muhammad, Bloomington, IN: Xlibris, 2012.

40.   Sahih al-Bukhari, p. 752, Hadith 3053. In other versions: Book of Jihad, 2016, Chapter 176, p. 1427, No. 3053. The Arabic word used is "Yah-Jur," which means "speaking nonsense." In other editions, the statement is presented as a question: "Is the messenger of Allah talking nonsense?" In other translations, the word "Yah-jur" has been translated to "sick." That is an incorrect translation, as the word "sick" in Arabic is "Mareedh," and not "Yah-jur."

41.   Sahih al-Bukhari, Book 3, p. 41, Hadith 114; Sahih Muslim, Book 25, Hadith 31.

42.   Sahih al-Bukhari, Book 3, p. 41, Hadith 114.

43.   Ibid.

44.   Sahih al-Bukari, Beirut, Lebanon: Dar Al-Kotob Al-Ilmiyah, 2014, Vol. 1, Book 4, No. 183.

45.   Ibid, Vol. 1, Book 4, No. 150.

46.   Ibid, Vol. 1, Book 4, No. 91.

47.   "'Standing Up Like Animals': Australian Islamic Preacher Warns Muslims Not to Use Public URINALS – Because They Are 'Exposing Their Private Parts to Others,'" The Daily Mail, April 10, 2017.

48. Ibid.

49. Sahih al-Bukhari, Vol. 1, Book 5, No. 268. In other narrations, there were nine wives.

50. Quran, 2:260.

51. Sahih al-Bukhari, Vol. 2, Book 12, No. 3372.

52. Sahih al-Bukhari, Vol. 1, Book 4, Section 70, No. 233, p. 64.

53. Imam Ibn Hajar al Askalani, Fath al Bari fi Sharh Sahih al Bukhari, Vol. 8, p. 5.

54. Sadiq Shirazi, Politics: The Very Heart of Islam, CreateSpace Publishing, 2016, p. 45.

55. Asma Afsaruddin, "'Ā'isha Bt. Abī Bakr" in Kate Fleet et al. (eds), Encyclopaedia of Islam, Leiden, Netherlands: Brill Online, 2018.

56. W. Montgomery Watt, "'Ā'isha Bint Abī Bakr " in P. Bearman et al. (eds) Encyclopaedia of Islam, 2nd edn, Leiden, Netherlands: Brill Online, 2018; Amira Sonbol, "Rise of Islam: 6th to 9th Century" in Joseph Suad (ed.), Encyclopedia of Women and Islamic Cultures, Leiden, Netherlands: Brill Publishers, 2003, pp. 3–9.

57. For further reading on this matter, see: Denise Spellberg, Politics, Gender, and the Islamic Past: The Legacy of A'isha bint Abi Bakr, New York: Columbia University Press, 1994.

58. Ibid, pp. 39–40.

59. Kathryn Kueny, The Rhetoric of Sobriety: Wine in Early Islam, Albany, NY: State University of New York Press, 2001, p. 59.

60. Sahaja Carimokam, Muhammad and the People of the Book, Bloomington, IN: Xlibris, 2011, p. 520.

61. Tom Holland, In the Shadow of the Sword, New York: Doubleday, 2012, p. 42; Gordon Darnell Newby and Muhammad Ibn Ishāq, The Making of the Last Prophet: A Reconstruction of the Earliest Biography of Muhammad, Columbia, SC: University of South Carolina Press, 1989, p. 9.

62. Sahih al-Bukhari, Book 67, Hadith 70.

63. Sadakat Kadri, Heaven on Earth, New York: Farrar, Straus & Giroux, 2012, p. 30.

64. Asma Barlas, "Believing Women" in Islam: Unreading Patriarchal Interpretations of the Qur'an, Austin, TX: University of Texas Press, 2012, p. 126.

65. Tarikh Sahih Islam, Muhammad Niknam Arabshahi, Vol. 1, p. 197.

66. Denise Spellberg, Politics, Gender, and the Islamic Past: The Legacy of A'isha bint Abi Bakr, New York: Columbia University Press, 1994, pp. 39–40.

67. Resit Haylamaz, Aisha, The Wife, The Companion, The Scholar, Clifton, NJ: Tughra Books, 2014.

68. Ibn Abi Shaybah, Musannaf Ibn Abi Shaybah, 2008, Vol. 6, p. 303.

69. Quran, 3:144, emphasis added.

70. Al Bukhari, Al-Adab al-Mufrad, Book 12, Hadith 6; Sahih al-Bukhari, Book 64, Hadith 450. See also: Imam Ibn Hajar al Askalani, Fath al Bari fi Sharh Sahih al Bukhari, Vol. 10, p. 245.

71. Sahih al-Bukhari, Book 64, Hadith 450; Sunan Abi Dawud, 4512, Book 41, Hadith 19.

72. Al-Naisapuri, Al Mustadrak, 1997, Vol. 4, p. 564, no. 8305.

73. Ibid, commentary section.

74. Tafsir Qomi, Exegesis on the Quran by Ali Ibn Ibrahim Qomi, 1968, Vol. 2, p. 376.

75. Sahih Muslim, Book 39, Hadith 115.

76. Sahih al-Bukhari, Book 64, Hadith 474; Book 87, Hadith 36.

77. Al-Bayhaqi, Dala'il al-Nubuwwah (The Signs of Prophethood), 1988, Vol. 7, p. 169.

78. Al-Darimi, Sunan al-Darimi, 2002, Vol. 1, p. 25.

79. Abu Nu`aym al-Isfahani, Ma`rifat al-Sahâba wa Fadâ'ilihim (Knowing the Companions and Their Merits), Salim Bin Ubaid, Report No. 494, 1998.

80. Al-Baladhuri, Ansaab al Ashraaf (Lineage of the Nobles), Cairo: Darul Ma'arif, 1996, Vol. 1, p. 567, Report No. 1151.

81. Abu Nu`aym al-Isfahani, Ma`rifat al-Sahâba wa Fadâ'ilihim (Knowing the Companions and Their Merits), Salim Bin Ubaid, Report No. 494, 1998.

82. Quran, 66:10.

83. Quran, 33:6.

84. Al-Qurtubi, Tafsir al-Qurtubi, Beirut, Lebanon: Al-Resalah Publishers, 2006, Vol. 17, p. 209.

85. Tafsir Qomi, Exegesis on the Quran by Ali Ibn Ibrahim Qomi, 1968, Vol. 2, pp. 377–378. In some editions, the author conceals the names of the adulterers for safety reasons, and writes "So and so" instead. Other scholars from Sunni and Shia Islamic denominations report the incident while mentioning their names: Aisha and Talha. See: Al-Qurtubi, Tafsir al-Qurtubi, Beirut, Lebanon: Al-Resalah Publishers, 2006, Vol. 17, p. 209.

86. Ibn Abi'l-Hadid, Sharh Nahj al-Balagha , 2007, Vol. 6, p. 314.

87. Ibid.

88. Sahih al-Bukhari, Book 52, Chapter 15, Hadith 25.

89. Sahih Muslim, Book 54, Chapter 16, Hadith 61.

90. Wiebke Walther, Women in Islam, Princeton, NJ: Wiener Publishers, 1993, pp. 64–65.

91. Sahih Muslim, Book 11, Chapter 35, Hadith 132. See the Arabic text. The English translation is not accurate.

92. Sahih Muslim, Book 2, Hadith 140.

93. Sunan Abi Dawud, Book of Purification, Book 1, Hadith 371.

94. Muhammad ibn Ya'qāb al-Kulaynd Al-Kdfā(The Sufficient Book), Vol. 5, p. 421.

95. Ibn Abi Shaybah, Musannaf Ibn Abi Shaybah , 2008, Vol. 6, p. 303. See also: Ibn Kathir, Al Bidayah wal-Nihaya .

96. Al-Dhahabi, Siyar a`lam al-nubala' (The Lives of Noble Figures), 1982, Vol. 2, p. 193; Al-Ghazali,Murtada al-Zabidi (The Revival of the Religious Sciences), 1993, Vol. 10, p. 333.

97. Aisha Abdurrahman Bewley, Mu'awiya: Restorer of the Muslim Faith, London: Dar Al Taqwa, 2002, p. 4.

98. Al-Nabati Al-Amuli, Al-Sirat al-Mustaqim, Vol. 3, pp. 45–46.

99. Mirza Husain Noori Tabarsi, Mustadrak al-Wasā'il wa-mustanbaṭ al-masā'il , 1987, Vol. 11, p. 60.

100. Musnad Ahmad bin Hanbal, Cairo: Dar al-Hadith, Vol. 43, pp. 342, 351–352.

101. Musa Shahin Lashin, Fat'h ul-Mun'im, Explaining Sahih Muslim, 2002, Vol. 5, p. 622.

102. L. Lavi, "Al-Azhar Lecturer Suspended after Issuing Controversial Fatwa Recommending Breastfeeding of Men by Women in the Workplace," Middle East Media Research Institute, June 3, 2007.

103. Sahih Muslim, Book 17, Hadith 34.

104. Ibn Maajah, Sunan Ibn Majah, Vol. 3, Book 9, Hadith 1944.

105. L. Lavi, "Al-Azhar Lecturer Suspended after Issuing Controversial Fatwa Recommending Breastfeeding of Men by Women in the Workplace," Middle East Media Research

Institute, June 3, 2007; Al-Masri Al-Yawm (Egypt), May 22, 2007; Al-Watani Al-Yawm (Egypt), May 15, 2007.

106. Abdul Rahman Shaheen, "Saudi Women Use Fatwa in Driving Bid," Gulf News, June 20, 2010.

107. Sahih al-Bukhari, Book 30, No. 34.

108. Sahih al-Bukhari, Book 30, Hadith 35.

109. "Markaz al-Fatwa" ("The Fatwa Department"), Fatwa.Islamweb.net, Fatwa No. 40160.

110. Sahih al-Bukhari, Book 5, No. 251.

111. Norman Stillman, The Jews of Arab Lands: A History and Source Book, Philadelphia, PA: Jewish Publication Society of America, 1979, pp. 13–14.

112. William Montgomery Watt, "Ka'b ibn al-Ashraf" in P.J. Bearman et al. (eds), Encyclopaedia of Islam Online, Leiden, Netherlands: Brill Academic Publishers, pp. 211–212.

113. William Montgomery Watt, Companion to the Qur'an, Based on the Arberry Translation, London: Allen and Unwin, 1967, p. 237.

114. Patricia Crone, Medieval Islamic Political Thought, Edinburgh: Edinburgh University Press, 2005, pp. 307–309.

115. AbdulShafi Mohammad Abdul Latif, The Prophetic Biography and Islamic History, Cairo: Dar-asSalam, Vol. 1, p. 91.

116. George F. Nafziger and Mark W. Walton, Islam at War: A History, Westport, CT: Praeger, 2003, p. 13; see also: William Muir, Life of Mahomet, Whitefish, MT: Kessinger Publishing, 2003, p. 454.

117. Sayyid Ali Ashgar Razwy, A Restatement of the History of Islam and Muslims, Middlesex, UK: World Federation of KSI Muslim Communities, 2014.

118. Ali ibn Abu-Talib, Nahjul-Balagha: Peak of Eloquence, 7th US edn, Elmhurst, NY: Tahrike Tarsile Qu'ran, 2009, Sermon 3, p. 314.

119. Ibid, p. 316.

120. Muhammad Al-Shahrastani, Book of Religious and Philosophical Sects, ed. William Cureton, Piscataway, NJ: Gorgias Press, 2002 p. 12.

121. Sahih al-Bukhari, Book 86, Hadith 57.

122. Sahih al-Bukhari, Chapter 176, Hadith 3053.

123. Shibli Nomani, Al-Farooq: The Life of Omar the Great, Lahore: Sh. Muhammad Ashraf, 1939, p. 89.

124. Ibn 'Abd al-Barr, The Comprehensive Compilation of the Names of the Prophet's Companions, Beirut, Lebanon: Dar el Fikr, 1992, Vol. 1, p. 47.

125. Sahih al-Bukhari, Hadith 1399, 1400.

126. Al-Baladhuri, Kitab Futuh al-Buldan (Book of the Conquests of the Lands), Vol. 1, p. 82.

127. Ibn Asakir, Tarikh Dimashiq (History of Damascus), 1995, Vol. 16, p. 258. See upcoming references in this section. Ibn al-Athir, Al-Kāmil fit-Tārīkh (The Complete History), 1987, Vol. 2, pp. 216–218; Ibn al-Athir, Usd al-ghābah fi ma'rifat al-ṣaḥābah (The Lions of the Forest and the Knowledge about the Companions), Beirut, Lebanon: Dar ibn Hazm, 2012, pp. 1078–1079, Report No. 4656 and 4657; Ibn 'Abd al-Barr, The Comprehensive Compilation of the Names of the Prophet's Companions, Beirut, Lebanon: Dar el Fikr, 2006, Vol. 2, p. 205.

128. John Bagot Glubb, The Great Arab Conquests, London: Hodder and Stoughton, 1963, p.

112.

129. Ibid.

130. Al-Waqidi, Kitab al Riddah, 1990, pp. 107–108.

131. Abu al-Fida,Concise History of Humanity, Vol. 1, p. 157; Al-Bidāya wa-n-Nihāya,
(The Beginning and the End), 1988, Vol. 6, pp. 321–322; Chief Judge Ibn Khallikan,
Wafayāt al-aʼyān wa-anbāʼ abnāʼ az-zamān (Deaths of Eminent Men and
History of the Sons of the Epoch), Vol. 6, p. 14; Al-Dhahabi, Tarikh al-Islam al-kabir (Major
History of Islam), 2003, Vol. 2, p. 24; Ibn Hajar al-Asqalani, Al-Isaba fi tamyiz al-Sahaba
(The Most Comprehensive Dictionary of the Companions), 1995, Vol. 5, p. 561.

132. John Bagot Glubb, The Great Arab Conquests, London: Hodder and Staughton, 1963, p.
112; Sayyid Ali Ashgar Razwy, A Restatement of the History of Islam and Muslims,
Middlesex, UK: World Federation of KSI Muslim Communities, p. 308; Ja'far Murtadha al-
Amili, Tragedy of al-Zahra': Doubts and Responses , pp. 62–63; Muhammad Ibrahim
Jannati, Ijtihad, pp. 72–73; Mujtaba Sabouri, Love and Hate for God's Sake, CreateSpace
Publishing, 2013, p. 12.

133. al-Tabari, The History of al-Tabari, Vol. 10: The Conquest of Arabia , Albany, NY: State
University of New York Press, 1993, p. 104.

134. Muhammad al-Tijani al-Samawi, Then I was Guided, 2012, p. 70.

135. Sahih al-Bukhari, Book 56, Hadith 3016.

136. Agha Ibrahim Akram, The Sword of Allah: Khalid bin al-Waleed – His Life and Campaigns ,
Oxford: Oxford University Press, 2004, pp. 89, 167.

137. Muhammad ibn Abd al-Wahhab, Mukhtasar Seerat ar-Rasul (Summarised Biography of
the Prophet), p. 291. See also: ʻAbd al-Razzaq al-Sanʻani, Musannaf of Abd al-Razzaq ,
1983, Vol. 10, pp. 174–175.

138. Ibid.

139. Ibid.

140. Ibn Kathir, Al-Bidḍya wa-n-Nihḍya (The Beginning and the End), 1998, Vol. 9, pp. 456-457;
Ibn al-Athir, Kāmil fī al-tārīkh (The Complete History), 1987, Vol. 2, p. 211; Al Tabari,
Tarikh al-Tabari (History of the Prophets and Kings), Vol. 3, pp. 264–265.

141. Ibn Asakir, Tarikh Dimashiq(History of Damascus), 1995, Vol. 30, p. 418.

142. Al Tabari, Tarikh al-Tabari (History of the Prophets and Kings), Vol. 3, p. 263.

143. Ibn al-Mulaqqin, Al Tawdheeh, Vol. 18, p. 61. See also: IslamQA, No. 227776,
https://islamqa.info/en/.

144. John Bentley, "Leon Panetta: U.S. 'Reaching the Limits of Our Patience' with Pakistan
Terror Safe Havens," CBS News, June 7, 2012; "Pakistan's Tribal Areas: A Safe Haven for
Terrorists," The Economist, April 12, 2007; Dean Nelson, "Nicolas Sarkozy Launches
Attack on Pakistan Over Terrorist Safe Havens," The Telegraph, December 7, 2010.

145. Agha Ibrahim Akram, The Sword of Allah: Khalid bin al-Waleed – His Life and Campaigns,
Oxford: Oxford University Press, 2004, p. 113.

146. Moshe Gil, A History of Palestine, 634–1099, Cambridge: Cambridge University Press,
1997, p. 32.

147. al-Muttaqi al-Hindi, Kanz al-ʻUmmḍl fāsunan al-aqwḍl waʼl afʻḍl (Treasure of the Doers of
Good Deeds), 1985, Vol. 10, p. 285.

148. Ibn al-Athir, Usd al-ghābah fi maʻrifat al-ṣaḥābah (The Lions of the Forest and the
Knowledge About the Companions), 1994, Vol. 7, p. 234.

149. Ibn Kathir, Al-Bidāya wa-n-Nihāya (The Beginning and the End), 1997, Vol. 8, p. 89.

150. Ibn Asakir, Tarikh Dimashiq (History of Damascus), 1996, Vol. 44, p. 250.

151. al-Muttaqi al-Hindi, Kanz al-'Ummāl fī sunan al-aqwāl wa'l af'āl (Treasure of the Doers of Good Deeds),

152. Muhammad al-Amin al-Shinqiti, Adhwa'ul Bayan , Beirut, Lebanon, 1995, Vol. 9, p. 63.

153. Ibid.

154. Al-Haythami, Majmau' al-Zawa'id wa Manba' al-Fawa'id , 1994, Vol. 7, p. 204, Hadith 11469; Al-Mawardi, Al-Hawi Al-Kabir (The Comprehensive Book), 1994, Vol. 13, p. 67.

155. Ibn al-Athir, al-Kāmil fit-Tārīkh (The Complete History), 1987, Vol. 1, p. 591.

156. Ali Muhammad as-Sallabi, Umar Ibn Al-Khattab: His Life and Times , 2007, Vol. 1, p. 48.

157. Ibn Hisham, Saheeh Al-Sirah al-Nabawiyah (The Authentic Traditions of the Prophetic Biography), compiled by Majdi Fathi As-Sayyid, 1995, p. 117;Ibn Sa'd, Kitab Tabaqat Al-Kubra (The Book of the Major Classes), 2001, Vol. 10, p. 244.

158. Al-Baladhuri, Ansaab al Ashraaf (Lineage of the Nobles), Cairo: Darul Ma'arif, 1996, Vol. 1, p. 195.

159. Ali Muhammad as-Sallabi, Umar Ibn Al-Khattab: His Life and Times , 2007, Vol. 2, p. 251.

160. Al-Hakim Nishapuri, Al-Mustadrak alaa al-Sahihain , 1997, Vol. 4, p. 291, Hadith 7420.

161. Muhammad Ibn Sa'd, The Women of Madina, London: Ta-Ha, 1995, p. 131.

162. Ali Muhammad as-Sallabi, Umar Ibn Al-Khattab: His Life and Times , 2009, Vol. 1, pp. 269–270.

163. Imam Malik, Muwaata Malik , 2004, Vol. 2, p. 875, Hadith 2248; English version: Imam Malik, Muwatta Imam Malik , Book 30, No. 30.2.13.

164. Ibn Sa'd, Kitab Tabaqat Al-Kabir (The Book of the Major Classes), 2001, Vol. 10, p. 252.

165. Ibn Abi Shaybah, Al-Musannaf , 2008, Vol. 3, p. 114, Hadith 6296.

166. Grand Imam Muhammad Nasiruddin al-Albani, Irwa al-Ghalil , Beirut, Lebanon, 1979, Vol. 6, p. 204.

167. Ibn Hajar al-Asqalani, al-Diraya fi Takhrij Ahadith al-Hidaya , Beirut, Lebanon: Dar-ul Ma'rifah, 2016, Vol. 1, p. 124.

168. The report is considered authentic by Imam Muslim in Sahih Muslim , which is one of the six major hadith collections in Islam, and is regarded as one of the two most authentic collections, alongside Sahih al-Bukhari . See: Grand Imam Muhammad Nasiruddin al-Albani, Irwa al-Ghalil , Beirut, Lebanon, 1979, Vol. 6, p. 204.

169. Al-Bayhaqi, Al-Sunan al-Kubra (commonly known as Sunan al-Bayhaqi), 2003, Vol. 2, pp. 320–321; Grand Imam Muhammad Nasiruddin al-Albani, Irwa al-Ghalil , Beirut, Lebanon, 1979, Vol. 6, p. 204.

170. Grand Imam Ahmad ibn Hanbal, Musnad , Vol. 4, pp. 30–31, Report No. 2127 and Vol. 5, p. 216, Report No. 3103; Grand Imam Muhammad ash-Shawkani, Nayl al-Awtar , 2004, p. 739, Report No. 1502; Al-Haythami, Majma al-Zawa'id , Lebanon, 2001, Vol. 3, p. 81, Report No. 4046; Al-Mawardi, Al-Hawi Al-Kabir (The Comprehensive Book), 1994, Vol. 3, p. 68; Al-Hakim Nishapuri, Al-Mustadrak alaa al-Sahihain , 1997, Vol. 1, pp. 531–532, Hadith 1403.

171. Ibn Hajar al-Asqalani, Fath al-Bārī fī Sharh Sahīh al-Bukhārī, 1959, Vol. 1, p. 74, Report No. 2420; Ibn Sa'd, Kitab Tabaqat Al-Kubra (The Book of the Major Classes), 2001, Vol. 3, p. 191; Al Tabari, Tarikh al-Tabari (History of the Prophets and Kings), Vol. 3, p. 423.

172. Al-Darimi, Sunan al-Darimi, Vol. 1, p. 67, Report No. 148.

173. Ibn Qayyim al-Jawziyya, *I'laam ul Muwaqqi'een 'an Rabb il 'Aalameen* (*Information for Those Who Write on Behalf of the Lord of the Worlds*), Vol. 4, p. 24.

174. Ibid, p. 25.

175. Ibid, p. 26.

176. Imam Muslim, *Sahih Muslim*, Hadith 2584 or Book 45, Hadith 81.

177. A link to this video can be found at www.ImamTawhidi.com/references

178. *Sahih al-Bukhari*, Book 8, Hadith 89.

179. Ibn Abi Shaybah, *Musannaf Ibn Abi Shaybah*, 2006, Vol. 12, p. 622, Report No. 25761.

180. Abd al-Razzaq al-San'ani, *Musannaf of Abd al-Razzaq*, 1983, Vol. 6, p. 77.

181. Ibn Khaldun, *Muqaddimah*, 2004, Vol. 1, p. 103.

182. Al-Bayhaqi, *Al-Sunan al-Kubra*, 2003, Vol. 8, p. 519, Hadith 17416.

183. Ibn Abi Shaybah, Musannaf Ibn Abi Shaybah, 2006, Vol. 12, pp. 221–222, Report No. 24372.

184. Al-Qurtubi, *Tafsir al-Qurtubi*, 2006, Vol. 12, p. 362; Al-Nisa'i, *Sunan Al-Kubra*, 2001, Vol. 6, p. 292, Hadith 6814.

185. Ibn Abi Shaybah, *Musannaf Ibn Abi Shaybah*, 2006, Vol. 14, pp. 431–432, Report No. 28991.

186. Al-Bayhaqi, *Al-Sunan al-Kubra*, 2003, Vol. 3, p. 161, Hadith 5256.

187. Imam Malik, *Muwatta Imam Malik*, English translation, 2004, Book 17, No. 17.5.11.

188. Ibid, Vol. 2, p. 1429, No. 3098.

189. Ibn al-Qayyim, *I'laam ul Muwaqqi'een 'an Rabb il 'Aalameen* (*Information for Those Who Write on Behalf of the Lord of the Worlds*), 2002, Vol. 4, p. 21. What's more noteworthy is the fact that Ibn Qayyim also affirmed in the reference section that this matter had been reported numerous times in both *Sahih al-Bukhari* and *Sahih Muslim*, in the editions and sources that were available to him in the thirteenth century.

190. Al-Bayhaqi, *Al-Sunan al-Kubra*, 2003, Vol. 1, p. 179, Hadith 540.

191. al-Muttaqi al-Hindi, *Kanz al-'Ummāl fī sunan al-aqwāl wa'l af'āl* (*Treasure of the Doers of Good Deeds*), 1985, Vol. 9, p. 588, Hadith 27547.

192. Ibid., Vol. 15, p. 428, Hadith 41694.

193. *Sahih Muslim*, Book 2, Hadith 1.

194. *Sahih al-Bukhari*, Hadith 6085, or Book 78, Chapter 68, Hadith 113.

195. Al-Tirmidhi, *Jami` at-Tirmidhi*, 1996, Vol. 6, p. 62, Hadith 3690.

196. David S. Margoliouth, *Mohammed and the Rise of Islam*, 3rd edn, New York: Putnam, 1905, pp. 163–164.

197. Al-Haythami, *Majmau' al-Zawa'id wa Manba' al-Fawa'id*, 2001, Vol. 9, pp. 49–50, Hadith 14463.

198. Ibn Taymiyah, *Minhaj Al-Sunnah Al-Nabawiyyah* (*The Way of the Prophet's Sunnah*), 1986, Vol. 6, p. 371.

199. Ibn Hibban, *Sahih Ibn Hibban*, Vol. 15, pp. 331–332, Hadith 6905.

200. Raihan Ismail, *Saudi Clerics and Shi'a Islam*, New York: Oxford University Press, 2016, p. 93.

201. Jean Calmard, "Shi'i Rituals and Power II. The Consolidation of Safavid Shi'ism: Folklore and Popular religion" in Charles Peter Melville (ed.), *Safavid Persia: The History and Politics of an Islamic Society*, London: I.B. Tauris, 1996, p. 161; India, Office of the Registrar

General, Census of India, 1961: Gujarat, Manager of Publications, 1965, p. 159; Afsaneh Nahavandi, "Cultural Mythology and Global Leadership in Iran" in E.H. Kessler and D.J. Wong-Mingji (eds), Cultural Mythology and Global Leadership, Cheltenham, UK: Edward Elgar Publishing, 2009, p. 255; Raihan Ismail, Saudi Clerics and Shi'a Islam, New York: Oxford University Press, 2016, pp. 92–93.

202. Abd al-Husain Zarrinkub, "The Arab Conquest of Iran and its Aftermath" in Peter Frye (ed.), The Cambridge History of Iran, Cambridge: Cambridge University Press, 1975, Vol. 4, p. 15.

203. Muhammad ibn Saad, The Women of Madina, trans. A. Bewley, London: Ta-Ha Publishers, 1995, Vol. 8, p. 25; Muhammad ibn Jarir al-Tabari, Biographies of the Prophet's Companions and Their Successors, trans. E. Landau-Tasseron, Albany, NY: State University of New York Press, 1998, Vol. 39, p. 162.

204. Muhammad ibn Umar al-Waqidi and Kitab al-Maghazi, The Life of Muhammad, trans. R. Faizer, A. Ismail and A. K. Tayob, Oxford: Routledge, 2011, p. 51.

205. Ahmad ibn Muhammad al-Sayyari, Revelation and Falsification: The Kitab al-qira'at of Ahmad b. Muhammad al-Sayyari: Critical Edition with an Introduction and Notes by Etan Kohlberg and Mohammad Ali Amir-Moezzi, ed. Etan Kohlberg and Mohammad Ali Amir-Moezzi, Leiden, Netherlands: Brill, 2009, Vol. 4, p. 248.

206. Grand Imam Ali bin Yunis Al-Nabaati Al-Amili, Al-Sirat Al-Mustakim, Vol. 3, p. 34; Faris Hasoun Karim, Al-Rawdh an Nadhir, 1995, p. 355; Center of Belief Researches, "Question: Did Othman kill Ruqayyah?", www.Aqaed.com.

207. Al-Suhayli, Raud al-Unuf, Beirut, Lebanon: Dar-al-Kutub al-Ilmiyah, Vol. 3, pp. 183–184.

208. Muhammad Taqi Shushtari (Allamah Shushtari), also known as Al-Tustari, Qamus al-rijal, 1959, reprinted in 2004, Vol. 12, p. 259. This book was written as a refutation of Tanqih al-maqal by Ayatollah Shaikh Abdullah Mamaqani.

209. Ja'far Murtaza Al-Ameli, Al-Sahih Min Sirat Al-Nabi Al-Azam, 2005, Vol. 6, p. 175.

210. Imam Malik, Muwaata Malik, 2004, Vol. 2, p. 1204, Hadith 2045; Al-Suyuti, Tafsir Dur al-Manthur(The Scattered Pearls: Intertextual Exegesis), 2003, Vol. 13, p. 323.

211. Al-Baladhuri, Ansab al-Ashraf (Genealogies of the Nobles), Beirut, Lebanon: Dar-al-Fikr, 1996, Vol. 6, p. 209.

212. Kitāb Taʾrīkh al-Madīna al-Munawwara (The History of Medina), pp. 1098–1099.

213. Valerie Jon Hoffman, The Essentials of Ibadi Islam, Syracuse: Syracuse University Press, 2012, p. 8.

214. Al Tabari, The History of al-Tabari, English version, Albany, NY: SUNY Press, 1997, Vol. 16, pp. 52–53.

215. Ibn Kathir, Al-Bidāya wa-n-Nihāya (The Beginning and the End), 1998, Vol. 10, pp. 315–316.

216. Al Tabari, The History of al-Tabari, English version, Albany, NY: SUNY Press, 1997, Vol. 15, p. 181.

217. Ali ibn Abu-Talib, Nahjul-Balagha: Peak of Eloquence, 7th US edn, Elmhurst, NY: Tahrike Tarsile Qu'ran, 2009, Sermon 3, p. 315.

218. William Muir, The Life of Mahomet: From Original Sources, London: Smith, Elder, 1877, pp. 259–260.

219. Ali ibn Abu-Talib, Nahjul-Balagha: Peak of Eloquence, 7th US edn, Elmhurst, NY: Tahrike Tarsile Qu'ran, 2009.

220. Sayyid Ali Ashgar Razwy, A Restatement of the History of Islam and Muslims , Middlesex, UK: World Federation of KSI Muslim Communities, 2014, pp. 430–431; Mohammad Ishaque, Journal of the Pakistan Historical Society , Vol 3, No. 1.

221. Sayyid Ali Ashgar Razwy, A Restatement of the History of Islam and Muslims , Middlesex, UK: World Federation of KSI Muslim Communities, 2014, p. 433.

222. Yasin T. Jibouri, Kerbalā and Beyond, Bloomington, IN: AuthorHouse, 2011, p. 30; Wilferd Madelung, The Succession to Muhammad: A Study of the Early Caliphate , Cambridge: Cambridge University Press, 1997, p. 177.

223. Sahih Muslim, Book 54, Hadith 61.

224. Al-Nabati Al-Amuli, Siraat Al-Mustaqeem , Vol. 3, p. 13.

225. Muhammad Tahir-Ul-Qadri, Virtues of Sayyedah Fatimah , Lahore: Tehreek-e-Minhaj-ul-Quran, 2006, p. 7.

226. Sahih al-Bukhari , Book 62, Hadith 114.

227. Al-Tabari, Tafsir al-Tabari , 2001, Vol. 22, pp. 517–519.

228. Quran, 59:7 [original emphasis].

229. Sahih Muslim, Book 32, Hadith 1759.

230. Mohammad Ali Al-Tabrizi Al-Ansari, Al-Lum'uah al Baydhaa' , Vol. 1, pp. 309–310.

231. Sahih al-Bukhari ,Book 62, Hadith 114.

232. Al-Farooq, The Life of Omar the Great, Vol. 1, pp. 94–95; Ibn Abi Shaybah, Musannaf Ibn Abi Shaybah, 2008, Vol. 13, p. 201.

233. Al-Tabari, The History of al-Tabari, Vol. 9, p. 189.

234. Yusuf al-Bahrani, Al-Hada'iq al Nadhirah , 1985, Vol. 5, p. 180.

235. Mohammed Raza Dungersi, A Brief Biography of Hazrat Fatima , Dar es Salaam: Bilal Muslim Mission of Tanzania, 1994, pp. 36–37; Hassan A. Nahim, The Division After Prophet Muhammad, Bloomington, IN: Xlibris, 2012, p. 83; Bridget Blomfield, "Fatimah," in John Andrew Morrow (ed.), Islamic Images and Ideas: Essays on Sacred Symbolism , Jefferson, NC: McFarland, 2013, p. 104.

236. Sulaym ibn Qays, The Book of Sulaym ibn Qays , English translation, Part 6, p. 42.

237. al-Tusi, Al-Amali, 2001, p. 292 [original emphasis].

238. Sahih Muslim, Book 32, Hadith 61, No. 1759.

239. Hassan Farhan al-Maliki, Qira'atun Fi Kutub Al-Aqa'id , 2001, p. 53.

240. Allamah Al-Majlisi, Bihar Al-Anwar, Vol. 43, pp. 198–199; Allamah Al-Majlisi, Rawdhatul Muttaqeen, Vol. 5, p. 342.

241. ShibliNu'mani,Al-Faruq,Lahore,p. 96.

242. Ibn al-Athir, Usd al-ghābah fi ma'rifat al-ṣahābah (The Lions of the Forest and the Knowledge about the Companions), Beirut, Lebanon: Dar ibn Hazm, 2012, Vol. 5, pp. 69–70, Person No. 4695.

243. Muḥibb al-Dīn Aḥmad al- Ṭabarī, Dhakha'ir Al-Uqba, p. 105.

244. Arthur F. Buehler, "Fatima," in Coeli Fitzpatrick and Adam Hani Walker (eds), Muhammad in History, Thought, and Culture: An Encyclopedia of the Prophet of God, Vol. 1, Santa Barbara, CA: ABC-CLIO, 2014, p. 186.

245. Bridget Blomfield, "Fatimah," in John Andrew Morrow (ed.), Islamic Images and Ideas: Essays on Sacred Symbolism, Jefferson, NC: McFarland, 2013, p. 104.

246. Ibid.

247. Ibn al-Mubarad, Al-Shajarah Al-Nabawiyya, 1997, p. 120 [original emphasis]

248. Ibn Shahrashub, Manaqib Al Abi Talib, 1991, Vol. 3, p. 407 [original emphasis].

249. Ibn Abd Rabbih, Al-ʿIqd al-Farīd, 1983, Vol. 5, p. 13.

250. Al-Tabari, Dala'il Al-Imamah, 1993, pp. 134–135.

251. Al-Tabari, Al-Mustarshid, 1995, p. 224, also referencing Sunni scholars Ibn Qutaybah and Ibn Abd Rabbih.

252. Al-Baladhuri, Ansab al-Ashraf (Genealogies of the Nobles), 1996, Vol. 2, p. 268.

253. This narration has been reported by three grand Islamic jurists: Al-Suyuti, Jami Al-Ahadeeth, 1994, Vol. 13, pp. 100–101, no. 352; Al-Baladhuri, Ansab al-Ashraf (Genealogies of the Nobles), 1996, Vol. 10, pp. 346–347; Al-Tabari, The History of Al-Tabari, 1993, Vol. 11, p. 149.

254. Ahmad ibn Hanbal, Kitab al-Zuhd(The Book of Abstinence), 1983, p. 139.

255. Ibn Abi al-Dunya, Al-Mutamanin, 1997, pp. 26–27.

256. Ibid; see also p. 71.

257. Al-Tabari, The History of Al-Tabari, 1993, Vol. 11, p. 149, commentary section.

258. Along with all of the aforementioned evidence, see also: Sayyid Ja'far Murtada Al-'Amili, Tragedy of Fatima Daughter of Prophet Muhammed: Doubts Cast and Rebuttals, trans. Yasin T. al-Jibouri, Bloomington, IN: AuthorHouse, 2013.

259. Baqir Shareef Qurashi, The Life of Fatima Az-Zahra, Qum, Iran: Ansariyan Publications, 2006, p. 248.

260. Mohammed Raza Dungersi, A Brief Biography of Hazrat Fatima (s.a.), Dar es Salaam: Bilal Muslim Mission of Tanzania, 1994, p. 43; Hassan A. Nahim, The Division After Prophet Muhammad, Bloomington, IN: Xlibris Corporation, 2012, p. 39; Sayyid Hussein Alamdar, Fatimeh Al-Zahra, Bloomington, IN: AuthorHouse, 2014.

261. Mousavi Zanjanrudi and Seyyed Mojtaba, The Missing Grave(in Persian), 2012.

262. Wilferd Madelung, The Succession to Muhammad: A Study of the Early Caliphate,Cambridge: Cambridge University Press, 1998, p. 52.

263. Sayyid Hussein Alamdar, Fatimeh Al-Zahra, Bloomington, IN: AuthorHouse, 2014.

264. Al-Majlisi, Rawdhatul Muttaqeen, Vol. 5, p. 347; Muhammad ibn Ya'qūb al-Kulaynī, Al-Kafi, Vol. 1, pp. 291–292, Hadith 3.

265. The entire incident is mentioned by Al-Tabari, Kamil Al-Baha'i, Vol. 1, pp. 396–397, and can also be found in numerous other sources on Islamic history which have shed light on this incident.

266. Sayyid Al-Himyari (died 173 AH) was acontemporary of Imam Al-Sadiq and Imam Al-Kadhim, the descendants and successors of Prophet Mohammad. Source:Al-Nabati Al-Amuli, Al-Sirat al-Mustaqim, Vol. 3, p. 13.

267. Ibid.

268. "Yazid I," in New World Encyclopedia, April 4, 2008, http://www.newworldencyclopedia.org/entry/Yazid_I

269. Ibrahim Ayati, A Probe into the History of Ashura', New York: Al-Khoei Foundation, 1991, p. 47.

270. Ahmad ibn A'tham, Kitab al-Futuh, 1991, Vol. 5, pp. 13–14 [original emphasis].

271. Ibid.

272. Ibid.

273.   Ibid.

274.   Ibid.

275.   Allamah Al-Majlisi, Bihar Al-Anwar, Vol. 44, p. 192.

276.   Prime Minister Narendra Modi, official Twitter page, September 14, 2018.

277.   Sayid Baqir Al-Hindi, Adab Al-Taff, 1989, Vol. 8, p. 223.

278.   Ingvild Flaskerud, Visualizing Belief and Piety in Iranian Shiism, London: Continuum International, 2010, pp. 134–139.

279.   Shaikh Abdullah al-Bahrani al-Isfahani, Awalim al-Uloom, 2004, Vol. 17, p. 117.

280.   Nafasul Mahmoom, Shaykh Abbas Qummi, Qum, Iran, Ansariyan Publications, 2005, pp. 388–389.

281.   Abd al Razzaq Al Muqarram, Maqtal Al Husayn: Martyrdom Epic of Imam al Husain , Beirut, Lebanon: Al-Kharsan Foundation, 2005, pp. 190–191.

282.   Ibid.

283.   Ibid.

284.   Abd al Razzaq Al Muqarram, Maqtal Al Husayn: Martyrdom Epic of Imam al Husain , Beirut, Lebanon: Al-Kharsan Foundation, 2005.

285.   Nafsul Mahmoom, part 3; Al-Sawa'iq-ul-Muharriqah , p. 199; Ilyas Attar Qadri, Marvels of Sayyiduna Imam Hussain , Maktaba-tul-Madina.

286.   For more information on this event, see: Mateen J. Charbonneau, Christians who Defended and Died for Prophet Muhammad and his Family , Roanoke, VA: Second Chance Books, 2012.

287.   Peter J. Chelkowski, Eternal Performance: Ta'ziyeh and Other Shiite Rituals, Chicago: University of Chicago Press, 2010, p. 2.

288.   A. Guillaume, The Life of Muhammad, Oxford: Oxford University Press, 1955, p. 385; Ibn 'Abdu l-Barr, al-Istī'āb.

289.   Edward Gibbon, The Decline and Fall of the Roman Empire , London: Dent, 1911, Vol. 5, pp. 391–392.

290.   Ignác Goldziher, Introduction to Islamic Theology and Law , trans. Andras and Ruth Hamori, Princeton, NJ: Princeton University Press, 1981, p. 179.

291.   Saifur Rahman al-Mubarakpuri, The Sealed Nectar, Riyadh, Saudi Arabia: Darussalam Publications, 2005, p. 192.

292.   Sunan Abu Dawud, The Book of Jihad, Hadith 2638.

293.   William Muir, The Life of Mahomet, London: Smith, Elder, 1861, Vol. 4, p. 83.

294.   'Abd Al-Husein Zarrinkub, "The Arab Conquest of Iran and its Aftermath," in William Bayne Fisher and Richard Nelson Frye (eds), The Cambridge History of Iran, Vol 4, Cambridge: Cambridge University Press, 1999, pp. 5–6.

295.   Spencer Tucker, Battles That Changed History: An Encyclopedia of World Conflict , Santa Barbara, CA: ABC-CLIO, 2010, p. 92.

296.   Dan Fratini, "The Battle of Yarmuk, 636," Military History Online, 2006, https://www.militaryhistoryonline.com/muslimwars/articles/yarmuk.aspx

297.   Sayyid Ali Ashgar Razwy, A Restatement of the History of Islam and Muslims , Middlesex, UK: World Federation of KSI Muslim Communities, 2014, p. 330.

298.   Zafar Ahmad Usmani, I'ilaa al- Sunan, 1981, Vol. 12, p. 550; Sayyid Hussain 'Afani, Fursan al-Nahar Min Al-Sahaba Al-Akhyar, Vol. 2, pp. 230–231; Sayyid Hussain 'Afani,

Anwar al-Fajr Fi Fadha'il Ahl Badr, 2006, Vol. 1, p. 365; Ibn al-Adim, Everything Desirable about the History of Aleppo, Arabic version, Vol. 1, p. 333.

299. Ibn al-Adim,Everything Desirable about the History of Aleppo, Arabic version, Vol. 1, p. 333.

300. Piers Paul Read, The Templars, London: Orion Publishing, 1999, pp. 50–51.

301. David Nicolle, Yarmuk AD 636, London: Osprey Publishing, 1994, pp. 47–49.

302. For more information on these events, see: Walter Emil Kaegi, Byzantium and the Early Islamic Conquests, Cambridge: Cambridge University Press, 1995.

303. David Nicolle, Yarmuk AD 636, London: Osprey Publishing, 1994.

304. Geoffery Regan, First Crusader: Byzantium's Holy Wars, New York: Palgrave Macmillan, 2003, p. 167.

305. Steven Runciman, A History of the Crusades, Vol. 1, Cambridge: Cambridge University Press, 1987, p. 3.

306. Walter Emil Kaegi, Byzantium and the Early Islamic Conquests, Cambridge: Cambridge University Press, 1995, pp. 2–3.

307. Daniel J. Sahas, John of Damascus on Islam: The "Heresy of the Ishmaelites", Leiden, Netherlands: Brill, 1972, p. 20.

308. Walter Emil Kaegi, Byzantium and the Early Islamic Conquests, Cambridge: Cambridge University Press, 1995, p. 67.

309. For more information on these barriers, see Al-'Awasim.

310. Hugh Kennedy, "Egypt as a Province in the Islamic Caliphate, 641–868," in M. W. Daly (ed.), The Cambridge History of Egypt, Cambridge: Cambridge University Press, 1998, p. 62.

311. For more about these events, see: A.I. Akram, The Muslim Conquest of Persia, Oxford: Oxford University Press, 1975.

312. Parvaneh Pourshariati, Decline and Fall of the Sasanian Empire: The Sasanian-Parthian Confederacy and the Arab Conquest of Iran, London: I. B. Tauris, 2008; M. Morony, "Bahman Jādūya " Encyclopaedia Iranica, 1988, p. 217.

313. Professor Masud-ul-Hasan, Hadrat Abu Bakr, Umar, Usman, Ali (ra), Lahore, Pakistan, 1982.

314. Kasim Javed, "The Battle of Buwaib and the Conquest of Persia," Hizb ut-Tahrir Britain, June 8, 2017, http://www.hizb.org.uk/ramadan/battle-buwaib-conquest-persia/

315. Ibid, citingMuhammad Sedeeq Al Minshawi, 100 Stories from the Life of 'Umar Ibn Al Khattab',Dubai: Dar Al Fadeela Publishing, 2002.

316. Muḥammad Abū al-Faḍl Ibrāhīm, Muḥammad Aḥmad Jād al-Mawlā and ʿAlī Muḥam-mad al-Bajāwī, Qiṣaṣ al-ʿArab, Bayrūt: al-Maktabah al-ʿAsriyah, 2003, p. 134. For more information, see: George Rawlinson, The Seven Great Monarchies of the Ancient Eastern World, Vol 7: The Sassanian the History, Geography and Antiquities of Chaldaea, Assyria, Babylon, Media, Persia, Parthia and Sassanian or New Persian Empire, Library of Alexandria, 2004.

317. Abd al-Husain Zarrinkub, "The Arab Conquest of Iran and its Aftermath," in R. N. Frye (ed.), The Cambridge History of Iran, Vol. 4: From the Arab Invasion to the Saljuqs, Cambridge: Cambridge University Press, 1975, pp. 1–57.

318. Chris Rice, Director of the Center for Reconciliation, said: "The Palestinian-Israeli divide

may be the most intractable conflict of our time." Quoted inSalim J. Munayer and Lisa Loden, *Through My Enemy's Eyes: Envisioning Reconciliation in Israel-Palestine*, Milton Keynes, UK: Paternoster, 2014, p. 24.

319.   David Brog, "Why Isn't There a Palestinian State?," *Prager University*, March 27, 2017, https://www.prageru.com/videos/why-isnt-there-palestinian-state

320.   Edward Gibbon, *The History of the Decline and Fall of the Roman Empire*, Philadelphia, PA: J.D. Morris Publishers, 1862, Vol. 6, p. 321; Steven Runciman, *A History of the Crusades, Vol. 1: The First Crusade and the Foundation of the Kingdom of Jerusalem*, Cambridge: Cambridge University Press, 1987, p. 17; Moshe Gil, *A History of Palestine, 634–1099*, Cambridge: Cambridge University Press, 1997, p. 51. See also: Adrian Fortescue, "Jerusalem," in *The Catholic Encyclopaedia*, New York: Robert Appleton Company, 1910.

321.   Jacob Rader Marcus, *The Jew in the Medieval World: A Source Book, 315–1791*,revised edn, Jerusalem: Hebrew Union College Press, 2000, pp. 13–15.

322.   Charles Mills, "The History of the Crusades for the Recovery and Possession of the Holy Land," *The Eclectic Review*, Vol. 13, 1820, pp. 497–525.

323.   Moshe Gil and Ethel Broido, *A History of Palestine*, Cambridge: Cambridge University Press, 1997, pp. 634–1099.

324.   *Sahih al-Bukhari*148, Book 4, Hadith 14 or Vol. 1, Book 4, Hadith 150; *Sahih al-Bukhari*149, Book 4, Hadith 15 or Vol. 1, Book 4, Hadith 151. Book of Ablutions (Wudu'), 'Chapter: To defecate in houses'.

325.   Al-Tabari, *Tafsir al-Tabari*, 2001, Vol. 6, p. 172.

326.   Ibn Hibban, *Sahih Ibn Hibban*, Vol. 15, pp. 498–500. Ibn Hibban was a prominent specialist in Islamic scripture and a prolific author whose compilation of reports on the history of Islam have been described by other leading Islamic scholars as "the most authentic hadith collection, after Sahih Bukhari."

327.   Al-Hakim Nishapuri, *Al-Mustadrak alaa al-Sahihain*, 2006, Vol. 3, p. 63. While numerous grand Islamic scholars have testified that the report of this incident is indeed authentic, Imam Bukhari and Imam Muslim did not include it in their compilations of "authentic reports" in *Sahih al-Bukhari* and *Sahih Muslim*. We can therefore assume that they wished to hide this incident from future generations of Muslims.

328.   Agha Ibrahim Akram,The Sword of Allah: Khalid bin al-Waleed – His Life and Campaigns, Oxford: Oxford University Press, 2004, p. 301.

329.   `Abdu'l-Bahá,*Some Answered Questions*, Wilmette, IL: Bahá'í Publishing Trust, 1990 [1908], pp. 51–69.

330.   H. U. Rahman, *A Chronology of Islamic History 570–1000 CE*, London: Ta-Ha Publishers, 1999, p. 128.

331.   For more information regarding this event, see:Will Durant, *The History of Civilization: Part IV – The Age of Faith*, New York: Simon and Schuster, 1950.

332.   Desmond J. Clark, Roland Anthony Oliver, J. D. Fage and A. D. Roberts, *The Cambridge History of Africa*, Cambridge: Cambridge University Press, 1978, p. 637.

333.   Edward Gibbon, *The History of the Decline and Fall of the Roman Empire*, London: Strahan & Cadell, 1776–1789.

334.   Ira Lapidus, *A History of Islamic Societies*, Cambridge: Cambridge University Press, 2002, p. 54.

335.   Hugh Chisholm, "Abbasids," in *Encyclopædia Britannica*,Vol. 1(11th ed.), Cambridge:

Cambridge University Press, 1911, p. 10.

336. Anon, Deutsche Literaturzeitung für Kritik der Internationalen Wissenschaft[German Weekly Literary Journal for Criticism of International Science] (in German),Vol.49, 1928, pp.27–52.

337. R. Ernest Dupuy and Trevor N. Dupuy, The Encyclopedia of Military History from 3500 B.C. to the Present, 2nd edn, New York: Harper & Row, 1986, p. 233.

338. Ibid, p. 265.

339. Ibid, p. 265.

340. Ibid, p. 266.

341. al-Ṭabarī, The History of al-Ṭabarī, Vol. 34: Incipient Decline, trans. Joel L. Kraemer, Albany, NY: State University of New York Press, 1989, p. 181.

342. Ibid, pp. 171–182, 184, 195; Hugh Kennedy, When Baghdad Ruled the Muslim World: The Rise and Fall of Islam's Greatest Dynasty , Cambridge, MA: Da Capo Press, 2006, pp. 264–267.

343. "Al-Kindi," In Our Time, BBC Radio, 28 June 2012; Kevin M. Dunn, Caveman Chemistry: 28 Projects, From the Creation of Fire to the Production of Plastics, Irvine, CA: Universal Publishers, 2003, p. 166.

344. Vartan Gregorian, Islam: A Mosaic, Not a Monolith, Washington, DC: Brookings Institution Press, 2003, pp. 26–38.

345. "Al-Kindi," In Our Time, BBC Radio, 28 June 2012.

346. David Matthews, "UK Research Council Budgets to 2019–20 Revealed," Times Higher Education, March 4, 2016.

347. Ibid.

348. John Docker, "Arabesques of the Cosmopolitan and International: Lucien Henry, Baroque Allegory and Islamophilia," Australian Humanities Review, issue 22, 2001, http://australianhumanitiesreview.org/2001/06/01/arabesques-of-the-cosmopolitan-and-international-lucien-henry-baroque-allegory-and-islamophilia/. See also: John Docker, 1492: The Poetics of Diaspora, London: Bloomsbury, 2001; Ammiel Alcalay, After Jews and Arabs: Remaking Levantine Culture , Minneapolis, MN: University of Minnesota Press, 1993; Ella Shohat, "Taboo Memories and Diasporic Visions: Columbus, Palestine and Arab-Jews," in May Joseph and Jennifer Natalya Fink (eds), Performing Hybridity, Minneapolis, MN: University of Minnesota Press, 1999, pp. 131–156; John Docker, "An Unbecoming Australian: Romancing a Lost Pre-1492 World," in Richard Nile and Michael Peterson (eds), Becoming Australia: The Woodford Forum, University of Queensland Press, St. Lucia, 1998, pp. 136–148.

349. Serge Trifkovic, The Sword of the Prophet, Salisbury, MA: Regina Orthodox Press, 2002.

350. Ira M. Lapidus, A History of Islamic Societies, Cambridge: Cambridge University Press, 2014, p. 125; Wael B. Hallaq, An Introduction to Islamic Law, Cambridge: Cambridge University Press, 2009, pp. 31–35; Knut S. Vikør, "Sharī'ah," in Emad El-Din Shahin (ed.), The Oxford Encyclopedia of Islam and Politics, Oxford: Oxford University Press, 2014.

351. Farhat J. Ziadeh, "Uṣūl al-fiqh," in John L. Esposito (ed.), The Oxford Encyclopedia of the Islamic World, Oxford: Oxford University Press, 2009.

352. Robert Tignor et al., Worlds Together, Worlds Apart, New York: Norton, 2011, p. 313; Justin Wintle, History of Islam, London: Rough Guides, 2003, pp. 136–137.

353. Eva Baer, Metalwork in Medieval Islamic Art, Albany, NY: SUNY Press,1983, p. 23.

354. Mirza Ghulam Ahmad, *The Essence of Islam*, Surrey, UK: Islam International Publications, 2005, Vol. 3, p. 279; Haqiqat-ul-Wahi, *Ruhani Khaza'in*, Vol. 22, p. 41.

355. Ahmad, Noor-ul-Haqq, Vol. 1, p. 106. Retrieved from *Idara Dawat-O-Irshad*, "Mirza Ghulam's Tirade against Jesus Christ".

356. Satt Bachan,*Ruhani Khaza'en: Collection of the Books of Mirza Ghulam Ahmad Qadiani*, Surrey, UK: Islam International Publications, 1984, Vol. 10, pp. 172, 296, 300.

357. Hazrat Mirza Ghulam Ahmad, *Victory of Islam*, trans. Zahid Aziz, New York: Ahmadiyya Anjuman Isha`at Islam Lahore, 2000, pp. 12–13.

358. Satt Bachan,*Ruhani Khaza'en: Collection of the Books of Mirza Ghulam Ahmad Qadiani*, Surrey, UK: Islam International Publications, 1984, Vol. 9, p. 442; Nur-ul-Quran, *Ruhani Khaza'en*, Vol. 9, p. 416.

359. Hazrat Mirza Ghulam Ahmad, *Noah's Ark: An Invitation to Faith*, Surrey, UK: Islam International Publications, 2016 [1902], p. 115.

360. *Ruhani Khaza'en: Collection of the Books of Mirza Ghulam Ahmad Qadiani*, Rabwah, Pakistan, 2008, Vol. 11, p. 329; *Anjam-i-Atham, Ruhani Khaza'en*, Vol. 11, p. 291, addenda;*Anjam-i-Atham*, p. 9, appendix.

361. *Anjam-i-Atham,Roohany Khazaen*, Vol. 11, p. 291, addenda. Retrieved from *Idara Dawat-O-Irshad*, "Mirza Ghulam's Tirade against Jesus Christ".

362. Mirza Ghulam Ahmad of Qādiān, *Lecture Ludhiana*, Surrey, UK: Islam International Publications, 2003, p. 59.

363. Satt Bachan,*Ruhani Khaza'en: Collection of the Books of Mirza Ghulam Ahmad Qadiani*, Surrey, UK: Islam International Publications, 1984, Vol. 9, p. 459 [original emphasis]. See also Nur-ul-Qur'an part 2, Ruhani Khaza'in, Vol. 9, pp. 429–436. Retrieved from *Idara Dawat-O-Irshad*, "Mirza Ghulam's Tirade against Jesus Christ".

364. Albadr, September 11, 1903. Retrieved from *Idara Dawat-O-Irshad*, "Mirza Ghulam's Tirade against Jesus Christ".

365. Stephanie Cronin, *The Making of Modern Iran: State and Society under Riza Shah, 1921–1941*, London: Routledge, 2012, p. 6.

366. "Ayatollah Sadegh Khalkhali," *The Daily Telegraph*, November 28, 2003.

367. Afshin Molavi, *The Soul of Iran: A Nation's Journey to Freedom*, New York: Norton and Co., 2005, p. 9.

368. Christopher M. Blanchard, "The Islamic Traditions of Wahhabism and Salafiyya" in Cofie D. Malbouisson (ed.), *Focus on Islamic Issues*, New York: Nova Science Publishers, 2007, p. 23; Harvey Tripp and Peter North, *Culture Shock, Saudi Arabia: A Guide to Customs and Etiquette*, Portland, OR: Times Media Private, 2003, p. 14.

369. "Saudi Arabia: Women Beheaded in Street, Corpses Dangling from Cranes," *News.com.au*, March 22, 2016.

370. Amnesty International, "The Death Penalty in 2017: Facts and Figures," *Amnesty International*, April 12, 2018, https://www.amnesty.org/en/latest/news/2018/04/death-penalty-facts-and-figures-2017/; Harriet Agerholm, "Outcry as Saudi Arabia Executes Six People in One Day to Bring 2017 Death Penalty Total to 44," *The Independent*, July 11, 2017.

371. Harriet Agerholm, "Outcry as Saudi Arabia Executes Six People in One Day to Bring 2017 Death Penalty Total to 44," *The Independent*, July 11, 2017.

372. Cornell Center on the Death Penalty Worldwide, "Saudi Arabia," *Death Penalty Database*,

April 4, 2011; Harry R. Dammer and Jay S. Albanese, *Comparative Criminal Justice Systems*, 4th edn, Belmont, CA: Wadsworth Cengage Learning, 2010, p. 56.

373. Justin Huggler, "German Vice-Chancellor Accuses Saudi Arabia of Funding Islamic Extremism in the West," *The Telegraph*(Berlin), December 6, 2015; "What is Wahhabism? The Reactionary Branch of Islam from Saudi Arabia Said to be 'the Main Source of Global Terrorism,'" *The Telegraph*, May 19, 2017.

374. Ibid.

375. Gitika Ahuja, "Saudi Prince Donates $40 Million to Harvard, Georgetown Universities," *ABC News*, December 13, 2005.

376. Ibid.

377. Mervyn Bendle, "National Security: Secret Saudi Funding of Australian Institutions," *News Weekly*, February 21, 2009.

378. Raif Badawi, "A Sheikh Offered to Take 200 Lashes on Behalf of Saudi Blogger," *StepFeed*, September 22, 2017.

379. Naim ibn Hammad, *'Kitab Al Fitan*, Beirut, Lebanon: Dar-Al-Fikr, 2003, p. 201. See also *Sahih Muslim*, Book 12, Hadith 206.

380. Will Drabold, "Donald Trump Says He'll Keep Calling Clinton and Obama the 'Founders of ISIS,'" *Time*, August 11, 2016.

381. Imam Khomeini, *Tafsir Ayat al-Basmalah*, 1992, p. 87.

382. Imam Khomeini, *Sharh Du'a al-Sahar: Commentary on Pre-Dawn Supplication*, Tehran, 1996, p. 103.

383. *The Quran in the Words of Imam Khomeini*, Al-Maaref Islamic Organisation, 2009, p. 84.

384. Ja'far Murtadha al-Amili, *Ibn Arabi is an Intolerant Sunni*, 2007, pp. 91–96.

385. Ibid.

386. Ibid.

387. Kamāl Sayyid and Jasim Rasheed, *Kumail Bin Zyyad*, Qum, Iran: Ansariyan, 2000.

388. Ali Ibn Abi Talib, *Nahjul Balagha; Peak of Eloquence: Sermons, Letters, and Sayings of Imam Ali Ibn Abu Talib*, ed. Mohammad Askari Jafery, Elmhurst, NY: Tahrike Tarsile Quran, 1984, p. 654.

389. Shaikh M. Tawhidi, "Islamic Unity: Realistic Aspects of Success," *Huffington Post*, April 11, 2016.

390. Emile Nakhleh, *A Necessary Engagement: Reinventing America's Relations with the Muslim World*, Princeton, NJ: Princeton University Press, 2008, p. 29.

391. "Al-Qaradhawi: Islamic Caliphate Should Look Like the EU," *Middle East Media Research Institute*, August 26, 2014, emphasis added.

392. Hassan Hassan, "Hatred, Violence and the Sad Demise of Yusuf Al Qaradawi," *The National*, January 28, 2014; European Council on Foreign Relations, *The Gulf and Sectarianism*, London: European Council on Foreign Relations, 2013, pp. 3, 11.

393. "Shiite's Are 'Invading' Sunni Societies: Qaradawi," *AFP*, September 19, 2008; "Influential Sunni Cleric Speaks of Shiite 'Invasion,'" *AFP*, September 18, 2008.

394. "Sheik Yousuf Al-Qaradhawi: If the Shiite Doctrine Is Preached in Egypt, There Will Be Civil Strife and Endless Massacres," *Middle East Media Research Institute*, August 31, 2006.

395. "Try to be Nice About Each Other, A Sunni Preacher Upsets the Shias," *The Economist*, September 25, 2008.

396.   Imam Khomeini, *Book of Purity(Kitab-ul-Taharah)*, Tehran, Iran: Imam Khomeini Publications, Vol. 3, p. 457.

397.   V. G. Julie Rajan, *Al Qaeda's Global Crisis: The Islamic State, Takfir and the Genocide of Muslims*, London: Routledge, 2015, pp. 121–122, 159.

398.   Ibn Khaldun, *The Muqaddimah: Abd Ar Rahman bin Muhammed ibn Khaldun*, trans. Franz Rosenthal.

399.   Muhammad Moj, *The Deoband Madrassah Movement: Countercultural Trends and Tendencies*, London: Anthem Press, 2015.

400.   Anders Jerichow, *Saudi Arabia: Outside Global Law and Order: A Discussion Paper*, Hove, UK: Psychology Press, 1997, p. 69.

401.   Israel Friedlaender, "The Heterodoxies of the Shiites in the Presentation of Ibn Hazm," *Journal of the American Oriental Society*, Vol. 29, 1908, p. 19.

402.   Hassan Abbas, "Pakistan" in Assaf Moghadam (ed.), *Militancy and Political Violence in Shiism: Trends and Patterns*, Abingdon, Oxon, UK: Routledge, 2011, p. 166.

403.   Nabil Mouline, *The Clerics of Islam: Religious Authority and Political Power in Saudi Arabia*, New Haven, CT: Yale University Press, 2014, p. 70.

404.   V. G. Julie Rajan, *Al Qaeda's Global Crisis: The Islamic State, Takfir and the Genocide of Muslims*, London: Routledge, 2015, p. 122.

405.   David A. Graham, "Iran's Beleaguered Sunnis," *The Atlantic*, January 6, 2016; Human Rights Watch,*Iran: Religious and Ethnic Minorities: Discrimination in Law and Practice*, New York: Human Rights Watch, 1997; Raihan Ismail, *Saudi Clerics and Shi'a Islam*, Oxford: Oxford University Press, 2016, p. 153; *Global Issues: Selections from CQ Researcher*, Thousand Oaks, CA: CQ Press, 2013, p. 34.

406.   Ershad Alijani, "Tehran's Authorities Destroy Sunni Worship Space," *France 24*, June 8, 2015.

407.   Bernard Rougier, *The Sunni Tragedy in the Middle East: Northern Lebanon from al-Qaeda to ISIS*, Princeton, NJ: Princeton University Press, 2015, p. 73; Sophie McNeill, "Saudi Arabia Cutting Diplomatic Ties with Iran – Fears of New Sectarian Clash," *AM*, ABC, January 4, 2016.

408.   "Where Was Khomeini?," *Iran Global*, November 1, 2011.

409.   Michael M. J. Fischer,*Iran: From Religious Dispute to Revolution*, Madison, WI: University of Wisconsin Press, 2003, p. 196.

410.   Mohammad Sahimi, "The Ten Days That Changed Iran,"*Frontline*, PBS, February 3, 2010.

411.   "Iran remembers Khomeini's return," *Al-Jazeera*, February 2, 2010, emphasis added.

412.   "Khomeini: 'We Shall Confront the World with Our Ideology,'" *Middle East Research and Information Project*, March 21, 1980, emphasis added.

413.   "Ayatullah Khomeini, Man of the Year," *Time*, January 7, 1980.

414.   The History Guy, "Iran-U.S. Hostage Crisis (1979–1981)," *historyguy.com*; Michael Köhler, "Two Nations, a Treaty, and the World Court – An Analysis of United States–Iranian Relations under the Treaty of Amity before the International Court of Justice," *Wisconsin International Law Journal*, Vol. 18, 2000, p. 287.

415.   Nicholas M. Nikazmerad, "A Chronological Survey of the Iranian Revolution," *Iranian Studies*, Vol. 13, No. 1/4, 1980, pp. 327–368.

416.   Dinesh D'Souza,*The Enemy at Home: The Cultural Left and Its Responsibility for 9/11*, New York: Broadway Books, 2008, p. 209.

417. "Khomeini Fatwa 'Led to Killing of 30,000 in Iran,'" *The Telegraph*, February 4, 2001.

418. Dudi Cohen, "Japanese Crane Manufacturer Cuts Ties with Iran," *YNet News*, July 15, 2011; Reut Cohen, "Crane Manufacturer, UNIC, Ends Business with Iran," *Neon Tommy*, August 8, 2011; United Against Nuclear Iran, "Construction Company Liebherr to End Its Business in Iran Following UANI Cranes Campaign," media release, August 24, 2011.

419. Ayatollah Khomeini, *Sayingsof the Ayatollah Khomeini*, trans. H. Salemson, 1979, p. 30.

420. Leaked audio file of Ayatollah Muntazeri, *BBC Persian*, 2009.

421. "Audio File of Ayatollah Muntazeri Regarding 1988 Executions Has Been Leaked," *BBC Persian*, 2016.

422. Majid Rafizadeh, "Iran's Massacre and Rising Crimes Against Humanity," *Gatestone Institute*, October 5, 2016.

423. "Cleric's Funeral Becomes Protest of Iran Leaders," *New York Times*, December 21, 2009.

424. "Ayatollah Montazeri's Son Receives a 21-Year Sentence for Disclosing Audio Tape About Mass Execution of Iranian Political Prisoners in 1988," *Payvand*, November 28, 2016.

425. Islam Asil Culture and Media Center, *YouTube*, uploaded February 17, 2014.

426. "BBC Profile: Ayatollah Ali Khamenei," *BBC News*, June 17, 2009.

427. "Grand Ayatollah Fayyad: Political Clerics Have no Value," *Shia-Documents*, September 9, 2016.

428. Karim Sadjadpour, "The Prince of Persia," *Foreign Policy Magazine*, July 21, 2011.

429. Ayatullah Muhammad Qaim Maqami, "Infallibility of the Islamic Leader," Farsi Lecture, 2015.

430. Mustapha Ajbaili, "Khamenei said 'Ya Ali' at Birth," *Al-Arabiya News*, April 16, 2011.

431. Quran 4:59, emphasis added.

432. Imam Khomeini, *Islamic Government: Governance of the Jurist*, trans.Hamid Algar,Tehran:Institute for Compilation and Publication of Imam Khomeini's Works, p. 18.

433. Ibid.

434. Ibid, p. 20.

435. Ibid, p.29.

436. Ibid.

437. US Department of State, *Iran Human Rights Report*, Washington, DC: 2015 and 2016.

438. Baqer Moin, *Khomeini: Life of the Ayatollah*, New York: Thomas Dunne Books, 1999, p. 158.

439. Muhammad Hussein Al Kashef Al-Ghetaa, *Al-Tabaqat al Ja'fariyah*, 1998, pp. 86–91.

440. Al-Amudi, *Ghurar al-Hikam wa Durar al-Kalim(Exalted Aphorisms and Pearls of Speech)*, Hadith 1133.

441. "The Family of Ayatollah Makarem, and the Mafia of Sugar," *Voice of America Farsi*, November 3, 2015.

442. "Poverty in Iran on the Rise," *Borgen Magazine*, July 23, 2014.

443. "Islamic Clerics Oppose Women's Presence in Football Stadiums," *BBC Persian*, April 26, 2006.

444. "Volleyball Ban for Female Fans Reignites Debate in Iran," *The Guardian*, June 20, 2015.

445. "Iran Cleric Says Dogs 'Unclean' and Not to Be Kept as Pets," *Reuters*, June 19, 2010.

446. Ibid.

447.   Parvaneh Vahidmanesh, "Sad Fate of Iran's Jews," Institute for War and Peace Reporting, May 11, 2010.

448.   "Senior Iranian Cleric Dismisses Nazi Holocaust as 'Superstition,'" Daily Mail, September 6, 2010.

449.   "Iranian Cleric Issues Fatwa Against the Internet," The Washington Post, September 2, 2014.

450.   Michael M. J. Fischer, Iran: From Religious Dispute to Revolution, Madison, WI: University of Wisconsin Press, 2003, pp. 34–35.

451.   Ibid, pp. 221–222.

452.   "Makarem Shirazi Sentences Taheri to Execution," France Médias Monde, August 25, 2015.

453.   Ayatollah Nasir Makarem Shirazi, "Prohibition of Smoking in Islam,"Islamic Insights, February 2, 2009.

454.   "Profile: Iran's 'Unremarkable' Supreme Leader Ayatollah Khamenei," BBC, August 4, 2011

455.   Colin Freeman, "The Rise of Prof 'Crocodile' – A Hardliner to Terrify Hardliners," The Telegraph, November 20, 2005.

456.   Vali Nasr, The Shia Revival: How Conflicts Within Islam Will Shape the Future ,New York: Norton, 2006, p. 216.

457.   Erich Follath, "Is War Between Iran and Israel Inevitable?,"Salon, June 23, 2009.

458.   "Obeying Ahmadinejad Like Obeying God: Cleric,"Global News, August 13, 2009.

459.   "Ganji Identified Fallahian as the 'Master Key' in Chain Murders,"Iran PressService, December 2000.

460.   "'Iranian Clerics' Angling Stirs Worry on Absolute Rule," The New York Times, September 25, 2006;Colin Freeman, "The Rise of Prof 'Crocodile' – A Hardliner to Terrify Hardliners," The Telegraph(London), November 20, 2005.

461.   Erich Follath, "Is War Between Iran and Israel Inevitable?,"Salon, June 23, 2009.

462.   "Ahmadinejad Isolated by Battle with Iran's Supreme Leader," The Atlantic, June 8, 2011.

463.   "Islamic Jurist Issued Death Fatwa Against Musavi and Karubi," Al-Arabiya, June 23, 2009.

464.   Thomas Erdbrink, "Ayatollah: Iran's President 'Bewitched' by Senior Aide," The Washington Post, May 15, 2011.

465.   Ibid.

466.   Asef Bayat, "Iran: A Green Wave for Life and Liberty," Open Democracy, July 7, 2009.

467.   Afshin Molavi, The Soul of Iran, New York: Norton, 2005, p. 105.

468.   Transcript of TV interview with Dr. Soroush by Dariush Sajjadi, Homa TV, March 9, 2006; Dr. Soroush (in Persian).

469.   Olivier Roy,The Politics of Chaos in the Middle East, London: Hurst, 2008, p. 132.

470.   Erich Follath, "Is War Between Iran and Israel Inevitable?,"Salon, June 23, 2009.

471.   Colin Freeman, "The Rise of Prof 'Crocodile' – A Hardliner to Terrify Hardliners," The Telegraph (London), November 20, 2005.

472.   Ibid.

473.   Ibid.

474.   Peter Beaumont, "Battle for Iran Shifts from the Streets to the Heart of Power," The Guardian, June 28, 2009;"The Assembly of Experts,"PBSTehran Bureau, June 24, 2009.

475. Jakob Skovgaard-Petersen, Defining Islam for the Egyptian State: Muftis and Fatwas of the Ddr Al-Iftd, Leiden: Brill, 1997, p. 172.

476. "Islamic Fatwa Decrees That Toilet Paper is Halal: Directorate of Religious Affairs Says Wiping is Acceptable," Daily Mail, April 8, 2015.

477. "Halal Certification in Australia is Big Business and Worth Millions to Certifiers," Daily Telegraph, August 16, 2015.

478. "A 'Four Corners' Investigation Looks into Halal Certification and its Impact on Australian Consumers," News.com.au, September 9, 2015.

479. Tehrani was then placed under house arrest and forced to erase this matter from his letter. The remainder of his letter is published in his memoirs. See: Shaikh Ali Tehrani, My Memoirs, from 1926–2002, France, p. 99; "A Testimony that Khamenei is Homosexual," Iran Global(Farsi), January 9, 2013.

480. "Iran has Detained Hussain Shirazi For Labelling Iran's Khamanei a 'Pharaoh,'" Al-Bawaba News, March 8, 2018.

481. Shmuel Bar, "The Religious Sources of Islamic Terrorism," Hoover Institution, June 1, 2004.

482. "NATO's Military Concept for Defence Against Terrorism," NATO, April 14, 2005.

483. Muhammad Asad, Sahih Al-Bukhari: The Early Years of Islam , Lahore: Arafat Publications, 1938.

484. Sahih al-Bukhari, Vol. 1, p. 64, Book 4, Section 70, No. 233.

485. Sahih al-Bukhari, Book 56, Hadith 1; Book 56, Hadith 34.

486. Ibid, Book 56, Hadith 10.

487. Ibid, Book 56, Hadith 15.

488. Ibid, Book 56, Hadith 27.

489. Sahih al-Bukhari, No. 2796, Book 56, Hadith 14.

490. Sahih al-Bukhari, No. 3849, Book 63, Hadith 75.

491. Al Bayhaqi, Shu`ab al-Iman (The Branches of Faith), 2000, Vol. 6, pp. 101–103.

492. "Jailhouse Jihad: Violent Inmates Forcing Prison Conversions to Islam," News.com.au, June 30, 2017.

493. "Muslim Boxer Anthony Mundine Says Men Can Beat Their Wives With a 'Little Stick as Long as They Don't Cause Injury,'" Daily Mail, April 28, 2017.

494. "2011: The Year That Saw the Issuing of Some of the Weirdest Fatwas," Al Arabiya News, December 30, 2011; "Top Saudi Sheikh Issues Bizarre Fatwa Allowing Men to EAT Their Wives if They Are Hungry," Mirror, April 10, 2015.

495. Ibn Arabi, Al-Futūhāt al-Makkiyya (The Meccan Illuminations), 1969, Vol. 1, p. 373.

496. "Arabs Denounce Cleric's Fatwa on 'Immoral' TV," USA Today, September 19, 2008; "Mickey Mouse Must Die, Says Saudi Arabian Cleric," The Telegraph, September 15, 2008.

497. Official Website of Imam Khaled Abdel-Alim, "The Law of Gifting Roses to Other People," Fatwa no. 1162, www.khaledabdelalim.com.

498. Zainuddin Ibn Nujaym, Al-Bahr al Ra'iq, 1997, Vol. 1, p. 60.

499. Ibn Qayyim al-Jawziyya, Badā`i` al-Fawā`id (Amazing Points of Benefit), Vol. 1, pp. 1471–1472.

500. Amrutha Gayathri, "Islamic Cleric Bans Women from Touching Bananas, Cucumbers to

       Avoid 'Sexual Thoughts,'" International Business Times, December 7, 2011.

501. "Fatwa Banning Muslim Women from Touching Bananas and Other Penis-Shaped Foods Makes Internet Rounds," New York Daily News, December 11, 2011.

502. Muna Khan, "Bananas, Cucumbers, Carrots, Oh My," Al Arabiya News, December 9, 2011.

503. "ISIS Extremists Order Mannequin Faces Covered in Mosul, Iraq," Jezebel, July 23, 2014.

504. Imam Abdul Jalil Isa Abu Nasr, Maa Iaa Yajuzu Fihi al Khilaf Bayn al Muslimeen (What None of the Muslims can Differ on), p. 96.

505. Al-Nawawi, Al Minhaj Be Sharh Sahih Muslim (Commentary on Sahih Muslim), 1929, Vol. 4, p. 41.

506. Ibn Hajar al-Haytami, Tuhfatu'l Muhtaj li Sharh Al-Minhaj, Vol. 1, p. 260.

507. Imam Alaa' al Din al Haskafi, Al Dur al Mukhtar, 2002, p. 76.

508. Ibn Hazm, Al-Muhalla, Vol. 11, p. 253 (citing Abu Hanifah).

509. Al-Khaṭīb ash-Shirbīniy, Mughni Al-Muhtaj, Book of Marriage (Nikah), 2000, Vol. 4, p. 300.

510. ibn Abidin, Radd al-Muhtar ala al-Dur al-Mukhtar , 2003, Vol. 5, p. 283.

511. Al-Nawawi, Al Minhaj Be Sharh Sahih Muslim (Commentary on Sahih Muslim), 1929, Vol. 9, p. 206.

512. Ibn Hajar al-Asqalani, Fatḥ al-Bārī fī Sharḥ Ṣaḥīḥ al-Bukhārī, 2005, Vol. 12, p. 347.

513. Ibn Qayyim al-Jawziyya, Badā'i' al-Fawā'id (Amazing Points of Benefit), Vol. 1, p. 1473.

514. Imam Khomeini, Tahrir al-Wasilah, 1998, Iran, Vol. 2, pp. 221–222.

515. "Sex Jihad Raging in Syria, Claims Minister," The Telegraph, September 20, 2013.

516. "Fatwas Preventing Women from Sleeping Beside Walls, Because It's Masculine," Albawaba News, March 22, 2007.

517. "Women Sitting on Chairs Become Apostates Because Evil Spirits Penetrate Them," Donia Al-Watan, April 29, 2013.

518. "Women Sitting on Chairs is Adultery, Without a Doubt," International Quranic Center, April 2, 2007.

519. "Syria: Islamists Forbid Women to Sit in Chairs," Clarion Project, January 14, 2014.

520. Burhan al-Din al-Marghinani, al-Hidayah (The Guidance), 1996, Vol. 4, p. 105.

521. "Syria: Islamists Forbid Women to Sit in Chairs," Clarion Project, January 14, 2014.

522. Imam Tawhidi, "Undercover Radicals: What's Stopping the Reformation of Islam?" The Huffington Post, June 18, 2017.

523. Imam Tawhidi, "Undercover Radicals: What's Stopping the Reformation of Islam?" The Huffington Post, June 18, 2017.

524. Steve Postal, "A Muslim Reformer Speaks Out About His Battle Against Islamism and PC," The Federalist, January 30, 2017.

525. "'Devout Moderate Muslim' Mohammed Zuhdi Jasser Whines About Being 'Bullied' By His Radical Mosque With CAIR Imam," Militant Islam Monitor, August 24, 2014.

526. Sean Holstege and Matthew Casey, 'Elton Simpson's Slow, Isolated Descent into ISIS, Jihad," AZCentral, May 9, 2015.

527. Anderson Cooper, "60 Minutes Investigates First ISIS-Claimed Attack in U.S. and What the FBI Knew," 60 Minutes, CBS, March 26, 2017.

528. Zuhdi Jasser, A Battle for the Soul of Islam: An American Muslim Patriot's Fight to Save his Faith, New York: Threshold Editions, 2012, p. 63.

529.   Alija Izetbegovic, *The Islamic Declaration: A Programme for the Islamization of Muslims and the Muslim Peoples*, Sarajevo, 1990.

530.   Steven L. Burg and Paul S. Shoup, *Ethnic Conflict and International Intervention: Crisis in Bosnia-Herzegovina, 1990–93*, New York: Taylor & Francis, 2015, p. 67.

531.   Vjekoslav Perica, *Balkan Idols: Religion and Nationalism in Yugoslav States*, Oxford: Oxford University Press, 2002, p. 77.

532.   Mehdi Hasan and Ryan Grim, "Leaked State Department Memo Advised Trump Administration to Push for 'Islamic Reformation,'" *The Intercept*, June 19, 2018.

533.   "American Islamic Forum for Democracy," *CitizenAudit.org*, 2018, https://www.citizenaudit.org/organization/710940051/american-islamic-forum-for-democracy/

534.   Lauren Markoe, "Muslims Call New Religious Freedom Appointee a 'Puppet' for Islam Foes," *The Washington Post*, March 27, 2012.

535.   Sheila Musaji, "Zuhdi Jasser and AIFD – Identified by Rep. King as the Ideal American Muslim Leadership," *The American Muslim*, March 28, 2012.

536.   Quran, 2:285.

537.   E. A. Wallis Budge (Aug 1, 2014). A History of Ethiopia: Volume I: Nubia and Abyssinia. Routledge. p. 7.; William Montgomery Watt (1961). Muhammad: Prophet and Statesman. Oxford University Press. p. 66.